SCHAUM'S OUTLINE OF

THEORY AND PROBLEMS

OF

BOOKKEEPING
and
ACCOUNTING
Third Edition

•

JOEL J. LERNER, M.S., P.D.
Professor of Business
Sullivan County Community College

•

SCHAUM'S OUTLINE SERIES
McGRAW-HILL, INC.

New York St. Louis San Francisco Auckland Bogotá Caracas
Lisbon London Madrid Mexico City Milan Montreal
New Delhi San Juan Singapore
Sydney Tokyo Toronto

JOEL J. LERNER is Professor and former Chairman of the Business Division at Sullivan County Community College, Loch Sheldrake, New York. He received his B.S. from New York University and his M.S. and P.D. from Columbia University. He has coauthored the Schaum's Outlines of *Principles of Accounting I, Principles of Accounting II,* and *Business Mathematics* and is the sole author of McGraw-Hill's publication of *Financial Planning for the Utterly Confused.* He is the president of MASTCA Publishing Corp. and is the editor of "The Middle/Fixed Income Letter," a monthly financial publication. Professor Lerner is also a financial lecturer to several Fortune 500 firms, has produced his own TV and radio series for eleven years, and addresses thousands of people annually on finances.

 This book is printed on recycled paper containing a minimum of 50% total recycled fiber with 10% postconsumer de-inked fiber. Soybean based inks are used on the cover and text.

Portions of this book have been taken from Schaum's Outline of *Principles of Accounting I,* 4th edition, © 1993.

Schaum's Outline of Theory and Problems of

BOOKKEEPING AND ACCOUNTING

1 2 3 4 5 6 7 8 9 10 11 12 13 14 15 16 17 18 19 20 BAW BAW 9 8 7 6 5 4

ISBN 0-07-037593-3

Sponsoring Editor, John Aliano
Production Supervisor, Fred Schulte
Editing Supervisor, Patty Andrews
Cover design by Amy E. Becker

Library of Congress Cataloging-in-Publication Data

Lerner, Joel J.
    Schaum's outline of theory and problems of bookkeeping and
accounting / Joel J. Lerner.—3rd ed.
        p.   cm.—(Schaum's outline series)
    Includes index.
    ISBN 0-07-037593-3
    1. Bookkeeping—Problems, exercises, etc.   2. Accounting—
Problems, exercises, etc.   I. Title   II. Title: Outline of theory
and problems of bookkeeping and accounting.   III. Title: Bookkeeping
and accounting.
HF5661.L46   1994b
657'.076—dc20   93-41304
                                                CIP

Preface

This third edition brings to the study of bookkeeping and accounting the same solved-problems approach that has proved so successful in the disciplines of engineering, mathematics, and accounting. In contrast to previous supplementary materials, which have been little more than summary textbooks, this book is organized around the practical application of basic bookkeeping and accounting concepts. By providing

1. Concise definitions and explanations, in easily understood terms,

2. Fully worked-out solutions to a large range of problems (against which students can check their own solutions),

3. Review questions,

4. Sample examinations typical of those used by high schools and 2- and 4-year colleges,

5. Comprehensive Review Problems in each category,

this book develops the student's ability to understand and solve bookkeeping and accounting problems.

JOEL J. LERNER

Contents

Chapter 1

Assets, Liabilities, and Capital

1.1 NATURE OF BOOKKEEPING AND ACCOUNTING

An understanding of the principles of bookkeeping and accounting is essential for anyone who is interested in a successful career in business. The purpose of bookkeeping and accounting is to provide information concerning the financial affairs of a business. This information is needed by owners, managers, creditors, and governmental agencies.

An individual who earns a living by recording the financial activities of a business is known as a *bookkeeper,* while the process of classifying and summarizing business transactions and interpreting their effects is accomplished by the *accountant.* The bookkeeper is concerned with techniques involving the recording of transactions, and the accountant's objective is the use of data for interpretation. Bookkeeping and accounting techniques will both be discussed.

1.2 BASIC ELEMENTS OF FINANCIAL POSITION: THE ACCOUNTING EQUATION

The financial condition or position of a business enterprise is represented by the relationship of assets to liabilities and capital.

Assets: properties that are owned and have money value—for instance, cash, inventory, buildings, equipment

Liabilities: amounts owed to outsiders, such as notes payable, accounts payable, bonds payable

Capital: the interest of the owners in an enterprise; also known as owners' equity

These three basic elements are connected by a fundamental relationship called *the accounting equation.* This equation expresses the equality of the assets on one side with the claims of the creditors and owners on the other side:

$$\text{Assets} \quad = \quad \text{Liabilities} \quad + \quad \text{Capital}$$

According to the accounting equation, a firm is assumed to possess its assets subject to the rights of the creditors and owners.

EXAMPLE 1

Assume that a business owned assets of $100,000, owed creditors $80,000, and owed the owner $20,000. The accounting equation would be:

Assets	=	Liabilities	+	Capital
$100,000	=	$80,000	+	$20,000

Suppose that $6,000 was used to reduce liabilities and the balance remained in assets. The equation would then be:

Assets	=	Liabilities	+	Capital
$94,000	=	$74,000	+	$20,000

We shall call any business event that alters the amount of assets, liabilities, or capital a *transaction.* In Example 1, the net changes in asset groups were discussed; in Example 2, we show how the accountant makes a meaningful record of a series of transactions, reconciling them step by step with the accounting equation.

1

EXAMPLE 2

During the month of January, Ted Drew, Lawyer,

(1) Invested $4,000 to open his practice.

(2) Bought supplies (stationery, forms, pencils, and so on) for cash, $300.

(3) Bought office furniture from Robinson Furniture Company on account, $2,000.

(4) Received $2,500 in fees earned during the month.

(5) Paid office rent for January, $500.

(6) Paid salary for part-time help, $200.

(7) Paid $1,200 to Robinson Furniture Company on account.

(8) After taking an inventory at the end of the month, Drew found that he had used $200 worth of supplies.

(9) Withdrew $400 for personal use.

These transactions might be analyzed and recorded as follows:

Transaction (1) **Mr. Drew invested $4,000 to open his practice.** Two accounts are affected:
January 1 the asset Cash is increased, and the capital of the firm is increased by the same amount.

	Assets	=	Liabilities	+	Capital
	Cash				T. Drew, Capital
(1)	+$4,000	=		+	+$4,000

Transaction (2) **Bought supplies for cash, $300.** In this case, Mr. Drew is substituting one asset
January 4 for another; he is receiving (+) the asset Supplies and paying out (−) the asset Cash. Note that the capital of $4,000 remains unchanged, and there is still equality.

	Assets			=	Liabilities	+	Capital
	Cash	+	Supplies				T. Drew, Capital
	$4,000						$4,000
(2)	−300		+$300				
	$3,700	+	$300	=		+	$4,000

Transaction (3) **Bought office furniture from Robinson Furniture Company on account,**
January 5 **$2,000.** Mr. Drew is receiving the asset Furniture but is not paying for it with the asset Cash. Instead, he will owe the money to the Robinson Furniture Company. Therefore, he is liable for this amount in the future, thus creating the liability Accounts Payable.

	Assets					=	Liabilities	+	Capital
	Cash	+	Supplies	+	Furniture		Accounts Payable		T. Drew, Capital
	$3,700		$300						$4,000
(3)					+$2,000		+$2,000		
	$3,700	+	$300	+	$2,000	=	$2,000	+	$4,000

Transaction (4)   **Received $2,500 in fees earned during the month.**   Because Mr. Drew received
January 15 $2,500, the asset Cash increased, and also his capital increased. It is important to
                      note that he labels the $2,500 *fees income* (revenue) to show its origin.

	Assets			=	Liabilities	+	Capital
Cash	+	Supplies	+ Furniture		Accounts Payable		T. Drew, Capital
$3,700		$300	$2,000		$2,000		$4,000
(4) +2,500							+2,500 Fees Income
$6,200	+	$300	+ $2,000	=	$2,000	+	$6,500

Transaction (5)   **Paid office rent for January, $500.**   When the word "paid" is stated, you know it
January 30   means a deduction from Cash, since Mr. Drew is paying out his asset Cash. Pay-
                      ment of expense is a reduction of capital. It is termed *rent expense*.

	Assets			=	Liabilities	+	Capital
Cash	+	Supplies	+ Furniture		Accounts Payable		T. Drew, Capital
$6,200		$300	$2,000		$2,000		$6,500
(5) −500							−500 Rent Expense
$5,700	+	$300	+ $2,000	=	$2,000	+	$6,000

Transaction (6)   **Paid salary for part-time help, $200.**   Again, the word "paid" means a deduction
January 30   of cash and a reduction in capital. This time it refers to *salaries expense*.

	Assets			=	Liabilities	+	Capital
Cash	+	Supplies	+ Furniture		Accounts Payable		T. Drew, Capital
$5,700		$300	$2,000		$2,000		$6,000
(6) −200							−200 Salaries Expense
$5,500	+	$300	+ $2,000	=	$2,000	+	$5,800

Transaction (7)   **Paid $1,200 to Robinson Furniture Company on account.**   Here Mr. Drew is
January 31   reducing the asset Cash because he is paying $1,200, and he is also reducing the lia-
                      bility Accounts Payable. He will now owe $1,200 less.

	Assets			=	Liabilities	+	Capital
Cash	+	Supplies	+ Furniture		Accounts Payable		T. Drew, Capital
$5,500		$300	$2,000		$2,000		$5,800
(7) −1,200					−1,200		
$4,300	+	$300	+ $2,000	=	$ 800	+	$5,800

Transaction (8)   **After taking an inventory at the end of the month, Mr. Drew found that he**
January 31   **had used $200 worth of supplies.**   The original amount of supplies purchased has
                      been reduced to the amount that was found to be left at the end of the month. There-
                      fore, the difference was the amount used ($300 − $100 = $200). This reduces the
                      asset Supplies by $200 and reduces capital by the same amount. It is termed *supplies
                      expense*.

	Assets			=	Liabilities	+	Capital
Cash	+	Supplies	+ Furniture		Accounts Payable		T. Drew, Capital
$4,300		$−300	$2,000		$800		$5,800
(8)		−200					−200 Supplies Expense
$4,300	+	$ 100	+ $2,000	=	$800	+	$5,600

Transaction (9) **Withdrew $400 for personal use.** The withdrawal of cash is a reduction not only
January 31 in Mr. Drew's cash position but also in his capital. This is *not an expense* but a personal withdrawal, a reduction of the amount invested.

	Assets				=	Liabilities	+	Capital	
	Cash	+	Supplies	+	Furniture	Accounts Payable		T. Drew, Capital	
	$4,300		$100		$2,000	$800		$5,600	
(9)	−400							−400	Drawing
	$3,900	+	$100	+	$2,000	=	$800	+	$5,200	

T. Drew, Attorney
Month of January 19X5

	Assets					=	Liabilities	+	Capital	
	Cash	+	Supplies	+	Furniture		Accounts Payable		T. Drew, Capital	
(1)	$4,000								$4,000	
(2)	−300	+	$300							
	$3,700	+	$300			=			$4,000	
(3)					$2,000		$2,000			
	$3,700	+	$300	+	$2,000	=	$2,000	+	$4,000	
(4)	+2,500							+	2,500	Fees Income
	$6,200	+	$300	+	$2,000	=	$2,000	+	$6,500	
(5)	−500								−500	Rent Expense
	$5,700	+	$300	+	$2,000	=	$2,000	+	$6,000	
(6)	−200								−200	Salaries Expense
	$5,500	+	$300	+	$2,000	=	$2,000	+	$5,800	
(7)	−1,200						−1,200			
	$4,300	+	$300	+	$2,000	=	$800	+	$5,800	
(8)			−200						−200	Supplies Expense
	$4,300	+	$100	+	$2,000	=	$800	+	$5,600	
(9)	−400								−400	Drawing
	$3,900	+	$100	+	$2,000	=	$800	+	$5,200	

Summary

1. The accounting equation is _____ = _____ + _____ .

2. Items owned by a business that have money value are known as _____ .

3. _____ is the interest of the owners in a business.

4. Money owed to an outsider is a _____ .

5. The difference between assets and liabilities is _____ .

6. An investment in the business increases _____ and _____ .

7. To purchase "on account" is to create a _____ .

8. When the word "paid" occurs, it means a deduction of _____ .

9. Income increases net assets and also _____ .

10. A withdrawal of cash reduces cash and _____ .

Answers: 1. assets, liabilities, capital; 2. assets; 3. Capital; 4. liability; 5. capital; 6. assets and capital; 7. liability; 8. cash; 9. capital; 10. capital

Solved Problems

1.1   Given any two known elements, the third can easily be computed. Determine the missing amount in each of the accounting equations below.

	Assets	=	Liabilities	+	Capital
(a)	$ 7,200	=	$2,800	+	?
(b)	7,200	=	?	+	$4,400
(c)	?	=	2,800	+	4,400
(d)	20,000	=	5,600	+	?
(e)	18,000	=	?	+	6,000
(f)	?	=	4,280	+	8,420

SOLUTION

	Assets	=	Liabilities	+	Capital
(a)	$ 7,200	=	$2,800	+	$4,400
(b)	7,200	=	2,800	+	4,400
(c)	7,200	=	2,800	+	4,400
(d)	20,000	=	5,600	+	14,400
(e)	18,000	=	12,000	+	6,000
(f)	12,700	=	4,280	+	8,420

1.2   Classify each of the following as elements of the accounting equation using the following abbreviations: A = Assets; L = Liabilities; C = Capital.

(*a*)   Cash

(*b*)   Accounts Payable

(*c*)   Owners' Investment

(*d*)   Accounts Receivable

(*e*)   Supplies

(*f*)   Notes Payable

(*g*)   Land

(*h*)   Equipment

SOLUTION

(*a*) A	(*c*) C	(*e*) A	(*g*) A
(*b*) L	(*d*) A	(*f*) L	(*h*) A

1.3   Determine the effect of the following transactions on capital.

(*a*)   Bought machinery on account.

(*b*)   Paid the above bill.

(*c*)   Withdrew money for personal use.

(*d*)   Received fees for services rendered.

(*e*)   Bought supplies for cash.

(*f*)   Inventory of supplies decreased by the end of the month.

SOLUTION

(*a*) No effect—only the asset (machinery) and liability are affected (accounts payable).
(*b*) No effect—same reason.
(*c*) Decrease in capital—capital is withdrawn.
(*d*) Increase in capital—fees are income that increases capital.
(*e*) No effect—the asset cash is decreased while the asset supplies is increased.
(*f*) Decrease in capital—supplies that are used represent an expense (reduction in capital).

1.4   Determine the net effect of the transactions listed below, using I = increase; D = decrease; NE = no effect.

(*a*)   Invested cash in a business.

(*b*)   Purchased equipment for cash.

(*c*)   Purchased supplies on account.

(*d*)   Paid creditors.

(*e*)   Borrowed $5,000 from bank.

(*f*)   Received fees.

(*g*)   Withdrew money for personal use.

	Assets	=	Liabilities	+	Capital
(*a*)	_____		_____		_____
(*b*)	_____		_____		_____

	(c)	———		———		———
	(d)	———		———		———
	(e)	———		———		———
	(f)	———		———		———
	(g)	———		———		———

SOLUTION

	Assets	=	Liabilities	+	Capital
(a)	I		NE		I
(b)	NE		NE		NE
(c)	I		I		NE
(d)	D		D		NE
(e)	I		I		NE
(f)	I		NE		I
(g)	D		NE		D

1.5 T. Drew invests in his new firm $8,600 cash, $4,000 worth of supplies, equipment, and machinery valued at $12,000, and a $5,000 note payable based on the equipment and machinery. What is the capital of the firm?

SOLUTION

Assets	=	Liabilities	+	Capital
$ 8,600				
4,000				
12,000				
$24,600	=	$5,000	+	$19,600

1.6 Record the following entry: Bought an automobile for $14,000, paying $3,000 cash and giving a note for the balance.

	Assets		=	Liabilities	+	Capital
	Cash	Equipment		Notes Payable		
Balance	$15,000					$15,000
Entry (?)	———			———		———
Balance (?)						

SOLUTION

	Assets		=	Liabilities	+	Capital
	Cash	Equipment		Notes Payable		
Balance	$15,000					$15,000
Entry	−3,000	+ $14,000		$11,000*		———
Balance	$12,000	+ $14,000		$11,000	+	$15,000

*Total value of auto	$14,000
Less cash deposit	3,000
Amount owed	$11,000

1.7 Record the following entry: The inventory of supplies at the end of the year is valued at $2,200.

	Assets	=	Liabilities	+	Capital
	Supplies				
Balance					
(Beginning of month)	$6,400	=		+	$6,400
Entry (?)	_____				_____
Balance (?)					
(End of month)					

SOLUTION

	Assets	=	Liabilities	+	Capital	
	Supplies					
Balance						
(Beginning of month)	$6,400			+	$6,400	
Entry	−4,200				−4,200	Supplies Expense
Balance	$2,200				$2,200	
(End of month)						

Supplies is an asset. Supplies expense ($4,200) represents the amount that has been used. This amount is applied as a reduction in capital.

1.8 The summary data of the Ellery's laundry are presented below. Describe each transaction.

	Assets			=	Liabilities	+	Capital	
	Cash	+ Supplies	+ Machinery	=	Accounts Payable	+		
(1)	$8,000 +	$4,000 +	$ 5,000			+	$17,000	
(2)	−3,000 +	3,000						
(3)	−2,000 ×		+ 9,000		+7,000			
(4)	+9,000					+	9,000	Laundry Income
(5)	−1,200						−1,200	Salaries Expense
(6)		−2,000					−2,000	Supplies Expense
(7)	−7,000				−7,000			
(8)	−1,000						−1,000	Withdrawal
	$2,800	$5,000	$14,000	=	—	+	$21,800	

SOLUTION

(1) Invested cash, supplies, and machinery into the firm.
(2) Bought additional supplies for cash.
(3) Bought a $9,000 machine, paying $2,000 down and owing the balance.
(4) Income for the period.
(5) Paid salaries expense.
(6) Supplies inventory was determined.
(7) Paid in full amount owed (see transaction 3).
(8) Owner withdrew cash for personal use.

1.9 Summary financial data of the Rag Time Band Co. for October are presented below in transaction form.

(1) Began operations by depositing $22,000 in a business bank account.

(2) Purchased musical equipment for $10,000, paying $4,000 in cash with the balance on account.

(3) Purchased supplies for cash, $500.

(4) Cash income received for musical engagement, $3,000.

(5) Paid salaries for the month, $1,200.

(6) Paid general expenses, $600.

(7) Paid $1,000 on account (see transaction 2).

(8) The inventory of supplies on hand at the end of the month was $200.

Record the transactions and running balances below.

	Assets			=	**Liabilities**	+	**Capital**
	Cash	+ Supplies +	Equipment		Accounts Payable		Rag Time Band Co.
(1)							
(2)	_____		_____		_____		_____
Balance				=			
(3)	_____	_____	_____		_____		_____
Balance				=			
(4)	_____	_____	_____		_____		_____
Balance				=			
(5)	_____	_____	_____		_____		_____
Balance				=			
(6)	_____	_____	_____		_____		_____
Balance				=			
(7)	_____	_____	_____		_____		_____
Balance				=			
(8)	_____	_____	_____		_____		_____
Balance	_____	_____	_____	=	_____		_____

SOLUTION

	Assets			=	Liabilities	+	Capital
	Cash	+ Supplies	+ Equipment		Accounts Payable		Rag Time Band Co.
(1)	$22,000						$22,000
(2)	−4,000		+$10,000		+$6,000		
Balance	$18,000		$10,000	=	$6,000	+	$22,000
(3)	−500	$+500		=			
Balance	$17,500 +	$500 +	$10,000	=	$6,000	+	$22,000
(4)	+3,000						+3,000 Fees Income
Balance	$20,500 +	$500 +	$10,000	=	$6,000	+	$25,000
(5)	−1,200						−1,200 Salaries Expense
Balance	$19,300 +	$500 +	$10,000	=	$6,000	+	$23,800
(6)	−600						−600 General Expense
Balance	$18,700 +	$500 +	$10,000	=	$6,000	+	$23,200
(7)	−1,000				−1,000		
Balance	$17,700 +	$500 +	$10,000	=	$5,000	+	$23,200
(8)		−300					−300 Supplies Expense
Balance	$17,700 +	$200 +	$10,000	=	$5,000	+	$22,900

1.10 Robert Lawn has just passed the law exam and started practicing. Below are his first month's transactions.

Jan. 1 Began business by investing $5,000 cash and land with a value of $4,500.
   4 Purchased $750 worth of supplies on account.
   9 Paid rent for the month, $300.
   15 Received $1,100 for legal fees.
   17 Paid salaries for month, $1,900.
   21 Purchased printing equipment for $1,000 cash.
   24 Paid $500 on account.
   27 Withdrew $500 for personal expenses.
   29 Made improvements to land, paying $1,500 cash.
   31 Supplies on hand, $400.

Record the transactions and running balances in the form below.

	Assets					Liabilities		Capital,
	Cash +	Supplies +	Equipment +	Land	=	Accounts Payable	+	R. Lawn
Jan. 1								
4	___	___	___	___		___		___
Balance					=			
Jan. 9	___	___	___	___		___		___
Balance					=			
Jan. 15	___	___	___	___		___		___
Balance					=			
Jan. 17	___	___	___	___		___		___
Balance					=			

	Assets Cash + Supplies + Equipment + Land				=	**Liabilities** Accounts Payable	+	**Capital,** **R. Lawn**
Jan. 21	___	___	___	___		___		___
Balance					=			
Jan. 24	___	___	___	___		___		___
Balance					=			
Jan. 27	___	___	___	___		___		___
Balance					=			
Jan. 29	___	___	___	___		___		___
Balance					=			
Jan. 31	___	___	___	___		___		___
Balance					=			

SOLUTION

	Assets Cash + Supplies + Equipment + Land				=	**Liabilities** **Accounts** Payable	+	**Capital, R. Lawn**
Jan. 1	$5,000			$4,500				$9,500
4	___	+$750	___	___	=	+$750		___
Balance	$5,000	$750		$4,500		$750		$9,500
Jan. 9	−300	___	___	___	=	___		−300 Rent Expense
Balance	$4,700	$750		$4,500		$750		$9,200
Jan. 15	+1,100	___		___	=	___		+1,100 Fees Earned
Balance	$5,800	$750		$4,500		$750		$10,300
Jan. 17	−1,900	___	___	___	=	___		−1,900 Salaries Expense
Balance	$3,900	$750		$4,500		$750		$8,400
Jan. 21	−1,000	___	+1,000	___	=	___		___
Balance	$2,900	$750	$1,000	$4,500		$750		$8,400
Jan. 24	−500	___	___		=	−500		
Balance	$2,400	$750	$1,000	$4,500		$250		$8,400
Jan. 27	−500				=			−500 Drawing
Balance	$1,900	$750	$1,000	$4,500		$250		$7,900
Jan. 29	−1,500	___	___	+1,500	=	___		___
Balance	$ 400	$750	$1,000	$6,000		$250		$7,900
Jan. 31		−350			=			−350 Supplies Expense
Balance	$ 400	$400	$1,000	$6,000		$250		$7,550

1.11 Financial information of B. Glatt, Carpenter, for December is presented below.

    (1)   Began business by investing $14,000 cash and $6,000 equipment in the business.

    (2)   Bought additional equipment for $2,000 on account.

    (3)   Purchased supplies, $600, for cash.

    (4)   Paid $500 to creditor on account.

    (5)   Received $2,400 in fees earned during the month.

    (6)   Paid salary of part-time assistant, $300.

    (7)   Paid general expenses, $400.

    (8)   Paid balance due on equipment.

    (9)   Withdrew $700 for personal use.

  (10)   Cost of supplies used during month, $450.

Enter each transaction in the form below.

	Assets			=	Liabilities	+	Capital
	Cash	+ Supplies	+ Equipment		Accounts Payable		B. Glatt, Capital
(1)							
(2)	_____	_____	_____		_____		_____
Balance				=			
(3)	_____	_____	_____		_____		_____
Balance				=			
(4)	_____	_____	_____		_____		_____
Balance				=			
(5)	_____	_____	_____		_____		_____
Balance				=			
(6)	_____	_____	_____		_____		_____
Balance				=			
(7)	_____	_____	_____		_____		_____
Balance				=			
(8)	_____	_____	_____		_____		_____
Balance				=			
(9)	_____	_____	_____		_____		_____
Balance				=			
(10)	_____	_____	_____		_____		_____
Balance	======	======	======	=	======		======

SOLUTION

	Assets			=	Liabilities	+	Capital	
	Cash	+ Supplies +	Equipment		Accounts Payable		B. Glatt, Capital	
(1)	$14,000		$6,000				$20,000	
(2)			+2,000	=	+$2,000			
Balance	$14,000 +	+	$8,000	=	$2,000	+	$20,000	
(3)	−600	$+600						
Balance	$13,400 +	$600 +	$8,000	=	$2,000	+	$20,000	
(4)	−500				−500			
Balance	$12,900 +	$600 +	$8,000	=	$1,500	+	$20,000	
(5)	+2,400						+2,400	Fees Income
Balance	$15,300 +	$600 +	$8,000	=	$1,500	+	$22,400	
(6)	−300						−300	Salaries Expense
Balance	$15,000 +	$600 +	$8,000	=	$1,500	+	$22,100	
(7)	−400						−400	General Expense
Balance	$14,600 +	$600 +	$8,000	=	$1,500	+	$21,700	
(8)	−1,500				−1,500			
Balance	$13,100 +	$600 +	$8,000	=	—	+	$21,700	
(9)	−700						−700	Drawing
Balance	$12,400 +	$600 +	$8,000	=	—	+	$21,000	
(10)		−450					−450	Supplies Expense
Balance	$12,400 +	$150 +	$8,000	=	—	+	$20,550	

1.12 M. Boyd operates a taxi company known as the Boyd Taxi Co. The balances of his accounts as of July 1 of the current year are as follows: cash, $6,400; supplies, $800; automobile, $4,500; accounts payable, $2,000; capital, $9,700. The transactions of the firm during the month of July appear below.

(1) Paid the balance owed to the creditor.

(2) Income (cash) for the month, $8,200.

(3) Paid wages for the month, $1,900.

(4) Paid for advertising, $200.

(5) Purchased an additional used taxi for $5,000, terms half in cash and the balance on account.

(6) Paid $425 for maintenance of automobiles.

(7) Sold $100 of our supplies at cost as an accommodation.

(8) Withdrew $800 for personal use.

(9) Inventory of supplies at the end of the month was $350.

Enter each transaction on the accompanying form.

	Assets				**=**	**Liabilities**	**+**	**Capital**
	Cash	+	Supplies	+	Automobiles	Accounts Payable		Capital
Balance	$ 6,400		$800		$4,500	$2,000		$ 9,700
(1)	_____		_____		_____	_____		_____
Balance						=	+	
(2)	_____		_____		_____	_____		_____
Balance						=	+	
(3)	_____		_____		_____	_____		_____
Balance						=	+	
(4)	_____		_____		_____	_____		_____
Balance						=	+	
(5)	_____		_____		_____	_____		_____
Balance						=	+	
(6)	_____		_____		_____	_____		_____
Balance						=	+	
(7)	_____		_____		_____	_____		_____
Balance						=	+	
(8)	_____		_____		_____	_____		_____
Balance						=	+	
(9)	_____		_____		_____	_____		_____
Balance	======		======		======	= ======	+	======

SOLUTION

	Assets			=	Liabilities	+ Capital	
	Cash	+ Supplies	+ Automobiles		Accounts Payable	Capital	
Balance	$ 6,400 +	$800 +	$4,500	=	$2,000	+ $ 9,700	
(1)	−2,000				−2,000		
Balance	$ 4,400 +	$800 +	$4,500	=	$ —	+ $ 9,700	
(2)	+8,200					+8,200	Fee Income
Balance	$12,600 +	$800 +	$4,500	=	$ —	+ $17,900	
(3)	−1,900					−1,900	Wages Expense
Balance	$10,700 +	$800 +	$4,500	=	$ —	+ $16,000	
(4)	−200					−200	Advertising Expense
Balance	$10,500 +	$800 +	$4,500	=	$ —	+ $15,800	
(5)	−2,500		+5,000		+$2,500		
Balance	$ 8,000 +	$800 +	$9,500	=	$2,500	+ $15,800	
(6)	−425					−425	Maintenance Expense
Balance	$ 7,575 +	$800 +	$9,500	=	$2,500	+ $15,375	
(7)	+100	−100					
Balance	$ 7,675 +	$700 +	$9,500	=	$2,500	+ $15,375	
(8)	−800					−800	Drawing
Balance	$ 6,875 +	$700 +	$9,500	=	$2,500	+ $14,575	
(9)		−350				350	Supplies Expense
Balance	$ 6,875 +	$350 +	$9,500	=	$2,500	+ $14,225	

Chapter 2

Debits and Credits: The Double-Entry System

2.1 INTRODUCTION

Preparing a new equation $A = L + C$ after each transaction would be cumbersome and costly, especially when there are a great many transactions in an accounting period. Also, information for a specific item such as cash would be lost as successive transactions were recorded. This information could be obtained by going back and summarizing the transactions, but that would be very time-consuming. Thus we begin with the *account*.

2.2 THE ACCOUNT

An account may be defined as *a record of the increases, decreases, and balances in an individual item of asset, liability, capital, income (revenue), or expense.*

The simplest form of the account is known as the "T" account because it resembles the letter "T." The account has three parts: (1) the name of the account and the account number, (2) the debit side (left side), and (3) the credit side (right side). The increases are entered on one side, the decreases on the other. The balance (the excess of the total of one side over the total of the other) is inserted near the last figure on the side with the larger amount.

							1 Account Number
			1 Account Title				
Date	Item	Ref.	Debit	Date	Item	Ref.	Credit

2   3

EXAMPLE 1

Cash

700	600
400	200
600	*800*
900 *1,700*	

Note that the left side of the account adds up to $1,700, while the right side totals $800. The $1,700 and $800 totals, respectively, are written in smaller type and are known as footings. The difference between the total amounts is $900 and is called the ending balance. Since the larger total $1,700 appears on the left side of the account, the ending balance of $900 is placed there. Had the right side total been greater than the left, the ending balance would have appeared on the right side.

2.3 DEBITS AND CREDITS

When an amount is entered on the left side of an account, it is a debit, and the account is said to be *debited*. When an amount is entered on the right side, it is a credit, and the account is said to be *credited*. The abbreviations for debit and credit are *Dr.* and *Cr.*, respectively.

Whether an increase in a given item is credited or debited depends on the category of the item. By convention, asset and expense increases are recorded as debits, whereas liability, capital, and income increases are recorded as credits. Asset and expense decreases are recorded as credits, whereas liability, capital, and income decreases are recorded as debits. The following tables summarize the rule.

Assets and Expenses		Liabilities, Capital, and Income	
Dr.	Cr.	Dr.	Cr.
+	−	−	+
(Increases)	(Decreases)	(Decreases)	(Increases)

EXAMPLE 2

Let us reexamine the transactions that occurred in T. Drew's practice during the first month of operation. These are the same as in Chapter 1, except that accounts are now used to record the transactions.

Transaction (1)
January 1

Mr. Drew opened his law practice, investing $4,000 in cash. The two accounts affected are Cash and Capital. Remember that an increase in an asset (cash) is debited, whereas an increase in capital is credited.

Cash			Capital		
Dr.	Cr.		Dr.	Cr.	
+	−		−	+	
(1) 4,000				4,000	(1)

Transaction (2)
January 4

Bought supplies for cash, $300. Here we are substituting one asset (cash) for another asset (supplies). We debit Supplies because we are receiving more supplies. We credit Cash because we are paying out cash.

Cash			Supplies		
Dr.	Cr.		Dr.	Cr.	
+	−		+	−	
4,000	300	(2)	(2) 300		

Transaction (3)
January 5

Bought furniture from Robinson Furniture Company on account, $2,000. We are receiving an asset and, therefore, debit Furniture to show the increase. We are not paying cash but creating a new liability, thereby increasing the liability account (Accounts Payable).

Furniture			Accounts Payable		
Dr.	Cr.		Dr.	Cr.	
+	−		−	+	
(3) 2,000				2,000	(3)

Transaction (4)
January 15

Received $2,500 in fees earned during the month. In this case, we are increasing the asset account Cash, since we have received $2,500. Therefore, we debit it. We are increasing the capital, yet we do not credit Capital. It is better temporarily to separate the income from the owners' equity (capital) and create a new account, Fees Income (also known as Revenue).

	Cash				Fees Income	
	Dr.	Cr.			Dr.	Cr.
	+	−			−	+
	4,000	300				2,500	(4)
(4)	2,500					

Transaction (5)
January 30

Paid office rent for January, $500. We must decrease the asset account Cash because we are paying out money. Therefore, we credit it. It is preferable to keep expenses separated from the owners' equity. Therefore, we open a new account for the expense involved, Rent Expense. The $500 is entered on the left side, since expense decreases capital.

	Cash				Rent Expense	
	Dr.	Cr.			Dr.	Cr.
	+	−			+	−
	4,000	300		(5)	500	
	2,500	500	(5)			

Transaction (6)
January 30

Paid salary for part-time help, $200. Again, we must reduce our asset account Cash because we are paying out money. Therefore, we credit the account. Drew's capital was reduced by an expense; thus we open another account, Salaries Expense. A debit to this account shows the decrease in capital.

	Cash				Salaries Expense	
	Dr.	Cr.			Dr.	Cr.
	+	−			+	−
	4,000	300		(6)	200	
	2,500	500				
		200	(6)			

Transaction (7)
January 31

Paid $1,200 to Robinson Furniture Company on account. This transaction reduced our asset account Cash since we are paying out money. We therefore credit Cash. We also reduce our liability account Accounts Payable by $1,200; we now owe that much less. Thus, we debit Accounts Payable.

	Cash				Accounts Payable	
	Dr.	Cr.			Dr.	Cr.
	+	−			−	+
	4,000	300		(7)	1,200	2,000
	2,500	500				
		200				
		1,200	(7)			

Transaction (8)
January 31

After taking inventory at the end of the month, Mr. Drew found that he had used $200 worth of supplies. We must reduce the asset account Supplies by crediting it for $200. Supplies Expense is debited for the decrease in capital. This is computed as follows: Beginning inventory of $300, less supplies on hand at the end of the month $100, indicates that $200 must have been used during the month.

Supplies				Supplies Expense	
Dr.	Cr.			Dr.	Cr.
+	–			+	–
300	200	(8)	(8)	200	

Transaction (9)
January 31

Withdrew $400 for personal use. The withdrawal of cash means that there is a reduction in the asset account Cash. Therefore, it is credited. The amount invested by the owner is also $400 less. We must open the account Drawing, which is debited to show the decrease in capital.

Cash				Drawing	
Dr.	Cr.			Dr.	Cr.
+	–			+	–
4,000	300	(9)		400	
2,500	500				
	200				
	1,200				
	400	(9)			

An account has a debit balance when the sum of its debits exceeds the sum of its credits; it has a credit balance when the sum of the credits is the greater. In *double-entry accounting,* which is in almost universal use, there are equal debit and credit entries for every transaction. Where only two accounts are affected, the debit and credit amounts are equal. If more than two accounts are affected, the total of the debit entries must equal the total of the credit entries.

2.4 THE LEDGER

The complete set of accounts for a business entry is called a *ledger.* It is the "reference book" of the accounting system and is used to classify and summarize transactions and to prepare data for financial statements. It is also a valuable source of information for managerial purposes, giving, for example, the amount of sales for the period or the cash balance at the end of the period.

2.5 THE CHART OF ACCOUNTS

It is desirable to establish a systematic method of identifying and locating each account in the ledger. The *chart of accounts,* sometimes called the *code of accounts,* is a listing of the accounts by title and numerical designation. In some companies, the chart of accounts may run to hundreds of items.

In designing a numbering structure for the accounts, it is important to provide adequate flexibility to permit expansion without having to revise the basic system. Generally, blocks of numbers are assigned to various groups of accounts, such as assets, liabilities, and so on. There are various systems of coding, depending on the needs and desires of the company.

EXAMPLE 3

A simple chart structure is to have the first digit represent the major group in which the account is located. Thus, accounts that have numbers beginning with 1 are assets; 2, liabilities; 3, capital; 4, income; and 5, expenses. The second or third digit designates the position of the account in the group.

In the two-digit system, assets are assigned the block of numbers 11–19, and liabilities 21–29. In larger firms, a three-digit (or higher) system may be used, with assets assigned 101–199 and liabilities 201–299. Following are the numerical designations for the account groups under both methods.

Account Group	Two-Digit	Three-Digit
1. Assets	11–19	101–199
2. Liabilities	21–29	201–299
3. Capital	31–39	301–399
4. Income	41–49	401–499
5. Expenses	51–59	501–599

Thus, Cash may be account 11 under the first system and 101 under the second system. The cash account may be further broken down as: 101, Cash—First National Bank; 102, Cash—Second National Bank; and so on.

2.6   THE TRIAL BALANCE

As every transaction results in an equal amount of debits and credits in the ledger, the total of all debit entries in the ledger should equal the total of all credit entries. At the end of the accounting period, we check this equality by preparing a two-column schedule called a *trial balance,* which compares the total of all debit balances with the total of all credit balances. The procedure is as follows:

1. List account titles in numerical order.
2. Record balances of each account, entering debit balances in the left column and credit balances in the right column.

    Note: Asset and expense accounts are debited for increases and normally would have debit balances. Liabilities, capital, and income accounts are credited for increases and normally would have credit balances.
3. Add the columns and record the totals.
4. Compare the totals. They must be the same.

If the totals agree, the trial balance is in balance, indicating that debits and credits are equal for the hundreds or thousands of transactions entered in the ledger. While the trial balance provides arithmetic proof of the accuracy of the records, it does not provide theoretical proof. For example, if the purchase of equipment was incorrectly charged to Expense, the trial balance columns may agree, but theoretically the accounts would be wrong, as Expense would be overstated and Equipment understated. In addition to providing proof of arithmetic accuracy in accounts, the trial balance facilitates the preparation of the periodic financial statements. Generally, the trial balance comprises the first two columns of a worksheet, from which financial statements are prepared. The worksheet procedure is discussed in Chapter 8.

EXAMPLE 4

The summary of the transactions for Mr. Drew (see Example 2), and their effect on the accounts, is shown below. The trial balance is then taken.

Assets

Cash			11
(1)	4,000	300	(2)
(4)	2,500	500	(5)
3,900	6,500	200	(6)
		1,200	(7)
		400	(9)
		2,600	

Supplies			12
(2)	300	200	(8)
100			

Furniture		13
(3)	2,000	

Liabilities

Accounts Payable			21
(7)	1,200	2,000	(3)
		800	

Capital

Capital			31
		4,000	(1)

Drawing		32
(9)	400	

Fees Income			41
		2,500	(4)

Rent Expense		51
(5)	500	

Salaries Expense		52
(6)	200	

Supplies Expense		53
(8)	200	

T. Drew
Trial Balance
January 31, 19X5

	Dr.	Cr.
Cash	$3,900	
Supplies	100	
Furniture	2,000	
Accounts Payable		$ 800
T. Drew, Capital		4,000
Drawing	400	
Fees Income		2,500
Rent Expense	500	
Salaries Expense	200	
Supplies Expense	200	
	$7,300	$7,300

Summary

1. To classify and summarize a single item of an account group, we use a form called an _____ .

2. The accounts make up a record called a _____ .

3. The left side of the account is known as the _____ , while the right side is the _____ .

4. Increases in all asset accounts are _____ .

5. Increases in all liability accounts are _____ .

6. Increases in all capital accounts are _____ .

7. Increases in all income accounts are _____ .

8. Increases in all expense accounts are _____ .

9. Expenses are debited because they decrease _____ .

10. The schedule showing the balance of each account at the end of the period is known as the _____ .

Answers: 1. account; 2. ledger; 3. debit side, credit side; 4. debited; 5. credited; 6. credited; 7. credited; 8. debited; 9. capital; 10. trial balance

Solved Problems

2.1 In each of the following types of T accounts, enter an increase (by writing +) and a decrease (by writing −).

Assets			Liabilities			Capital	
Dr.	Cr.		Dr.	Cr.		Dr.	Cr.

Income			Expense	
Dr.	Cr.		Dr.	Cr.

SOLUTION

Assets			Liabilities			Capital	
Dr.	Cr.		Dr.	Cr.		Dr.	Cr.
+	−		−	+		−	+

Income			Expense	
Dr.	Cr.		Dr.	Cr.
−	+		+	−

2.2   Below is a list of accounts. Rearrange the accounts as they would appear in the ledger and assign a numerical designation for each one from these numbers: 17, 22, 32, 59, 12, 51, 41, 11, 21, 31.

Accounts

Accounts Payable

Accounts Receivable

Capital

Cash

Drawing

Equipment

Fees Income

Miscellaneous Expense

Notes Payable

Rent Expense

SOLUTION

Accounts	Designated Number
Cash	11
Accounts Receivable	12
Equipment	17
Accounts Payable	21
Notes Payable	22
Capital	31
Drawing	32
Fees Income	41
Rent Expense	51
Miscellaneous Expense	59

2.3 Indicate in the columns below the increases and decreases in each account by placing a check mark in the appropriate column.

		Debit	Credit
(a)	Capital is increased		
(b)	Cash is decreased		
(c)	Accounts Payable is increased		
(d)	Rent Expense is increased		
(e)	Equipment is increased		
(f)	Fees Income is increased		
(g)	Capital is decreased (through drawing)		

SOLUTION

(a) Cr. (b) Cr. (c) Cr. (d) Dr. (e) Dr. (f) Cr. (g) Dr.

2.4 For each transaction in the table below, indicate the account to be debited and the account to be credited by placing the letter representing the account in the appropriate column.

Name of Account		Transaction	Dr.	Cr.
(a)	Accounts Payable	1. Invested cash in the firm		
(b)	Capital	2. Paid rent for month		
(c)	Cash	3. Received cash fees for services		
(d)	Drawing	4. Paid salaries		
(e)	Equipment	5. Bought equipment on account		
(f)	Fees Income	6. Paid balance on equipment		
(g)	Notes Payable	7. Bought supplies on account		
(h)	Rent Expense	8. Borrowed money from bank, giving a note in exchange		
(i)	Salaries Expense	9. Supplies inventory showed one-third used during the month		
(j)	Supplies	10. Withdrew cash for personal use		
(k)	Supplies Expense			

SOLUTION

	Dr.	Cr.
1.	(c)	(b)
2.	(h)	(c)
3.	(c)	(f)
4.	(i)	(c)
5.	(e)	(a)
6.	(a)	(c)
7.	(j)	(a)
8.	(c)	(g)
9.	(k)	(j)
10.	(d)	(c)

2.5 Record each *separate transaction* in the accompanying accounts.

(a) Bought supplies on account for $600.

(b) Bought equipment for $2,700, paying one-third down and owing the balance.

(c) Gave a note in settlement of transaction (b).

(d) Received $500 in plumbing fees.

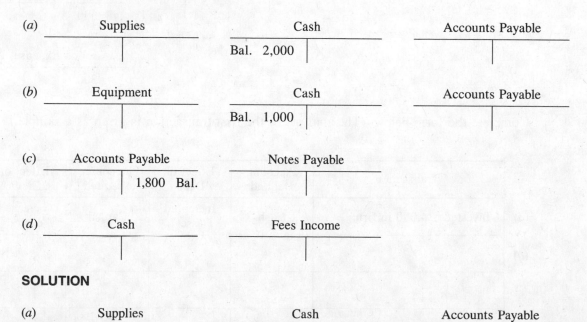

SOLUTION

(a)
Supplies		Cash		Accounts Payable	
600		Bal. 2,000			600

(b)

Equipment		Cash		Accounts Payable	
2,700		Bal. 1,000	900		1,800

(c)

Accounts Payable		Notes Payable	
1,800	1,800 Bal.		1,800

(d)

Cash		Fees Income	
500			500

2.6 The ten accounts that follow summarize the first week's transactions of the Charles Taxi Company.

	Cash		
(a)	14,000	10,000	(b)
(e)	1,000	200	(d)
		300	(f)
		500	(g)
		100	(h)
		2,000	(i)
		300	(j)

	Supplies	
(d)	200	

	Equipment	
(b)	10,000	
(c)	6,000	

	Accounts Payable		
(i)	2,000	6,000	(c)

Capital		
	14,000	(a)

	Drawing	
(h)	100	

Fees Income		
	1,000	(e)

	Salaries Expense	
(f)	300	

	Rent Expense	
(g)	500	

	Gasoline Expense	
(j)	300	

Complete the form below. (The analysis of the first transaction is given as a sample.)

	Transaction	Account Debited	Effect of Debit	Account Credited	Effect of Credit
(a)	Invested $14,000 in firm	Cash	Increased asset	Capital	Increased capital
(b)					
(c)					
(d)					
(e)					

	Transaction	Account Debited	Effect of Debit	Account Credited	Effect of Credit
(f)					
(g)					
(h)					
(i)					
(j)					

SOLUTION

	Transaction	Account Debited	Effect of Debit	Account Credited	Effect of Credit
(a)	Invested $14,000 in firm	Cash	Increased asset	Capital	Increased capital
(b)	Bought $10,000 of equipment of cash	Equipment	Increased asset	Cash	Decreased asset
(c)	Bought $6,000 of additional equipment on account	Equipment	Increased asset	Accounts Payable	Increased liability
(d)	Paid $200 for supplies	Supplies	Increased asset	Cash	Decreased asset
(e)	Received $1,000 in fees	Cash	Increased asset	Fees Income	Increased income
(f)	Paid $300 for salaries	Salaries Expense	Increased expense	Cash	Decreased asset
(g)	Paid $500 for rent	Rent Expense	Increased expense	Cash	Decreased asset
(h)	Withdrew $100 for personal use	Drawing	Decreased capital	Cash	Decreased asset
(i)	Paid $2,000 on account	Accounts Payable	Decreased liability	Cash	Decreased asset
(j)	Paid $300 for gasoline	Gasoline Expense	Increased expense	Cash	Decreased asset

2.7 Rearrange the following alphabetical list of the accounts and produce a trial balance.

Accounts Payable	$ 9,000	General Expense	1,000
Accounts Receivable	14,000	Notes Payable	11,000
Capital, P. Henry	32,000	Rent Expense	5,000
Cash	20,000	Salaries Expense	8,000
Drawing, P. Henry	4,000	Supplies	6,000
Equipment	18,000	Supplies Expense	2,000
Fees Income	26,000		

SOLUTION

	Dr.	Cr.
Cash	$20,000	
Accounts Receivable	14,000	
Supplies	6,000	
Equipment	18,000	
Accounts Payable		$ 9,000
Notes Payable		11,000
P. Henry, Capital		32,000
P. Henry, Drawing	4,000	
Fees Income		26,000
Salaries Expense	8,000	
Rent Expense	5,000	
Supplies Expense	2,000	
General Expense	1,000	
	$78,000	$78,000

2.8 The M. Ramirez Company's trial balance appears below. Certain accounts have been recorded improperly from the ledger to the trial balance, causing it not to balance. Present a corrected trial balance based on normal balances of each account.

M. Ramirez
Trial Balance
January 31, 19X5

	Dr.	Cr.
Cash	$29,000	
Accounts Receivable		$ 4,000
Accounts Payable	3,000	
Capital		12,500
Drawing		500
Fees Income	33,000	
Rent Expense	1,000	
Salaries Expense	10,000	
General Expense		4,000
	$76,000	$21,000

SOLUTION

M. Ramirez
Trial Balance
January 31, 19X5

	Dr.	Cr.
Cash	$29,000	
Accounts Receivable	4,000	
Accounts Payable		$ 3,000
Capital		12,500
Drawing	500	
Fees Income		33,000
Rent Expense	1,000	
Salaries Expense	10,000	
General Expense	4,000	
	$48,500	$48,500

2.9 The trial balance of P. Johnson does not balance as presented. In reviewing the ledger, you discover the following:

(1) The debits and credits in the cash account total $24,100 and $21,400, respectively.

(2) The $400 received in settlement of an account was not posted to the Accounts Receivable account.

(3) The balance of the Salaries Expense account should be $200 less.

(4) No balance should exist in the Notes Payable account.

(5) Each account should have a normal balance.

Prepare a corrected trial balance.

P. Johnson
Trial Balance
December 31, 19X5

	Dr.	Cr.
Cash	$ 3,000	
Accounts Receivable	11,800	
Supplies		$ 800
Equipment	18,500	
Accounts Payable		1,500
Notes Payable		300
Johnson, Capital		15,400
Johnson, Drawing		500
Fees Income		29,000
Salaries Expense	8,200	
Rent Expense	3,000	
Supplies Expense		200
General Expense		800
	$44,500	$48,500

SOLUTION

P. Johnson
Trial Balance
December 31, 19X5

	Dr.	Cr.
Cash	$ 2,700	
Accounts Receivable	11,400	
Supplies	800	
Equipment	18,500	
Accounts Payable		$ 1,500
Notes Payable		
Johnson, Capital		15,400
Johnson, Drawing	500	
Fees Income		29,000
Salaries Expense	8,000	
Rent Expense	3,000	
Supplies Expense	200	
General Expense	800	
	$45,900	$45,900

2.10 Using the information of Problem 1.11, record the entries in the accounts below for B. Glatt, labeling each item by number as in Problem 1.11. Then prepare a trial balance.

Cash	Equipment	Fees Income

	Accounts Payable	Supplies Expense

	Capital	Salaries Expense

Supplies	Drawing	General Expense

B. Glatt
Trial Balance
December 31, 19X5

Cash		
Supplies		
Equipment		
Accounts Payable		
Capital		
Drawing		
Fees Income		
Rent Expense		
Salaries Expense		

SOLUTION

Cash				
(1)	14,000	600	(3)
(5)	2,400	500	(4)
12,400	16,400	300	(6)
		400	(7)
		1,500	(8)
		700	(9)
		4,000	

Equipment		
(1)	6,000	
(2)	2,000	
	8,000	

Accounts Payable			
(4)	500	2,000	(2)
(8)	1,500		

Capital		
	20,000	(1)

Fees Income		
	2,400	(5)

Supplies Expense		
(10)	450	

Salaries Expense		
(6)	300	

Supplies			
(3)	600	450	(10)
	150		

Drawing		
(9)	700	

General Expense		
(7)	400	

B. Glatt
Trial Balance
December 31, 19X5

Cash	$12,400	
Supplies	150	
Equipment	8,000	
Capital		$20,000
Drawing	700	
Fees Income		2,400
Supplies Expense	450	
Salaries Expense	300	
General Expense	400	
	$22,400	$22,400

2.11 For each transaction below, record the entry in the T accounts furnished.

(1) The Nu-Look Dry Cleaning Company opened a business bank account by depositing $12,000 on Nov. 1.

(2) Purchased supplies for cash, $220.

(3) Purchased dry cleaning equipment for $3,500, paying $1,500 in cash with the balance on account.

(4) Paid rent for the month, $425.

(5) Cash sales for the month totaled $1,850.

(6) Paid salaries of $375.

(7) Paid $500 on account.

(8) The cost of supplies used was determined to be $60.

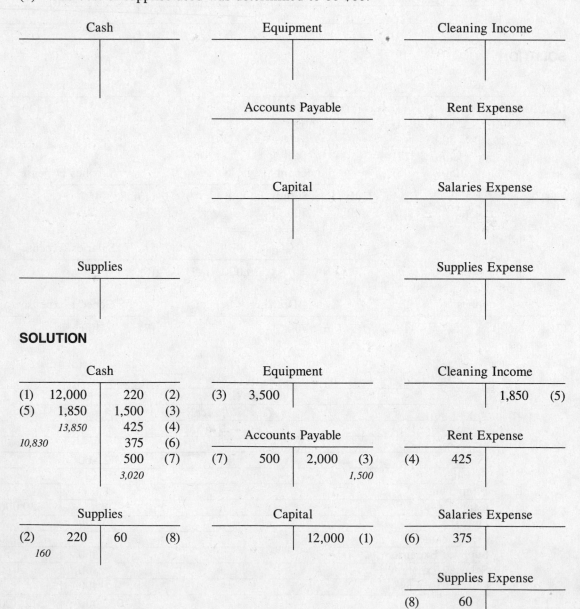

SOLUTION

2.12 Prepare a trial balance as of November 30 for the Nu-Look Dry Cleaning Company, using the account balances in Problem 2.11.

Nu-Look Dry Cleaning Company		
Trial Balance		
November 30, 19X5		
Cash		
Supplies		
Equipment		
Accounts Payable		
Nu-Look Dry Cleaning Company, Capital		
Cleaning Income		
Rent Expense		
Salaries Expense		
Supplies Expense		

SOLUTION

Nu-Look Dry Cleaning Company		
Trial Balance		
November 30, 19X5		
Cash	$10,830	
Supplies	160	
Equipment	3,500	
Accounts Payable		$ 1,500
Nu-Look Dry Cleaning Company, Capital		12,000
Cleaning Income		1,850
Rent Expense	425	
Salaries Expense	375	
Supplies Expense	60	
	$15,350	$15,350

Chapter 3

Journalizing and Posting Transactions

3.1 INTRODUCTION

In the preceding chapters, we discussed the nature of business transactions and the manner in which they are analyzed and classified. The primary emphasis was the "why" rather than the "how" of accounting operations; we aimed at an understanding of the reason for making the entry in a particular way. We showed the effects of transactions by making entries in T accounts. However, these entries do not provide the necessary data for a particular transaction, nor do they provide a chronological record of transactions. The missing information is furnished by the use of an accounting form known as the *journal*.

3.2 THE JOURNAL

The *journal,* or *day book,* is the book of original entry for accounting data. Afterward, the data is transferred or posted to the ledger, the book of subsequent or secondary entry. The various transactions are evidenced by sales tickets, purchase invoices, check stubs, and so on. On the basis of this evidence, the transactions are entered in chronological order in the journal. The process is called *journalizing.*

A number of different journals may be used in a business. For our purposes, they may be grouped into (1) general journals and (2) specialized journals. The latter type, which are used in businesses with a large number of repetitive transactions, are described in Chapter 6. To illustrate journalizing, we here use the *general journal,* whose standard form is shown below.

	General Journal			Page J-1*
Date (1)	Description (2)	P.R. (3)	Debit (4)	Credit (5)
19X5 Oct. 7	Cash	11	$10,000	
	Barbara Ledina, Capital	31		$10,000
	(6) Invested cash in the business			

*Denotes general journal, page 1.

3.3 JOURNALIZING

We describe the entries in the general journal according to the numbering in the table above.

(1) **Date.** The year, month, and day of the first entry are written in the date column. The year and month do not have to be repeated for the additional entries until a new month occurs or a new page is needed.

(2) **Description.** The account title to be debited is entered on the first line, next to the date column. The name of the account to be credited is entered on the line below and indented.

34

(3) **P.R. (Posting Reference).**   Nothing is entered in this column until the particular entry is posted, that is, until the amounts are transferred to the related ledger accounts. The posting process will be described in Section 3.4.

(4) **Debit.**   The debit amount for each account is entered in this column. Generally, there is only one item, but there could be two or more separate items.

(5) **Credit.**   The credit amount for each account is entered in this column. Here again, there is generally only one account, but there could be two or more accounts involved with different amounts.

(6) **Explanation.**   A brief description of the transaction is usually made on the line below the credit. Generally, a blank line is left between the explanation and the next entry.

EXAMPLE 1

To help in understanding the operation of the general journal, let us journalize the transactions previously described for Mr. Drew's law practice on page 2. They are printed again below.

During the month of January, Ted Drew, Lawyer,

Jan. 1   Invested $4,000 to open his practice.
    4   Bought supplies (stationery, forms, pencils, and so on) for cash, $300.
    5   Bought office furniture from Robinson Furniture Company on account, $2,000.
   15   Received $2,500 in fees earned during the month.
   30   Paid office rent for January, $500.
   30   Paid salary for part-time help, $200.
   31   Paid $1,200 to Robinson Furniture Company on account.
   31   After taking an inventory at the end of the month, Drew found that he had used $200 worth of supplies.
   31   Withdrew $400 for personal use.

Date	Description	P.R.	Debit	Credit
19X5				
Jan. 1	Cash		4,000	
	T. Drew, Capital			4,000
	Investment in law practice			
4	Supplies		300	
	Cash			300
	Bought supplies for cash			
5	Furniture		2,000	
	Accounts Payable			2,000
	Bought furniture from Robinson Furniture Co.			
15	Cash		2,500	
	Fees Income			2,500
	Received payment for services			
30	Rent Expense		500	
	Cash			500
	Paid rent for month			

(continued)

Date	Description	P.R.	Debit	Credit
30	Salaries Expense		200	
	Cash			200
	Paid salaries of part-time help			
31	Accounts Payable		1,200	
	Cash			1,200
	Payment on account to Robinson Furniture Co.			
31	Supplies Expense		200	
	Supplies			200
	Supplies used during month			
31	T. Drew, Drawing		400	
	Cash			400
	Personal withdrawal			

3.4 POSTING

The process of transferring information from the journal to the ledger for the purpose of summarizing is called *posting* and is ordinarily carried out in the following steps:

(1) *Record the amount and date.* The date and the amounts of the debits and credits are entered in the appropriate accounts.

General Journal   Page J-1

Date	Description	P.R.	Dr.	Cr.
Jan. 1	Cash		4,000	
	T. Drew, Capital			4,000

      Cash   11   T. Drew, Capital   31

Jan. 1 4,000   Jan. 1 4,000

(2) *Record the posting reference in the account.* The number of the journal page is entered in the account (broken arrows below).

(3) *Record the posting in the journal.* For cross-referencing, the code number of the account is now entered in the P.R. column of the journal (solid arrows). These numbers are called post reference or folio numbers.

General Journal   Page J-1

Date	Description	P.R.	Dr.	Cr.
Jan. 1	Cash	11	4,000	
	T. Drew, Capital	31		4,000

      Cash   11   T. Drew, Capital   31

J-1   4,000   J-1   4,000

EXAMPLE 2

The results of the posting from the journal appear below.

Assets	=	Liabilities	+	Capital

Cash   11

Jan. 1	4,000	Jan. 4	300
15	2,500	30	500
3,900	*6,500*	30	200
		31	1,200
		31	400
			2,600

Supplies   12

Jan. 4	300	Jan. 31	200
100			

Furniture   13

Jan. 5	2,000

Accounts Payable   21

Jan. 31	1,200	Jan. 5	2,000
			800

T. Drew, Capital   31

	Jan. 1	4,000

T. Drew, Drawing   32

Jan. 31	400	

Fees Income   41

	Jan. 15	2,500

Rent Expense   51

Jan. 30	500	

Salaries Expense   52

Jan. 30	200	

Supplies Expense   53

Jan. 31	200	

T. Drew
Trial Balance
January 31, 19X5

	Debit	Credit
Cash	$3,900	
Supplies on Hand	100	
Furniture	2,000	
Accounts Payable		$ 800
T. Drew, Capital		4,000
T. Drew, Drawing	400	
Fees Income		2,500
Rent Expense	500	
Salaries Expense	200	
Supplies Expense	200	
	$7,300	$7,300

Summary

1. The initial book for recording all transactions is known as the _____ .

2. Another name and description of the journal is _____ .

3. The process of transferring information from the journal to the ledger is known as
   _____ .

4. The list of code numbers that identifies the entries in the journal is called the
   _____ .

5. Asset account numbers begin with the number _____ , whereas liabilities begin
   with _____ .

6. All capital account numbers begin with the number _____ .

7. All income account numbers begin with _____ , whereas expense account numbers
   begin with _____ .

8. The process of recording transactions in the journal is termed _____ .

9. The complete process of accounting is called the _____ .

10. Journals may be grouped into two different classifications. They are _____ and
    _____ .

Answers: 1. journal; 2. book of original entry; 3. posting; 4. chart of accounts; 5. 1, 2; 6. 3; 7. 4, 5;
            8. journalizing; 9. accounting cycle; 10. general, specialized

Solved Problems

3.1   On the line below each entry, write a brief explanation of the transaction that might appear
          in the general journal.

		Debit	Credit
(a)	Equipment	10,000	
	Cash		2,000
	Accounts Payable, William Smith		8,000
(b)	Accounts Payable, William Smith	8,000	
	Notes Payable		8,000
(c)	Notes Payable	8,000	
	Cash		8,000

SOLUTION

		Debit	Credit
(a)	Equipment	10,000	
	Cash		2,000
	Accounts Payable, William Smith		8,000
	Purchase of equipment, 20% for cash, balance		
	on account		
(b)	Accounts Payable, William Smith	8,000	
	Notes Payable		8,000
	Notes Payable in settlement of accounts payable		
(c)	Notes Payable	8,000	
	Cash		8,000
	Settlement of the notes payable		

3.2 Dr. R. Berg, Dentist, began his practice, investing in the business the following assets:

Cash	$12,000
Supplies	1,400
Equipment	22,600
Furniture	10,000

Record the opening entry in the journal.

	Debit	Credit

SOLUTION

	Debit	Credit
Cash	12,000	
Supplies	1,400	
Equipment	22,600	
Furniture	10,000	
R. Berg, Capital		46,000

3.3 If, in Problem 3.2, Dr. Berg owed a balance of $3,500 on the equipment, what would the opening entry then be?

	Debit	Credit

SOLUTION

	Debit	Credit
Cash	12,000	
Supplies	1,400	
Equipment	22,600	
Furniture	10,000	
Accounts Payable		3,500
R. Berg, Capital		42,500

3.4 Record the following entries in the general journal for the Stephenson Cleaning Company:

(*a*) Invested $10,000 cash in the business.

(*b*) Paid $2,000 for office furniture.

(*c*) Bought equipment costing $6,000, on account.

(*d*) Received $2,200 in cleaning income.

(*e*) Paid one-fourth of the amount owed on the equipment.

	Debit	Credit
(*a*)		
(*b*)		
(*c*)		
(*d*)		
(*e*)		

SOLUTION

		Debit	Credit
(*a*)	Cash	10,000	
	Stephenson, Capital		10,000
(*b*)	Office Furniture	2,000	
	Cash		2,000
(*c*)	Equipment	6,000	
	Accounts Payable		6,000
(*d*)	Cash	2,200	
	Cleaning Income		2,200
(*e*)	Accounts Payable	1,500	
	Cash		1,500

3.5 Record the following entries in the general journal for the Gavis Medical Group.

(a) Invested $18,000 in cash, $4,800 in supplies, and $12,200 in equipment (of which there is owed $7,000) to begin the Medical Group.

(b) Received $2,400 from cash patients for the week.

(c) Invested additional cash of $5,000 in the firm.

(d) Paid one-half of the amount owed.

		Debit	Credit
(a)			
(b)			
(c)			
(d)			

SOLUTION

		Debit	Credit
(a)	Cash	18,000	
	Supplies	4,800	
	Equipment	12,200	
	Accounts Payable		7,000
	Gavis, Capital		28,000
(b)	Cash	2,400	
	Fees Income		2,400
(c)	Cash	5,000	
	Gavis, Capital		5,000
(d)	Accounts Payable	3,500	
	Cash		3,500

3.6   If, in Problem 3.5, the Gavis Medical Group billed patients for the month for $2,400, and a month later received $1,000, present the necessary journal entries to record each transaction.

		Debit	Credit
(a)			
(b)			

SOLUTION

		Debit	Credit
(a)	Accounts Receivable	2,400	
	Fees Income		2,400
	To record services rendered on account		
(b)	Cash	1,000	
	Accounts Receivable		1,000
	Received cash on account		

Note: Fees Income had already been recorded in the previous month, when the service had been rendered. On the accrual basis, income as well as expense is recorded in the period of service or use, not in the period of payment.

3.7   On January 1, 19X5, Mr. Ling started a dry cleaning service. Record the following entries for the month of January in general journal form. Disregard post reference numbers at this time.

Jan. 1   Invested $5,000 cash and equipment valued at $4,100 to start business.
    12   Paid first month's rent, $400.
    13   Purchased supplies on account, $700.
    16   Received $1,700 for cleaning fees.
    19   Purchased supplies paying $550 cash.
    21   Paid creditors $500 from Jan. 13 transaction.
    22   Paid electric bill, $275.
    23   Withdrew $500 for personal use.
    25   Received $1,100 for cleaning fees.
    26   Purchased equipment, paying $900 cash.
    28   Sent bills to customers totaling $500 for cleaning fees.
    30   Received $300 from Jan. 28 transaction.
    30   Paid creditor the balanced owed.

General Journal

Date	Description	P.R.	Debit	Credit
Jan. 1				
12				
13				
16				
19				
21				
22				
23				
25				
26				
28				
30				
30				

SOLUTION

General Journal

Date	Description	P.R.	Debit	Credit
Jan. 1	Cash		5,000	
	Equipment		4,100	
	Capital			9,100
12	Rent Expense		400	
	Cash			400
13	Supplies		700	
	Accounts Payable			700
16	Cash		1,700	
	Cleaning Fees			1,700
19	Supplies		550	
	Cash			550
21	Accounts Payable		500	
	Cash			500
22	Utilities Expense		275	
	Cash			275
23	Drawing		500	
	Cash			500
25	Cash		1,100	
	Cleaning Fees			1,100
26	Equipment		900	
	Cash			900
28	Accounts Receivable		500	
	Cleaning Fees			500
30	Cash		300	
	Accounts Receivable			300
30	Accounts Payable		200	
	Cash			200

3.8   Post the following journal entries for the Charles Taxi Company to the T accounts below. Disregard post reference numbers at this time.

		P.R.	Debit	Credit
(a)	Cash		9,000	
	Charles, Capital			9,000
(b)	Equipment		8,000	
	Accounts Payable			4,000
	Cash			4,000
(c)	Accounts Payable		3,000	
	Cash			3,000
(d)	Cash		1,500	
	Fares Income			1,500
(e)	Salaries Expense		600	
	Cash			600

Cash	Equipment	Accounts Payable

Charles, Capital	Fares Income	Salaries Expense

SOLUTION

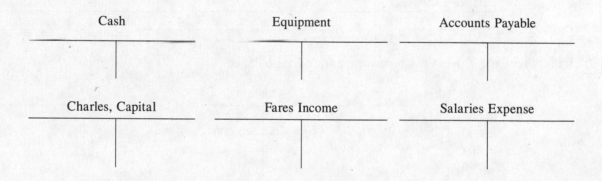

	Cash				Equipment			Accounts Payable		
(a)	9,000	4,000	(b)	(b)	8,000		(c)	3,000	4,000	(b)
(d)	1,500	3,000	(c)							
		600	(e)							

Charles, Capital			Fares Income			Salaries Expense		
	9,000	(a)		1,500	(d)	(e)	600	

3.9 Use the balances of the T accounts in Problem 3.8 to prepare a trial balance.

<table>
<tr><td colspan="3" align="center">*Charles Taxi Company*
Trial Balance</td></tr>
<tr><td>Cash</td><td></td><td></td></tr>
<tr><td>Equipment</td><td></td><td></td></tr>
<tr><td>Accounts Payable</td><td></td><td></td></tr>
<tr><td>Charles, Capital</td><td></td><td></td></tr>
<tr><td>Fares Income</td><td></td><td></td></tr>
<tr><td>Salaries Expense</td><td></td><td></td></tr>
</table>

SOLUTION

Charles Taxi Company *Trial Balance*		
Cash	$2,900	
Equipment	8,000	
Accounts Payable		$ 1,000
Charles, Capital		9,000
Fares Income		1,500
Salaries Expense	600	
	$11,500	$11,500

3.10 From the T accounts below, prepare a trial balance.

Cash		Capital		Drawing	
10,000	1,000		15,500	1,000	
5,000			2,000		
6,000					
500					

Rent Expense		Accounts Payable		Notes Payable	
500		500	500		1,000
			600		500
			1,000		

Equipment		Land		Accounts Receivable	
2,500		5,000		500	500
				5,000	
				200	

Supplies		Fees Income		Wages Expense	
300			7,000	1,450	
150			9,000		

	Ace Hardware Store Trial Balance December 31, 19X5	
Cash		
Accounts Receivable		
Supplies		
Land		
Equipment		
Accounts Payable		
Notes Payable		
Capital		
Drawing		
Fees Income		
Rent Expense		
Wages Expense		

SOLUTION

	Ace Hardware Store Trial Balance December 31, 19X5	
Cash	$20,500	
Accounts Receivable	5,200	
Supplies	450	
Land	5,000	
Equipment	2,500	
Accounts Payable	1,000	
Notes Payable		$17,500
Capital		1,600
Drawing		1,500
Fees Income		16,000
Rent Expense	500	
Wages Expense	1,450	
	$36,600	$36,600

3.11 The trial balance for Dampman Playhouse on October 31, 19X5, was as follows:

Dampman Playhouse
Trial Balance
October 31, 19X5

Cash	$ 2,400	
Accounts Receivable	1,500	
Supplies	350	
Equipment	11,200	
Building	10,000	
Accounts Payable		$ 9,450
Notes Payable		12,000
Dampman Playhouse, Capital		4,000
	$25,450	$25,450

Selected transactions for November were as follows:

(*a*) Nov. 2 Paid $1,000 due on the notes payable.
(*b*)   8 Paid $3,000 on account.
(*c*)   15 Receipts for the 2-week period totaled $8,400.
(*d*)   22 Bought an additional projector at a cost of $15,500 with a cash down payment of $5,000, the balance to be paid within 1 year.
(*e*)   30 Paid salaries of $1,600.

Using this data, (1) transfer the October 31 balances to the ledger accounts, (2) prepare journal entries for the month of November, (3) post to the ledger accounts, and (4) prepare a trial balance.

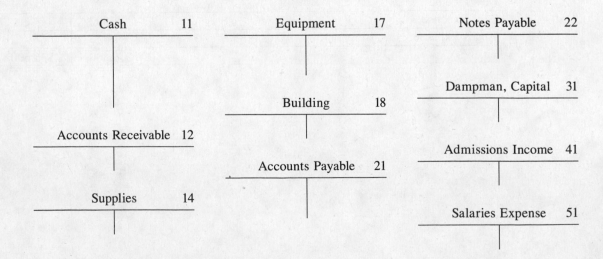

Journal   Page J-6

Date	Description	P.R.	Debit	Credit

Dampman Playhouse
Trial Balance
November 30, 19X5

Cash		
Accounts Receivable		
Supplies		
Equipment		
Building		
Accounts Payable		
Notes Payable		
Dampman, Capital		
Admissions Income		
Salaries Expense		

SOLUTION

Journal Page J-6

	Date	Description	P.R.	Debit	Credit
	19X5				
(a)	Nov. 2	Notes Payable	22	1,000	
		Cash	11		1,000
		Payment of installment note			
(b)	8	Accounts Payable	21	3,000	
		Cash	11		3,000
		Payment on outstanding accounts			
(c)	15	Cash	11	8,400	
		Admissions Income	41		8,400
		Receipts for the 2-week period to date			
(d)	22	Equipment	17	15,500	
		Cash	11		5,000
		Accounts Payable	21		10,500
		Purchase of a projector with cash			
		payment, balance due in 1 year			
(e)	30	Salaries Expense	51	1,600	
		Cash	11		1,600
		Salaries paid to employees			

Cash 11

Bal. 2,400	J-6 1,000 (a)
(c) J-6 8,400	J-6 3,000 (b)
	J-6 5,000 (d)
	J-6 1,600 (e)

Accounts Receivable 12

Bal. 1,500	

Supplies 14

Bal. 350	

Equipment 17

Bal. 11,200	
(d) J-6 15,500	

Buildings 18

Bal. 10,000	

Accounts Payable 21

(b) J-6 3,000	Bal. 9,450
	J-6 10,500 (d)

Notes Payable 22

(a) J-6 1,000	Bal. 12,000

Dampman, Capital 31

	Bal. 4,000

Admissions Income 41

	J-6 8,400 (c)

Salaries Expense 51

(e) J-6 1,600	

Dampman Playhouse		
Trial Balance		
November 30, 19X5		
Cash	$ 200	
Accounts Receivable	1,500	
Supplies	350	
Equipment	26,700	
Building	10,000	
Accounts Payable		$16,950
Notes Payable		11,000
Dampman, Capital		4,000
Admissions Income		8,400
Salaries Expense	1,600	
	$40,350	$40,350

Chapter 4

Financial Statements

4.1 INTRODUCTION

The two principal questions that the owner of a business asks periodically are:

(1) What is my net income (profit)?

(2) What is my capital?

The simple balance of assets against liabilities and capital provided by the accounting equation is insufficient to give complete answers. For (1) we must know the type and amount of income and the type and amount of each expense for the period in question. For (2) it is necessary to obtain the type and amount of each asset, liability, and capital account at the end of the period. The information to answer (1) is provided by the income statement and to answer (2) by the balance sheet. Also, you will note that each heading of a financial statement answers the questions "who," "what," and "when."

4.2 INCOME STATEMENT

The *income statement* may be defined as *a summary of the revenue (income), expenses, and net income of a business entity for a specific period of time.* This may also be called a profit and loss statement, an operating statement, or a statement of operations. Let us review the meanings of the elements entering into the income statement.

Revenue. The increase in capital resulting from the delivery of goods or rendering of services by the business. In amount, the revenue is equal to the cash and receivables gained in compensation for the goods delivered or services rendered.

Expenses. The decrease in capital caused by the business's revenue-producing operations. In amount, the expense is equal to the value of goods and services used up or consumed in obtaining revenue.

Net income. The increase in capital resulting from profitable operation of a business; it is the excess of revenue over expenses for the accounting period.

It is important to note that a *cash receipt* qualifies as revenue only if it serves to increase capital. Similarly, a *cash payment* is an expense only if it decreases capital. Thus, for instance, borrowing cash from a bank does not contribute to revenue.

EXAMPLE 1

Mr. T. Drew's total January income and the totals for his various expenses can be obtained by analyzing the transactions. The income from fees amounted to $2,500, and the expenses incurred to produce this income were: rent, $500; salaries, $200; and supplies, $200. The formal income statement can now be prepared.

T. Drew
Income Statement
Month of January 19X5

Fees Income		$2,500
Operating Expenses		
Rent Expense	$500	
Salaries Expense	200	
Supplies Expense	200	
Total Operating Expenses		900
Net Income		$1,600

In many companies, there are hundreds and perhaps thousands of income and expense transactions in a month. To lump all these transactions under one account would be very cumbersome and would, in addition, make it impossible to show relationships among the various items. For example, we might wish to know the relationship of selling expenses to sales and whether the ratio is higher or lower than in previous periods. To solve this problem, we set up a temporary set of income and expense accounts. The net difference of these accounts, the net profit or net loss, is then transferred as one figure to the capital account.

4.3 ACCRUAL BASIS AND CASH BASIS OF ACCOUNTING

Because an income statement pertains to a definite period of time, it becomes necessary to determine just when an item of revenue or expense is to be accounted for. Under the *accrual basis* of accounting, revenue is recognized only when it is earned and expense is recognized only when it is incurred. This differs significantly from the *cash basis* of accounting, which recognizes revenue and expense generally with the receipt and payment of cash. Essential to the accrual basis is the matching of expenses with the revenue that they helped produce. Under the accrual system, the accounts are adjusted at the end of the accounting period to properly reflect the revenue earned and the cost and expenses applicable to the period.

Most business firms use the accrual basis, whereas individuals and professional people generally use the cash basis. Ordinarily, the cash basis is not suitable when there are significant amounts of inventories, receivables, and payables.

4.4 BALANCE SHEET

The information needed for the balance sheet items are the net balances at the end of the period, rather than the total for the period as in the income statement. Thus, management wants to know the balance of cash in the bank, the balance of inventory, equipment, and so on, on hand at the end of the period.

The *balance sheet* may thus be defined as *a statement showing the assets, liabilities, and capital of a business entity at a specific date.* This statement is also called a statement of financial position or a statement of financial condition.

In preparing a balance sheet, it is not necessary to make any further analysis of the data. The needed data—that is, the balances of the asset, liability, and capital accounts—are already available.

EXAMPLE 2   Report Form

T. Drew
Balance Sheet
January 31, 19X5

ASSETS

Cash		$3,900
Supplies		100
Furniture		2,000
Total Assets		$6,000

LIABILITIES AND CAPITAL

Liabilities			
Accounts Payable			$ 800
Capital			
Balance, January 1, 19X5		$4,000	
Net Income for January	$1,600		
Less: Withdrawals	400		
Increase in Capital		1,200	
Total Capital			5,200
Total Liabilities and Capital			$6,000

The close relationship of the income statement and the balance sheet is apparent. The net income of $1,600 for January, shown as the final figure on the income statement of Example 1, is also shown as a separate figure on the balance sheet of Example 2. The income statement is thus the connecting link between two balance sheets. As discussed earlier, the income and expense items are actually a further analysis of the capital account.

The balance sheet of Example 2 is arranged in report form, with the liabilities and capital sections shown below the asset section. It may also be arranged in account form, with the liabilities and capital sections to the right of, rather than below, the asset section, as shown in Example 3.

EXAMPLE 3   Account Form

T. Drew
Balance Sheet
January 31, 19X5

ASSETS		LIABILITIES AND CAPITAL			
Cash	$3,900	Liabilities			
Supplies	100	Accounts Payable			$ 800
Furniture	2,000	Capital			
		Balance, January 1, 19X5		$4,000	
		Net Income for January	$1,600		
		Less: Withdrawals	400		
		Increase in Capital		1,200	
		Total Capital			5,200
Total Assets	$6,000	Total Liabilities and Capital			$6,000

4.5   CAPITAL STATEMENT

Instead of showing the details of the capital account in the balance sheet, we may show the changes in a separate form called the *capital statement*.

EXAMPLE 4

T. Drew
Capital Statement
January 31, 19X5

Capital, January 1, 19X5		$4,000
Net Income for January	$1,600	
Less: Withdrawals	400	
Increase in Capital		1,200
Total Capital		$5,200

4.6   FINANCIAL STATEMENT SUMMARY

The three financial statements from Examples 2, 3, and 4 are interrelated as shown in Example 5.

EXAMPLE 5

Income Statement

Fees Income		$ 2,500
Expenses		
Rent Expense	$ 500	
Salaries Expense	200	
Supplies Expense	200	
Total Expenses		900
Net Income		$ 1,600

Capital Statement

Capital, January 1, 19X5		$4,000
Add: Net Income	$ 1,600 ◄— Note 1	
Less: Drawing	400	
Increase in Capital		1,200
Capital, January 31, 19X5		$ 5,200

Balance Sheet

ASSETS

Cash	$3,900	
Supplies	100	
Furniture	2,000	
Total Assets		$ 6,000

LIABILITIES AND CAPITAL

Accounts Payable	$ 800	
Capital, January 31, 19X5	5,200 ◄— Note 2	
Total Liabilities and Capital		$ 6,000

Note 1. The net income of the income statement, $1,600, is transferred to the capital statement.

Note 2. The capital is summarized in the capital statement and the final balance included in the balance sheet.

4.7 CLASSIFIED FINANCIAL STATEMENTS

Financial statements become more useful when the individual items are classified into significant groups for comparison and financial analysis. The classifications relating to the balance sheet will be discussed in this section. The classifications relating to the income statement will be discussed in Chapter 9.

The Balance Sheet

The balance sheet becomes a more useful statement for comparison and financial analysis if the asset and liability groups are classified. For example, an important index of the financial state of a business, which can be derived from the classified balance sheet, is the ratio of current assets to current liabilities. This current ratio ought, generally, to be at least 2:1; that is, current assets should be twice current liabilities. For our purposes, we will designate the following classifications:

Assets

Current assets
Property, plant, and equipment
Other assets

Liabilities

Current liabilities
Long-term liabilities

Current assets.   Assets reasonably expected to be converted into cash or used in the current operation of the business. (The current period is generally taken as 1 year.) Examples are cash, notes receivable, accounts receivable, inventory, and prepaid expenses (prepaid insurance, prepaid rent, and so on). List these current assets in order of liquidity.

Property, plant, and equipment.   Long-lived assets used in the production of goods or services. These assets, sometimes called *fixed assets* or *plant assets,* are used in the operation of the business rather than being held for sale, as are inventory items.

Other assets.   Various assets other than current assets, fixed assets, or assets to which specific captions are given. For instance, the caption "Investments" would be used if significant sums were invested. Often, companies show a caption for intangible assets such as patents or goodwill. In other cases, there may be a separate caption for deferred charges. If, however, the amounts are not large in relation to total assets, the various items may be grouped under one caption, "Other Assets."

Current liabilities.   Debts that must be satisfied from current assets within the next operating period, usually 1 year. Examples are accounts payable, notes payable, the current portion of long-term debt, and various accrued items such as salaries payable and taxes payable.

Long-term liabilities.   Liabilities that are payable beyond the next year. The most common examples are bonds payable and mortgages payable. Example 6 shows a classified balance sheet of typical form.

EXAMPLE 6

F. Saltzmann
January 31, 19X5
Balance Sheet

ASSETS

Current Assets

Cash	$5,400	
Accounts Receivable	1,600	
Supplies	500	
Total Current Assets		$ 7,500

Fixed Assets

Land	$4,000	
Building	8,000	
Equipment	2,000	
Total Fixed Assets		14,000
Total Assets		$21,500

LIABILITIES AND CAPITAL

Current Liabilities

Accounts Payable	$2,000	
Notes Payable	1,750	
Total Current Liabilities		$ 3,750

Long-Term Liabilities

Mortgage Payable		12,000
Total Liabilities		$15,750

Capital

F. Saltzmann, Capital, January 1		$4,750	
Net Income for the Year	$3,000*		
Less: Withdrawals	2,000		
Increase in Capital		1,000	
F. Saltzmann, Capital, December 31			5,750
Total Liabilities and Capital			$21,500

*Assumed.

Summary

1. Another term for an accounting report is an _____ .

2. The statement that shows net income for the period is known as the _____ statement.

3. The statement that shows net loss for the period is known as the _____ statement.

4. Two groups of items that make up the income statement are _____ and _____ .

5. The difference between income and expense is known as _____ .

6. Withdrawal of money by the owner is not an expense but a reduction of _____ .

7. To show the change in capital of a business, the _____ statement is used.

8. The balance sheet contains _____ , _____ , and _____ .

9. Assets must equal _____ .

10. Expense and income must be matched in the same _____ .

Answers: 1. accounting statement; 2. income; 3. income; 4. income, expense; 5. net income; 6. capital; 7. capital; 8. assets, liabilities, capital; 9. liabilities and capital; 10. year or period

Solved Problems

4.1 Place a check mark in the appropriate box below to indicate the name of the account group in which each account belongs.

	Income Statement		Balance Sheet		
	Income	Expense	Assets	Liability	Capital
Accounts Payable					
Accounts Receivable					
Building					
Capital					
Cash					
Drawing					

(continued)

	Income Statement		Balance Sheet		
	Income	Expense	Assets	Liability	Capital
Equipment					
Fees Income					
General Expense					
Interest Expense					
Interest Income					
Land					
Notes Payable					
Other Income					
Rent Expense					
Rent Income					
Salaries Expense					
Supplies					
Supplies Expense					
Tax Expense					

SOLUTION

	Income Statement		Balance Sheet		
	Income	Expense	Assets	Liability	Capital
Accounts Payable				✔	
Accounts Receivable			✔		
Building			✔		
Capital					✔
Cash			✔		
Drawing					✔
Equipment			✔		
Fees Income	✔				
General Expense		✔			
Interest Expense		✔			
Interest Income	✔				

	Income Statement		Balance Sheet		
	Income	Expense	Assets	Liability	Capital
Land			✔		
Notes Payable				✔	
Other Income	✔				
Rent Expense		✔			
Rent Income	✔				
Salaries Expense		✔			
Supplies			✔		
Supplies Expense		✔			
Tax Expense		✔			

4.2   Below is an income statement with some of the information missing. Fill in the information needed to complete the income statement.

Sales Income		(b)
Operating Expenses:		
Wages Expense	$16,910	
Rent Expense	(a)	
Utilities Expense	3,150	
Total Operating Expenses		32,150
Net Income		$41,300

SOLUTION

(a) 12,090; (b) $73,450

4.3   Based on the following information, determine the capital as of December 31, 19X5. Net Income for period, $18,000; Drawing, $6,000; Capital (January 1, 19X5), $20,000.

SOLUTION

Capital, January 1, 19X5		$20,000
Net Income	$18,000	
Less: Drawing	6,000	
Increase in Capital		12,000
Capital, December 31, 19X5		$32,000

4.4   The following information was taken from an income statement:

Fees Income	$14,000
Rent Expense	2,000
Salaries Expense	5,000
Miscellaneous Expense	1,000

If the owner withdrew $2,000 from the firm, what is the increase or decrease in capital?

SOLUTION

There are two steps to solving this problem:

1.   Prepare an income statement.
2.   Determine increases or decreases in capital by subtracting the drawing (withdrawal) from the net income.

Fees Income		$14,000
Expenses		
Rent Expense	$2,000	
Salaries Expense	5,000	
Miscellaneous Expense	1,000	
Total Expenses		8,000
Net Income		$ 6,000
Net Income	6,000	
Less: Drawing	2,000	
Increase in Capital	$4,000	

4.5   Based on the information in Problem 4.4, if the withdrawal were $9,000 instead of $2,000, what would the increase (decrease) become?

SOLUTION

If the withdrawal is larger than the net income, a decrease in capital will result.

Net Income	$6,000
Drawing	9,000
Decrease in Capital	$3,000

4.6 If the capital account has a balance of $32,000 on January 1, what will be the balance by December 31: (*a*) based on Problem 4.4? (*b*) based on Problem 4.5?

(*a*)

(*b*)

SOLUTION

(*a*)	Capital, January 1		$32,000
	Net Income	$6,000	
	Less: Drawing	2,000	
	Increase in Capital		4,000
	Capital, December 31		$36,000
(*b*)	Capital, January 1		$32,000
	Net Income	6,000	
	Less: Drawing	9,000	
	Decrease in Capital		(3,000)
	Capital, December 31		$29,000

4.7 Eccleston Company had a capital balance as of January 1, 19X5, of $43,000. During its first year of operation, it had produced a net loss of $13,000 and drawings of $6,000. What is the capital balance of the company as of December 31, 19X5?

SOLUTION

Capital, January 1, 19X5		$43,000
Net loss	($13,000)	
Drawing	(6,000)	
Decrease in Capital		(19,000)
Capital, December 31, 19X5		$24,000

Note: Net loss and drawing are *added* together and then subtracted from capital, because both reduce the capital of the firm.

4.8   Based on the following information, determine the capital on December 31.

Cash	$6,000
Supplies	400
Equipment	8,000
Accounts Payable	4,500
Notes Payable	2,500

SOLUTION

ASSETS

Cash	$ 6,000
Supplies	400
Equipment	8,000
	$14,400

LIABILITIES AND CAPITAL

Accounts Payable	$4,500	
Notes Payable	2,500	
Total Liabilities		7,000
Capital		7,400*
Total Liabilities and Capital		$14,400

*$14,400	Assets
−7,000	Liabilities
$ 7,400	Capital

4.9   Prepare a balance sheet as of December 31, 19X5, from the following data:

Accounts Payable	$ 3,000
Cash	4,000
Equipment	16,000
Notes Payable	12,000
Supplies	200
Net Income	11,400
Drawing	10,200
Capital, January 1, 19X5	4,000

ASSETS		
Cash		
Supplies		
Equipment		
Total Assets		
LIABILITIES AND CAPITAL		
Accounts Payable		
Notes Payable		
Total Liabilities		
Capital, December 31, 19X5*		
Total Liabilities and Capital		
* **CAPITAL STATEMENT**		

SOLUTION

ASSETS		
Cash		$ 4,000
Supplies		200
Equipment		16,000
Total Assets		$20,200
LIABILITIES AND CAPITAL		
Accounts Payable	$ 3,000	
Notes Payable	12,000	
Total Liabilities		$15,000
Capital, December 31, 19X5*		5,200
Total Liabilities and Capital		$20,200
* **CAPITAL STATEMENT**		
Capital, January 1, 19X5		$ 4,000
Net Income	$11,400	
Less: Drawing	10,200	
Increase in Capital		1,200
Capital, December 31, 19X5		$ 5,200

4.10 Classify the following accounts by placing a check mark in the appropriate column.

		Current Asset	Fixed Asset	Current Liability	Long-Term Liability
(a)	Accounts Receivable				
(b)	Accounts Payable				
(c)	Notes Payable				
(d)	Mortgage Payable				
(e)	Cash				
(f)	Supplies				
(g)	Salaries Payable				
(h)	Bonds Payable				
(i)	Equipment				
(j)	Land				

SOLUTION

		Current Asset	Fixed Asset	Current Liability	Long-Term Liability
(a)	Accounts Receivable	✔			
(b)	Accounts Payable			✔	
(c)	Notes Payable			✔	
(d)	Mortgage Payable				✔
(e)	Cash	✔			
(f)	Supplies	✔			
(g)	Salaries Payable			✔	
(h)	Bonds Payable				✔
(i)	Equipment		✔		
(j)	Land		✔		

4.11 From the information that follows, prepare a classified balance sheet as of December 31.

Cash	$ 6,000	Accounts Payable	$ 2,500
Accounts Receivable	3,000	Notes Payable	1,500
Supplies	1,000	Mortgage Payable	12,000
Equipment	14,000	Capital, December 31	8,000

ASSETS		
Current Assets		
Total Current Assets		
Fixed Assets		
Total Assets		
LIABILITIES AND CAPITAL		
Current Liabilities		
Total Current Liabilities		
Long-Term Liabilities		
Total Liabilities		
Capital		
Total Liabilities and Capital		

SOLUTION

ASSETS		
Current Assets		
Cash	$6,000	
Accounts Receivable	3,000	
Supplies	1,000	
Total Current Assets		$10,000
Fixed Assets		
Equipment		14,000
Total Assets		$24,000
LIABILITIES AND CAPITAL		
Current Liabilities		
Accounts Payable	$2,500	
Notes Payable	1,500	
Total Current Liabilities		$ 4,000
Long-Term Liabilities		
Mortgage Payable		12,000
Total Liabilities		$16,000
Capital		8,000
Total Liabilities and Capital		$24,000

4.12 Below are account balances as of December 31, 19X5, of R. Dames, owner of a movie theater.

Accounts Payable	$11,400	Film Rental Expense	$ 6,000
Admissions Income	34,200	Miscellaneous Expense	4,000
Capital, January 1, 19X5	16,000	Notes Payable	1,000
Cash	7,500	Rent Expense	10,000
Drawing	5,400	Salaries Expense	7,000
Equipment	18,500	Supplies	4,200

Prepare (a) an income statement, (b) a capital statement, (c) a balance sheet.

(a)

R. Dames
Income Statement
Year Ended December 31, 19X5

(b)

R. Dames
Capital Statement
Year Ended December 31, 19X5

(c)

R. Dames
Balance Sheet
December 31, 19X5

SOLUTION

(a)

R. Dames		
Income Statement		
Year Ended December 31, 19X5		
Admissions Income		$34,200
Expenses		
Film Rental Expense	$ 6,000	
Rent Expense	10,000	
Salaries Expense	7,000	
Miscellaneous Expense	4,000	
Total Expenses		27,000
Net Income		$ 7,200

(b) The capital statement is needed to show the capital balance at the end of the year. Mr. Dames' capital balance above is at the beginning. Net income increases capital, and drawing reduces capital.

R. Dames		
Capital Statement		
Year Ended December 31, 19X5		
Capital, January 1, 19X5		$16,000
Add: Net Income	$7,200	
Less: Drawing	5,400	
Increase in Capital		1,800
Capital, December 31, 19X5		$17,800

(c)

R. Dames		
Balance Sheet		
December 31, 19X5		
ASSETS		
Cash	$ 7,500	
Supplies	4,200	
Equipment	18,500	
Total Assets		$30,200
LIABILITIES AND CAPITAL		
Accounts Payable	$11,400	
Notes Payable	1,000	
Total Liabilities		$12,400
Capital		17,800
Total Liabilities and Capital		$30,200

4.13 Wilbur Wright owns and operates an airplane repair shop. Listed below are the year-end balances for the shop. Prepare an income statement, capital statement, and balance sheet in good report form.

Cash	$12,200
Supplies	5,150
Accounts Receivable	3,100
Prepaid Insurance	1,150
Equipment	15,920
Accounts Payable	3,200
Wages Payable	2,600
W. Wright, Capital (January)	26,575
W. Wright, Drawing	9,500
Repair Shop Income	98,800
Wages Expense	41,500
Rent Expense	28,200
Utilities Expense	10,100
Supplies Expense	3,980
Miscellaneous Expense	375

Wilbur Wright Repair Shop
Income Statement
Year Ended December 31, 19X5

Wilbur Wright Repair Shop
Capital Statement
Year Ended December 31, 19X5

Wilbur Wright Repair Shop
Balance Sheet
December 31, 19X5

ASSETS		
LIABILITIES		
CAPITAL		

SOLUTION

Wilbur Wright Repair Shop
Income Statement
Year Ended December 31, 19X5

Repair Shop Income		$98,800
Operating Expenses:		
Wages Expense	$41,500	
Rent Expense	28,200	
Utilities Expense	10,100	
Supplies Expense	3,980	
Miscellaneous Expense	375	
Total Operating Expenses		84,155
Net Income		$14,645

Wilbur Wright Repair Shop
Capital Statement
Year Ended December 31, 19X5

Capital, January 1, 19X5		$26,575
Net Income for Year	$14,645	
Less Drawing	9,500	
Increase in Capital		5,145
Capital, December 31, 19X5		$31,720

Wilbur Wright Repair Shop		
Balance Sheet		
December 31, 19X5		
ASSETS		
Current Assets		
Cash	$12,200	
Accounts Receivable	3,100	
Supplies	5,150	
Prepaid Insurance	1,150	
Total Current Assets		$21,600
Plant Assets		
Equipment		15,920
Total Assets		$37,520
LIABILITIES		
Current Liabilities		
Accounts Payable	$ 3,200	
Wages Payable	2,600	
Total Liabilities		$ 5,800
CAPITAL		
Wilbur Wright, Capital		31,720
Total Liabilities and Capital		$37,520

4.14 Given the information in Problem 4.13, if revenues were only $84,000, drawing was $10,200, and Wright's beginning capital balance was $42,075, what affect would this have on the financial statements? Prepare new financial statements with these changes.

Wilbur Wright Repair Shop		
Income Statement		
Year Ended December 31, 19X5		

Wilbur Wright Repair Shop
Capital Statement
Year Ended December 31, 19X5

Wilbur Wright Repair Shop
Balance Sheet
December 31, 19X5

ASSETS		
LIABILITIES		
CAPITAL		

SOLUTION

Wilbur Wright Repair Shop		
Income Statement		
Year Ended December 31, 19X5		
Repair Shop Income		$84,000
Operating Expenses		
Wages Expense	$41,500	
Rent Expense	28,200	
Utilities Expense	10,100	
Supplies Expense	3,980	
Miscellaneous Expense	375	
Total Operating Expenses		84,155
Net Loss		$ (155)

Wilbur Wright Repair Shop		
Capital Statement		
Year Ended December 31, 19X5		
Capital, January 1, 19X5		$42,075
Net Loss	$ (155)	
Drawing	(10,200)	
Decrease in Capital		(10,355)
Capital, December 31, 19X5		$31,720

Wilbur Wright Repair Shop		
Balance Sheet		
December 31, 19X5		
ASSETS		
Current Assets		
Cash	$12,200	
Accounts Receivable	3,100	
Supplies	5,150	
Prepaid Insurance	1,150	
Total Current Assets		$21,600
Plant Assets		
Equipment		15,920
Total Assets		$37,520

(continued)

Wilbur Wright Repair Shop		
Balance Sheet		
December 31, 19X5		
LIABILITIES		
Current Liabilities		
Accounts Payable	$ 3,200	
Wages Payable	2,600	
Total Liabilities		$ 5,800
CAPITAL		
Wilbur Wright, Capital		31,720
Total Liabilities and Capital		$37,520

4.15 The balances of the accounts of Dr. C. Moss, Psychologist, are as follows:

Accounts Payable	$ 2,800
Accounts Receivable	3,600
Building	12,000
Capital, January 1, 19X5	19,000
Cash	12,200
Drawing	6,000
Equipment	15,000
Fees Income	38,000
Furniture	3,000
Mortgage Payable	10,000
Miscellaneous Expense	2,000
Notes Payable	2,000
Salaries Expense	8,000
Supplies	6,000
Supplies Expense	4,000

Using the forms provided below, prepare (a) an income statement, (b) a capital statement, and (c) a classified balance sheet.

(a)

Dr. C. Moss		
Income Statement		
Year Ended December 31, 19X5		
Fees Income		
Expenses		
Total Expenses		
Net Income		

(b)

Dr. C. Moss
Capital Statement
Year Ended December 31, 19X5

Capital, January 1, 19X5		
Net Income		
Less: Drawing		
Increase in Capital		
Capital, December 31, 19X5		

(c)

Dr. C. Moss
Balance Sheet
December 31, 19X5

ASSETS		
Current Assets		
Total Current Assets		
Fixed Assets		
Total Fixed Assets		
Total Assets		
LIABILITIES AND CAPITAL		
Current Liabilities		
Total Current Liabilities		
Long-Term Liabilities		
Total Liabilities		
Capital		
Total Liabilities and Capital		

SOLUTION

(a)

Dr. C. Moss
Income Statement
Year Ended December 31, 19X5

Fees Income		$38,000
Expenses		
Salaries Expense	$8,000	
Supplies Expense	4,000	
Miscellaneous Expense	2,000	
Total Expenses		14,000
Net Income		$24,000

(b)

Dr. C. Moss
Capital Statement
Year Ended December 31, 19X5

Capital, January 1, 19X5		$19,000
Net Income	$24,000	
Less: Drawing	6,000	
Increase in Capital		18,000
Capital, December 31, 19X5		$37,000

(c)

Dr. C. Moss
Balance Sheet
December 31, 19X5

ASSETS		
Current Assets		
Cash	$12,200	
Accounts Receivable	3,600	
Supplies	6,000	
Total Current Assets		$21,800
Fixed Assets		
Building	$12,000	
Equipment	15,000	
Furniture	3,000	
Total Fixed Assets		30,000
Total Assets		$51,800
LIABILITIES AND CAPITAL		
Current Liabilities		
Accounts Payable	$ 2,800	
Notes Payable	2,000	
Total Current Liabilities		4,800
Long-Term Liabilities		
Mortgage Payable		10,000
Total Liabilities		$14,800
Capital		37,000
Total Liabilities and Capital		$51,800

Chapter 5

Adjusting and Closing Procedures

5.1 INTRODUCTION: THE ACCRUAL BASIS OF ACCOUNTING

Accounting records are kept on an accrual basis, except in the case of very small businesses. *To accrue* means *to collect or accumulate.* This means that revenue is recognized when it is earned, regardless of when cash is actually collected, and expense is matched to the revenue, regardless of when cash is paid out. Most revenue is earned when goods or services are delivered. At this time, title to the goods or services is transferred, and there is created a legal obligation to pay for such goods or services. Some revenue, such as rental income, is recognized on a time basis and is earned when the specified period of time has passed. The accrual concept demands that expenses be kept in step with revenue, so that each month sees only that month's expenses applied against the revenue for that month. The necessary matching is brought about through a type of journal entry. In this chapter, we shall discuss these adjusting entries and also the closing entries through which the adjusted balances are ultimately transferred to balance sheet accounts at the end of the fiscal year.

5.2 ADJUSTING ENTRIES COVERING RECORDED DATA

To adjust expense or income items that have already been recorded, only a reclassification is required; that is, amounts have only to be transferred from one account (for example, Prepaid Insurance) to another (Insurance Expense). The following examples will show how adjusting entries are made for the principal types of recorded expenses.

EXAMPLE 1 Prepaid Insurance

Assume that a business paid a $1,200 premium on April 1 for 1 year's insurance in advance. This represents an increase in one asset (prepaid expense) and a decrease in another asset (cash). Thus, the entry would be:

Prepaid Insurance	1,200	
Cash		1,200

At the end of April, one-twelfth of the $1,200, or $100, had expired (been used up). Therefore, an adjustment has to be made, decreasing or crediting Prepaid Insurance and increasing or debiting Insurance Expense. The entry would be:

Insurance Expense	100	
Prepaid Insurance		100

Thus, $100 would be shown as Insurance Expense in the income statement for April, and the balance of $1,100 would be shown as Prepaid Insurance in the balance sheet.

EXAMPLE 2 Prepaid Rent

Assume that on March 1 a business paid $1,500 to cover rent for the balance of the year. The full amount would have been recorded as a debit to prepaid expense in March. Since there is a 10-month period

77

involved, the rent expense each month is $150. The balance of Prepaid Rent would be $1,350 at the beginning of April. The adjusting entry for April would be:

Rent Expense	150	
Prepaid Rent		150

At the end of April, the balance in the prepaid rent account would be $1,200.

EXAMPLE 3 Supplies on Hand

A type of prepayment that is somewhat different from those previously described is the payment for office or factory supplies. Assume that $400 worth of supplies were purchased on April 1. At the end of April, when expense and revenue are to be matched and statements prepared, a count of the amount on hand will be made. Assume that the inventory count shows that $250 of supplies are still on hand. Then the amount consumed during April was $150 ($400 − $250). The two entries would be as follows:

Apr. 1	Supplies	400	
	Cash		400
30	Supplies Expense	150	
	Supplies		150

Supplies Expense of $150 will be included in the April income statement; Supplies on Hand of $250 will be included as an asset on the balance sheet of April 30.

In each of the above examples, the net effect of the adjusting entry is to credit the same account as was originally debited. The following examples illustrate what are called *valuation or offset accounts*.

EXAMPLE 4 Accumulated Depreciation

In the previous three adjusting entries, the balances of the assets mentioned (Prepaid Insurance, Prepaid Rent, and Supplies) were all reduced. These assets usually lose their value in a relatively short period of time. However, assets that have a longer life expectancy (such as a building, equipment, etc.) are treated differently because the accounting profession wants to keep a balance sheet record of the equipment's original (historical) cost. Thus the adjusting entry needed to reflect the true value of the long-term asset each year must allocate (spread) the cost of its original price. This spreading concept is known as *depreciation*. In order to accomplish the objectives of keeping the original cost of the equipment and also maintaining a running total of the depreciation allocated, we must create a new account entitled Accumulated Depreciation. This account is known as a *contra asset* (which has the opposite balance of its asset), and it summarizes and accumulates the amount of depreciation over the equipment's total useful life. Assume that machinery costing $15,000 was purchased on February 1 of the current year and was expected to last 10 years. With the straight-line method of accounting (i.e., equal charges each period), the depreciation would be $1,500 a year, or $125 a month. The adjusting entry would be:

Depreciation Expense	125	
Accumulated Depreciation		125

At the end of April, Accumulated Depreciation would have a balance of $375, representing 3 months' accumulated depreciation. The account would be shown in the balance sheet as follows:

Machinery	$15,000	
Less: Accumulated Depreciation	375	$14,625

EXAMPLE 5   Allowance for Uncollectible Accounts

A business with many accounts receivable will reasonably expect to have some losses from uncollectible accounts. It will not be known which specific accounts will not be collected, but past experience furnishes an estimate of the total uncollectible amount.

Assume that a company estimates that 1 percent of sales on account will be uncollectible. Then, if such sales are $10,000 for April, it is estimated that $100 will be uncollectible. The actual loss may not definitely be determined for a year or more, but the loss attributed to April sales would call for an adjusting entry:

Uncollectible Accounts Expense	100	
Allowance for Uncollectible Accounts		100

If the balance in Accounts Receivable at April 30 was $9,500 and the previous month's balance in Allowance for Uncollectible Accounts was $300, the balance sheet at April 30 would show the following:

Accounts Receivable	$9,500	
Less: Allowance for Uncollectible Accounts	400	$9,100

5.3   ADJUSTING ENTRIES COVERING UNRECORDED DATA

In the previous section we discussed various kinds of adjustments to accounts to which entries had already been made. Now we consider those instances in which an expense has been incurred. For example, if salaries are paid on a weekly basis, the last week of the month may apply to 2 months. If April ends on a Tuesday, then the first 2 days of the week will apply to April and be an April expense, while the last 3 days will be a May expense. To arrive at the proper total for salaries for the month of April, we must include, along with the April payrolls that were paid in April, the 2 days' salary that was not paid until May. Thus, we make an entry to accrue the 2 days' salary. As mentioned earlier, to accrue means to collect or accumulate.

The following example shows an adjusting entry for the most common type of unrecorded expenses (accrued expenses).

EXAMPLE 6   Accrued Salaries

Assume that April 30 falls on Tuesday for the last weekly payroll period. Then, 2 days of that week will apply to April and 3 days to May. The payroll is $500 per day, for the week, or $2,500. For this example, $1,000 would apply to April (Monday and Tuesday) and $1,500 to May (Wednesday, Thursday, and Friday). The entries would be as follows:

Apr. 30	Salaries Expense	1,000	
	Salaries Payable		1,000

When the payment of the payroll is made—say, on May 3—the entry would be as follows:

May 3	Salaries Expense	1,500	
	Salaries Payable	1,000	
	Cash		2,500

As can be seen, $1,000 was charged to expense in April and $1,500 in May. The debit to Salaries Payable of $1,000 in May merely canceled the credit entry made in April, when the liability was set up for the April salaries expense.

5.4 CLOSING ENTRIES

After the income statement and balance sheet have been prepared, a summary account—variously known as Expense and Income Summary, Profit and Loss Summary, and so on—is set up. Then, by means of closing entries, each expense account is credited so as to produce a zero balance, and the total amount for the closed-out accounts is debited to Expense and Income Summary. Similarly, the individual revenue accounts are closed out by debiting, and the total amount is credited to the summary account. Thus, the new fiscal year starts with zero balances in the income and expense accounts, whereas the Expense and Income Summary balance gives the net income or the net loss for the old year.

EXAMPLE 7

To illustrate the closing procedure, we refer to the accounts of T. Drew (see Chapter 1).

T. Drew
Trial Balance
January 31, 19X5

Cash	$3,900	
Supplies	100	
Furniture	2,000	
Accounts Payable		$ 800
T. Drew, Capital		4,000
T. Drew, Drawing	400	
Fees Income		2,500
Rent Expense	500	
Salaries Expense	200	
Supplies Expense	200	
	$7,300	$7,300

The closing entries are as follows.

(1) **Close out income accounts.** Debit the individual income accounts and credit the total to Expense and Income Summary. Here, there is only one income account.

Jan. 31	Fees Income	2,500	
	Expense and Income Summary		2,500

(2) **Close out expense accounts.** Credit the individual expense accounts and debit the total to Expense and Income Summary.

Jan. 31	Expense and Income Summary	900	
	Rent Expense		500
	Salaries Expense		200
	Supplies Expense		200

(3) **Close out the Expense and Income Summary account.** If there is a profit, the credit made for total income in (1) above will exceed the debit made for total expense in (2) above. Therefore, to close out the balance to zero, a debit entry will be made to Expense and Income Summary. A credit

will be made to the capital account to transfer the net income for the period. If expenses exceed income, then a loss has been sustained, and a credit is made to Expense and Income Summary and a debit to the capital account. Based on the information given, the entry is:

Jan. 31	Expense and Income Summary	1,600	
	T. Drew, Capital		1,600

(4) *Close out the Drawing account.*   The drawing account would be credited for the total amount of the drawings for the period and the capital account would be debited for that amount. The difference between net income and drawing for the period represents the net change in the capital account for the period. The net income of $1,600, less drawings of $400, results in a net increase of $1,200 in the capital account. The closing entry for the drawing account is:

Jan. 31	T. Drew, Capital	400	
	T. Drew, Drawing		400

In summary, the procedure is as follows:

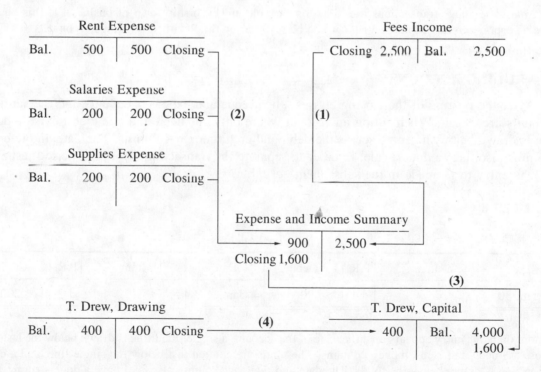

After the closing entries (1) through (4) are made,

    (1)   Close Fees Income account to Expense and Income Summary
    (2)   Close all expense accounts to Expense and Income Summary
    (3)   Close Expense and Income Summary to the Capital account
    (4)   Close the Drawing account to the Capital account

the various accounts will appear as shown on the following page. The income and expense accounts and the drawing account are ruled off or closed out, thus showing no balance. The net profit for the period and the drawing account balance were transferred to T. Drew, Capital, a balance sheet account.

	Cash			Furniture			T. Drew, Capital	
Bal.	3,900		Bal.	2,000		(4)	400	Bal. 4,000
								1,600 (3)

	Supplies			Accounts Payable			T. Drew, Drawing	
Bal.	100			Bal. 800		Bal.	400	400 (4)

	Fees Income				Salaries Expense		Expense and Income Summary	
(1)	2,500	Bal.	2,500	Bal. 200	200 (2)	(2)	900	2,500 (1)
						(3)	1,600	
							2,500	2,500

	Rent Expense			Supplies Expense	
Bal.	500	500 (2)	Bal. 200	200 (2)	

Note: The above transactions are based on the sole proprietorship form of business. If this business were a corporation the Capital account would be replaced by the Retained Earnings account.

5.5 RULING ACCOUNTS

After the posting of the closing entries, all revenue and expense accounts and the summary accounts are closed. When ruling an account where only one debit and one credit exist, a double rule is drawn below the entry across the debit and credit money columns. The date and reference columns also have a double rule, in order to separate the transactions from the period just ended and the entry to be made in the subsequent period.

EXAMPLE 8

Salaries Expense

Date	Item	P.R.	Debit	Date	Item	P.R.	Credit
Jan. 30		J-1	200	Jan. 31		J-2	200

If more than one entry appears on either side of the account, a single ruled line is drawn below the last entry across the debit and credit money columns. The totals are entered just below the single line, and a double ruling line is drawn below the totals. The date and reference column also will have a double ruling line.

EXAMPLE 9

Expense and Income Summary

Date	Item	P.R.	Debit	Date	Item	P.R.	Credit
Jan. 31		J-2	900	Jan. 31		J-1	2,500
31		J-2	1,600				
			2,500				2,500

The assets, liabilities, and capital accounts will have balances. These open accounts are ruled so that their balances are carried forward to the new fiscal year.

EXAMPLE 10

Cash

Date	Item	P.R.	Debit	Date	Item	P.R.	Credit
Jan. 4			4,000	Jan. 4			300
15			2,500	30			500
				30			200
Balance of				31			1,200
the account.	→ *3,900*			31			400
Pencil footing			6,500				2,600
					Bal.		3,900
			6,500				6,500
Feb. 1	Bal.		3,900				

The balance of the account is entered on the first day of the following month.

Note: When there are several entries on each side, both the debit column and the credit column are pencil-footed. The pencil footing of one side is subtracted from the other side. The difference is written in the "Item" column on the side of the account that has the larger total.

5.6 POST-CLOSING TRIAL BALANCE

After the closing entries have been made and the accounts ruled, only balance sheet accounts—assets, liabilities, and capital—remain open. It is desirable to produce another trial balance to ensure that the accounts are in balance. This is known as a *post-closing trial balance*.

EXAMPLE 11

T. Drew
Post-Closing Trial Balance
January 31, 19X5

Cash	$3,900	
Supplies	100	
Furniture	2,000	
Accounts Payable		$ 800
T. Drew, Capital		5,200
	$6,000	$6,000

5.7 BOOKKEEPING AND ACCOUNTING CYCLE

Figure 5-1 illustrates the steps involved in recording transactions of a business.

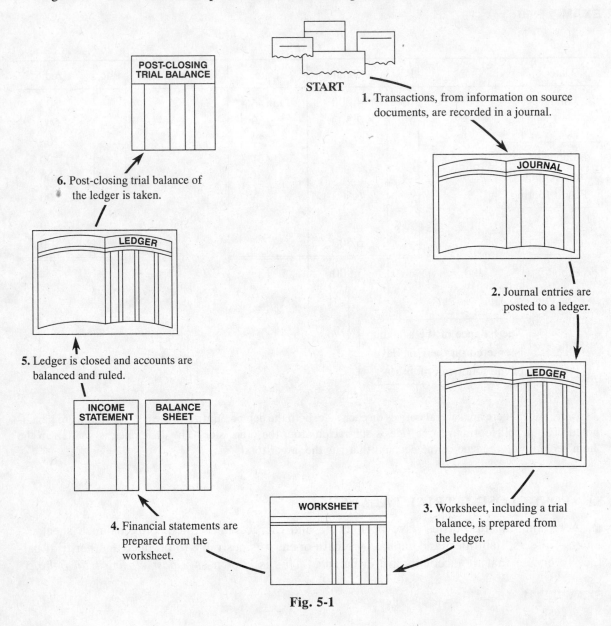

Fig. 5-1

Summary

1. The basis of accounting that recognizes revenue when it is earned, regardless of when cash is received, and matches the expenses to the revenue, regardless of when cash is paid out, is known as the _____.

2. An adjusting entry that records the expired amount of prepaid insurance would create the _____ account.

3. Supplies on hand is classified as an _____ and appears in the _____, whereas supplies expense is an _____ and appears in the _____.

4. Accrued salaries is treated in the balance sheet as a _____, whereas Salaries Expense appears in the income statement as an _____.

5. Both Allowance for Uncollectible Accounts and Accumulated Depreciation appear in the balance sheet as _____ from their related assets.

6. The related accounts discussed in Question 5 are _____ and _____.

7. An expense paid in advance is known as a _____.

8. The revenue and expense accounts are closed out to the summary account known as _____.

9. Eventually, all income, expense, and drawing accounts, including summaries, are closed into the _____ account.

10. The post-closing trial balance involves only _____, _____, and _____ accounts.

Answers: 1. accrual basis; 2. insurance expense; 3. asset, balance sheet, expense, income statement; 4. liability account, expense account; 5. deductions; 6. Accounts Receivable, Equipment; 7. Prepaid Expense; 8. Expense and Income Summary; 9. Capital; 10. asset, liability, capital

Solved Problems

5.1 A business pays weekly salaries of $10,000 on Friday for the 5-day week. Show the adjusting entry when the fiscal period ends on (a) Tuesday; (b) Thursday.

(a)		
(b)		

SOLUTION

(a)	Salaries Expense	4,000	
	Salaries Payable		4,000
(b)	Salaries Expense	8,000	
	Salaries Payable		8,000

5.2   An insurance policy covering a 2-year period was purchased on November 1 for $600. The amount was debited to Prepaid Insurance. Show the adjusting entry for the 2-month period ending December 31.

SOLUTION

Insurance Expense	50*	
Prepaid Insurance		50

$* \dfrac{\$600}{2 \text{ years}} \times \dfrac{2}{12} \text{ years} = \$50$

5.3   Office supplies purchases of $900 were debited to Office Supplies. A count of the supplies at the end of the period showed $500 on hand. Make the adjusting entry at the end of the period.

SOLUTION

Office Supplies Expense	400	
Office Supplies		400

5.4   Machinery costing $12,000, purchased November 30, is being depreciated at the rate of 10 percent per year. Show the adjusting entry for December 31.

SOLUTION

Depreciation Expense—Machinery	100*	
Accumulated Depreciation—Machinery		100

$*\$12,000 \times 10\% \text{ per year} \times \dfrac{1}{12} \text{ year} = \$100$

5.5   A large tractor costing $60,000 was purchased on September 30, is being depreciated by the straight-line method over 5 years, and has no salvage value. Show the year-end adjusting entry. (The tractor was put into use on October 1.)

SOLUTION

Depreciation	3,000*	
Accumulated Depreciation		3,000

$$\frac{*\text{Cost} - \text{salvage value}}{\text{Depreciation period}} \times \text{months in use} = \frac{\$60,000 - 0}{60 \text{ mo.}} = \$1,000 \times 3 \text{ mo.} = \$3,000$$

5.6 Salaries paid to employees are $500 per day. The weekly payroll ends on Friday, but Tuesday is the last day of the accounting period. Show the necessary adjusting entry (5-day week).

SOLUTION

Salaries Expense	1,000*	
Salaries Payable		1,000

*$500 × 2 = $1,000

5.7 On June 1, Dry Lake camps purchased a 3-year fire insurance policy costing $9,000. This was debited to a Prepaid Insurance account. The camp's year ends on November 30. (*a*) Show the necessary adjusting entry. (*b*) Show the entry if the above insurance policy was debited to an Insurance Expense account.

(*a*)			

(*b*)			

SOLUTION

(*a*)	Insurance Expense	1,500*	
	Prepaid Insurance		1,500

$$*\frac{\$9,000}{36 \text{ mo.}} = \$250 \times 6 \text{ mo.} = \$1,500$$

(*b*)	Prepaid Insurance	7,500*	
	Insurance Expense		7,500

$$*\frac{\$9,000}{36 \text{ mo.}} = \$250 \times 30 \text{ mo.} = \$7,500$$

Note that here we are concerned with how much is left of the policy amount.

5.8   Supplies costing $2,000 were debited to Supplies. The year-end inventory showed $1,150 of supplies on hand. (*a*) Show the necessary year-end adjusting entry. (*b*) Show the above adjusting entry if the supplies were debited to a Supplies Expense account when purchased.

(*a*)

(*b*)

SOLUTION

(*a*)
Supplies Expense	850*	
Supplies		850

*2,000 − $1,150 = $850

(*b*)
Supplies	1,150	
Supplies Expense		1,150

5.9   (*a*)   The balance in the Prepaid Insurance account, before adjustments, is $1,800, and the amount expired during the year is $1,200. The amount needed for the adjusting entry required is _____ .

(*b*)   A business pays weekly salaries (5-day week) of $4,000 on Friday. The amount of the adjusting entry necessary at the end of the fiscal period ending on Wednesday is _____ .

(*c*)   On December 31, the end of the fiscal year, the supplies account had a balance before adjustment of $650. The fiscal supply inventory account on December 31 is $170. The amount of the adjusting entry is _____ .

(*d*)   The supplies account on December 31 has an inventory of $500. The supplies used during the year is $200. The amount of the adjusting entry to record this information is _____ .

SOLUTION

(*a*) $1,200
(*b*) $2,400 ($4,000 ÷ 5 days = $800 per day; $800 × 3 days = $2,400)
(*c*) $480 ($650 − $170)
(*d*) $200

5.10   Listed are the T accounts of Douglas Money, financial advisor. The year-end adjustments necessary to bring the accounts up to date are as follows:

(*a*) Inventory of supplies at end of year was $395.

(*b*) Depreciation for the year was $900.

(*c*) Wages owed but not paid were $725.

(*d*) Utilities owed but not paid were $215.

(*e*) Insurance expense for the year was $1,150.

(*f*) Cash sales not yet posted were $2,175.

Cash		Accounts Receivable		Supplies		D. Money, Drawing	
7,555		1,750		915		1,250	

Accounts Payable		D. Money, Capital		Wages Expense	
	975		17,000	20,665	

Prepaid Insurance		Fees Income		Utilities Expense	
1,575			16,450	715	

First, prepare the adjusting journal entries. Then, make the necessary adjustments to the T accounts.

Adjusting Entries

(a)

(b)

(c)

(d)

(e)

(f)

Cash		Accounts Receivable		Supplies		Accounts Payable	
7,555		1,750		915			975

D. Money, Capital		Wages Expense		Prepaid Insurance		Fees Income	
	17,000	20,665		1,575			16,450

Utilities Expense		Supplies Expense		Depreciation Expense		Accumulated Depreciation	
715							

Wages Payable		Insurance Expense		D. Money, Drawing	

SOLUTION

Adjusting Entries

(a)	Supplies Expense	520	
	Supplies		520
(b)	Depreciation Expense	900	
	Accumulated Depreciation		900
(c)	Wages Expense	725	
	Wages Payable		725
(d)	Utilities Expense	215	
	Accounts Payable		215
(e)	Insurance Expense	1,150	
	Prepaid Insurance		1,150
(f)	Cash	2,175	
	Sales Income		2,175

Cash		Accounts Receivable		Supplies		Accounts Payable	
7,555		1,750		915	520 (a)		975
(f)2,175							215(d)

D. Money, Capital		Wages Expense		Prepaid Insurance		Fees Income	
	17,000	20,665		1,575	1,150 (e)		26,450
		(c) 725					2,175 (f)

Utilities Expense		Supplies Expense		Depreciation Expense		Accumulated Depreciation	
715		(a) 520		(b) 900			900 (b)
(d) 215							

Wages Payable		Insurance Expense		D. Money, Drawing	
	725 (c)	(e) 1,150		1,250	

5.11 From the preceding problem about Douglas Money, prepare the closing entries from the T accounts after you made the necessary adjustments.

Closing Entries

(1) _____

(2) _____

(3) _____

(4) _____

SOLUTION

Closing Entries

(1)	Fees Income	28,625	
	Expense and Income Summary		28,625
(2)	Expense and Income Summary	24,890	
	Wages Expense		21,390
	Insurance Expense		1,150
	Depreciation Expense		900
	Supplies Expense		520
	Utilities Expense		930
(3)	Expense and Income Summary	3,735	
	D. Money, Capital		3,735
(4)	D. Money, Capital	1,250	
	D. Money, Drawing		1,250

5.12 Prior to the adjustment on December 31, the Salaries Expense account had a debit of $200,000. Salaries owed, but not yet paid, totaled $5,000. Present the entries required to record the following:

(*a*) Accrued salary as of December 31

(*b*) The closing of the salary expense account

(*a*)			
(*b*)			

SOLUTION

(*a*)	Salaries Expense	5,000	
	Salaries Payable		5,000
(*b*)	Expense and Income Summary	205,000	
	Salaries Expense		205,000

5.13 Selected accounts from the ledger are presented in T-account form below. Journalize the adjusting entries that have been posted to the accounts.

Cash		Salaries Payable	
36,860			4,000

Prepaid Insurance		Capital	
600	200		32,000

Supplies		Expense and Income Summary	
540	240		

Equipment		Fees Income	
6,000			12,000

Accumulated Depreciation		Salaries Expense	
	1,800	4,000	

		Insurance Expense	
		200	

		Depreciation Expense	
		1,800	

		Supplies Expense	
		240	

SOLUTION

Insurance Expense	200	
Prepaid Insurance		200
Supplies Expense	240	
Supplies		240
Depreciation Expense	1,800	
Accumulated Depreciation		1,800
Salaries Expense	4,000	
Salaries Payable		4,000

5.14 From the information in Problem 5.13, present the necessary closing entries.

(a)

(b)

(c)

SOLUTION

(a)	Fees Income	12,000	
	Expense and Income Summary		12,000
(b)	Expense and Income Summary	6,240	
	Salaries Expense		4,000
	Insurance Expense		200
	Depreciation Expense		1,800
	Supplies Expense		240
(c)	Expense and Income Summary	5,760	
	Capital		5,760

5.15 From the information in Problem 5.14, prepare a post-closing trial balance.

Account	Dr.	Cr.

SOLUTION

Post Closing Trial Balance

Account	Dr.	Cr.
Cash	36,860	
Prepaid Insurance	400	
Supplies	300	
Equipment	6,000	
Accumulated Depreciation		1,800
Salaries Payable		4,000
Capital		37,760
	43,560	43,560

5.16 The trial balance before closing shows service income of $10,000 and interest income of $2,000. The expenses are: salaries, $6,000; rent, $2,000; depreciation, $1,500; and interest, $500. Give the closing entries to be made to Expense and Income Summary for (*a*) income and (*b*) expenses.

(*a*)

(*b*)

SOLUTION

(*a*)	Service Income	10,000	
	Interest Income	2,000	
	Expense and Income Summary		12,000
(*b*)	Expense and Income Summary	10,000	
	Salaries Expense		6,000
	Rent Expense		2,000
	Depreciation Expense		1,500
	Interest Expense		500

5.17 Using the solution to Problem 5.16, prepare the closing entry for net income, and post the transactions to the Expense and Income Summary and to the capital account, which had a prior balance of $20,000. Finally, close out the applicable account.

Expense and Income Summary				Capital		
(b)	10,000	12,000	(a)		Bal.	20,000
(c)	?					

SOLUTION

Expense and Income Summary	2,000	
Capital		2,000

Expense and Income Summary				Capital		
(b)	10,000	12,000	(a)		Bal.	20,000
(c)	2,000					2,000 (c)
	12,000	12,000				

5.18 After all revenue and expense accounts were closed at the end of the fiscal year, the Expense and Income Summary had a debit total of $100,000 and a credit total of $150,000. The capital account for Laura Anthony had a credit balance of $50,000; and Laura Anthony, Drawing, had a debit balance of $35,000. Journalize the closing entries.

SOLUTION

Expense and Income Summary	50,000	
Laura Anthony, Capital		50,000
Laura Anthony, Capital	35,000	
Laura Anthony, Drawing		35,000

5.19 Based on the balances below, prepare entries to close out (a) income accounts, (b) expense accounts, (c) Expense and Income Summary, (d) drawing account.

P. Silvergold, Capital		$22,000
P. Silvergold, Drawing	$6,000	
Service Income		12,000
Interest Income		1,500
Wages and Salaries Expense	8,000	
Rent Expense	4,000	
Depreciation Expense	3,000	
Interest Expense	2,000	

(a)			
(b)			
(c)			
(d)			

SOLUTION

(a)	Service Income	12,000	
	Interest Income	1,500	
	Expense and Income Summary		13,500
(b)	Expense and Income Summary	17,000	
	Wages and Salaries Expense		8,000
	Rent Expense		4,000
	Depreciation Expense		3,000
	Interest Expense		2,000
(c)	P. Silvergold, Capital	3,500*	
	Expense and Income Summary		3,500
(d)	P. Silvergold, Capital	6,000	
	P. Silvergold, Drawing		6,000

*$3,500 represents a net loss and is debited to the capital account.

Comprehensive Review Problem: Bookkeeping Cycle

1. Journalize the following transactions and post them to their respective accounts: (a) Sylvia Ellery opened a dry cleaning store on March 1, 19X5, investing $12,000 cash, $6,000 in equipment, and $4,000 worth of supplies; (b) bought $2,600 worth of equipment on account from J. Laym, Inc., Invoice 101; (c) received $2,800 from cash sales for the month; (d) paid rent, $200; (e) paid salaries, $600; (f) paid $1,600 on account to J. Laym, Inc.; (g) withdrew $500 for personal use; (h) used $1,000 worth of supplies during the month.

Page J-4

		P.R.	Debit	Credit
(a)				
(b)				
(c)				
(d)				
(e)				
(f)				
(g)				
(h)				

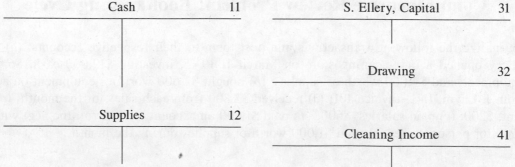

Cash	11	S. Ellery, Capital	31
		Drawing	32
Supplies	12		
		Cleaning Income	41

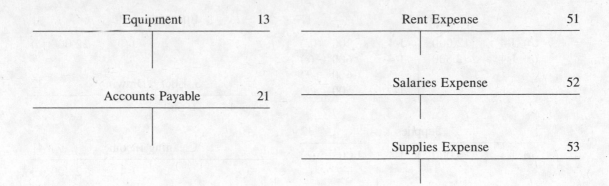

Equipment	13		Rent Expense	51
Accounts Payable	21		Salaries Expense	52
			Supplies Expense	53

SOLUTION

Page J-4

		P.R.	Debit	Credit
(a)	Cash	11	12,000	
	Supplies	12	4,000	
	Equipment	13	6,000	
	Sylvia Ellery, Capital	31		22,000
	Investment in business			
(b)	Equipment	13	2,600	
	Accounts Payable	21		2,600
	J. Laym, Inc., Invoice 101			
(c)	Cash	11	2,800	
	Cleaning Income	41		2,800
	Sales for month			
(d)	Rent Expense	51	200	
	Cash	11		200
	Rent for month			
(e)	Salaries Expense	52	600	
	Cash	11		600
	Salaries for month			
(f)	Accounts Payable	21	1,600	
	Cash	11		1,600
	Paid J. Laym, Inc., on account			
(g)	Sylvia Ellery, Drawing	32	500	
	Cash	11		500
	Personal withdrawal			
(h)	Supplies Expense	53	1,000	
	Supplies	12		1,000
	Supplies used during month			

	Cash				11
(a) J-4	12,000	J-4	200	(d)	
(c) J-4	2,800	J-4	600	(e)	
		J-4	1,600	(f)	
		J-4	500	(g)	

	Supplies				12
(a) J-4	4,000	J-4	1,000	(h)	

	Equipment		13
(a) J-4	6,000		
(b) J-4	2,600		

	Accounts Payable				21
(f) J-4	1,600	J-4	2,600	(b)	

	S. Ellery, Capital				31
		J-4	22,000	(a)	

	S. Ellery, Drawing		32
(g) J-4	500		

	Cleaning Income				41
		J-4	2,800	(c)	

	Rent Expense		51
(d) J-4	200		

	Salaries Expense		52
(e) J-4	600		

	Supplies Expense		53
(h) J-4	1,000		

2. Prepare a trial balance from the information for Ellery Dry Cleaners.

S. Ellery Dry Cleaning Company *Trial Balance*		
Cash		
Supplies		
Equipment		
Accounts Payable		
S. Ellery, Capital		
S. Ellery, Drawing		
Cleaning Income		
Rent Expense		
Salaries Expense		
Supplies Expense		

SOLUTION

S. Ellery Dry Cleaning Company
Trial Balance

Cash	$11,900	
Supplies	3,000	
Equipment	8,600	
Accounts Payable		$ 1,000
S. Ellery, Capital		22,000
S. Ellery, Drawing	500	
Cleaning Income		2,800
Rent Expense	200	
Salaries Expense	600	
Supplies Expense	1,000	
	$25,800	$25,800

3. Prepare all financial statements needed to reflect the information in the Ellery Dry Cleaners accounts.

S. Ellery Dry Cleaning
Income Statement
For the Year Ended December 31, 19X5

Income:		
Operating Expenses		
Total Operating Expenses		
Net Income		

S. Ellery Dry Cleaning
Capital Statement
For the Year Ended December 31, 19X5

Capital, January 1, 19X5		
Net Income		
Less: Drawing		
Increase in Capital		
Capital, December 31, 19X5		

S. Ellery Dry Cleaning Company
Balance Sheet
December 31, 19X5

ASSETS

Total Assets		
LIABILITIES AND CAPITAL		
Liabilities		
Capital, December 31, 19X5		
Total Liabilities and Capital		

SOLUTION

S. Ellery Dry Cleaning
Income Statement
For the Year Ended December 31, 19X5

Income:		
Cleaning Income		$2,800
Operating Expenses		
Rent Expense	$ 200	
Salaries Expense	600	
Supplies Expense	1,000	
Total Operating Expenses		1,800
Net Income		$1,000

S. Ellery Dry Cleaning
Capital Statement
For the Year Ended December 31, 19X5

Capital, January 1, 19X5		$22,000
Net Income	$1,000	
Less: Drawing	500	
Increase in Capital		500
Capital, December 31, 19X5		$22,500

S. Ellery Dry Cleaning Company		
Balance Sheet		
December 31, 19X5		
ASSETS		
Cash		$11,900
Supplies		3,000
Equipment		8,600
Total Assets		$23,500
LIABILITIES AND CAPITAL		
Liabilities		
Accounts Payable		$ 1,000
Capital, December 31, 19X5		22,500
Total Liabilities and Capital		$23,500

4. Prepare closing entries and post them.

	Journal			Page J-5
Date	Description	P.R.	Debit	Credit
	Closing Entries			
Dec. 31				

Cash					11
(a) J-4	12,000	J-4	200	(d)	
(c) J-4	2,800	J-4	600	(e)	
		J-4	1,600	(f)	
		J-4	500	(g)	

Supplies					12
(a) J-4	4,000	J-4	1,000	(h)	

S. Ellery, Capital					31
		J-4	22,000	(a)	

S. Ellery, Drawing					32
(g) J-4	500				

Cleaning Income					41
		J-4	2,800	(c)	

Equipment		13
(a) J-4 6,000		
(b) J-4 2,600		

Rent Expense		51
(d) J-4 200		

Accounts Payable		21
(f) J-4 1,600	J-4 2,600 (b)	

Salaries Expense		52
(e) J-4 600		

Cleaning Income		41
	J-4 2,800 (c)	

Supplies Expense		53
(h) J-4 1,000		

Expense and Income Summary		33

SOLUTION

Journal   Page J-5

Date	Description	P.R.	Debit	Credit
	Closing Entries			
Dec. 31				
	Cleaning Income		2,800	
	Expense and Income Summary			2,800
	Expense and Income Summary		1,800	
	Rent Expense			200
	Salaries Expense			600
	Supplies Expense			1,000
	Expense and Income Summary		1,000	
	S. Ellery, Capital			1,000
	S. Ellery, Capital		500	
	S. Ellery, Drawing			500

Cash		11
(a) J-4 12,000	J-4 200 (d)	
(c) J-4 2,800	J-4 600 (e)	
11,900	J-4 1,600 (f)	
	J-4 500 (g)	

S. Ellery, Capital		31
J-5 1,800	J-4 22,000 (a)	
J-5 500	J-5 2,800	
	23,500	

Supplies		12
(a) J-4 4,000	J-4 1,000 (h)	
3,000		

S. Ellery, Drawing		32
(g) J-4 500	J-5 500	

Cleaning Income		41
J-5 2,800	J-4 2,800 (c)	

Equipment		13
(a) J-4	6,000	
(b) J-4	2,600	
	8,600	

Accounts Payable		21
(f) J-4	1,600	J-4 2,600 (b)
		1,000

Rent Expense		51
(d) J-4	200	J-5 200

Salaries Expense		52
(e) J-4	600	J-5 600

Supplies Expense		53
(h) J-4	1,000	J-5 1,000

Expense and Income Summary		33
J-5	1,800	J-5 2,800
J-5	1,000	
	2,800	2,800

5. Prepare a Post Closing Trial Balance.

S. Ellery Dry Cleaning Company
Post-Closing Trial Balance
December 31, 19X5

Cash		
Supplies		
Equipment		
Accounts Payable		
S. Ellery, Capital		

SOLUTION

S. Ellery Dry Cleaning Company
Post-Closing Trial Balance
December 31, 19X5

Cash	$11,900	
Supplies	3,000	
Equipment	8,600	
Accounts Payable		$ 1,000
S. Ellery, Capital		22,500
	$23,500	$23,500

Examination I

Part I: Multiple Choice

1. The statement that presents assets, liabilities, and capital of a business entity as of a specific date is termed the (*a*) balance sheet, (*b*) income statement, (*c*) capital statement, (*d*) funds statement.

2. A business paid creditors on account. The effect of this transaction on the accounting equation was to (*a*) increase one asset, decrease another asset; (*b*) increase an asset, increase a liability; (*c*) decrease an asset, decrease a liability; (*d*) decrease an asset, decrease capital.

3. Which of the following applications of the rules of debit and credit is false?

		Recorded in Account as	Normal Balance of Account
(*a*)	Increase in drawing	Credit	Credit
(*b*)	Increase in salaries expense account	Debit	Debit
(*c*)	Increase in supplies account	Debit	Debit
(*d*)	Decrease in accounts payable account	Debit	Credit
(*e*)	Decrease in accounts receivable account	Credit	Debit

4. Which of the following errors, each considered individually, would cause the trial balance totals to be unequal? (*a*) A payment of $600 to a creditor was posted as a debit of $600 to Accounts Payable and a credit of $60 to Cash. (*b*) Cash received from customers on account was posted as a debit of $200 to Cash and a debit of $200 to Accounts Receivable. (*c*) A payment of $285 for equipment was posted as a debit of $285 to Equipment and a credit of $258 to Cash. (*d*) All of the above. (*e*) None of the above.

5. Entries journalized at the end of an accounting period to remove the balances from the temporary accounts so that they will be ready for use in accumulating data for the following accounting period are termed: (*a*) adjusting entries, (*b*) closing entries, (*c*) correcting entries, (*d*) all of the above, (*e*) none of the above.

6. If the effect of the debit portion of an adjusting entry is to increase the balance of an expense account, which of the following describes the effect of the credit portion of the entry? (*a*) decreases the balance of an asset account, (*b*) increases the balance of an asset account, (*c*) decreases the balance of a liability account, (*d*) increases the balance of a revenue account, (*e*) decreases the balance of the capital account.

7. Which of the following accounts should be closed to Expense and Income Summary at the end of the year? (*a*) depreciation expense, (*b*) sales income, (*c*) supplies expense, (*d*) rent income, (*e*) all of the above.

8. The adjusting entry to record depreciation of equipment is: (a) debit depreciation expense, credit depreciation payable; (b) debit depreciation payable, credit depreciation expense; (c) debit depreciation expense, credit accumulated depreciation; (d) debit equipment, credit depreciation expense.

9. The difference between the balance of a plant asset account and the related contra-asset account is termed: (a) expired cost, (b) accrual, (c) book value, (d) depreciation, (e) none of the above.

10. At the end of the preceding fiscal year, the usual adjusting entry for accrued salaries owed to employees was inadvertently omitted. This error was not corrected, but the accrued salaries were included in the first salary payment in the current fiscal year. Which of the following statements is true? (a) Salary expense was understated, and net income was overstated for the preceding year. (b) Salary expense was overstated, and net income was understated for the current year. (c) Salaries payable was understated at the end of the preceding fiscal year. (d) All of the above. (e) None of the above.

11. If total assets decreased by $5,000 during a period of time and capital increased by $15,000 during the same period, the amount and direction (increase or decrease) of the period's change in total liabilities is: (a) $10,000 increase, (b) $10,000 decrease, (c) $20,000 increase, (d) $20,000 decrease.

12. The total assets and total liabilities of a particular business enterprise at the beginning and at the end of the year appear below. During the year, the owner had withdrawn $18,000 for personal use and had made an additional investment in the enterprise of $5,000.

	Assets	Liabilities
Beginning of year	$166,000	$72,000
End of year	177,000	99,000

The amount of net income or net loss for the year was (a) net income of $11,000; (b) net income of $13,000; (c) net loss of $27,000; (d) net loss of $3,000.

13. The balance in the prepaid insurance account before adjustment at the end of the year is $1,840, and the amount of insurance expired during the year is $720. The adjusting entry required is: (a) debit insurance expense, $720; credit prepaid insurance, $720; (b) debit prepaid insurance, $720; credit insurance expense, $720; (c) debit insurance expense, $1,120; credit prepaid insurance, $1,120; (d) debit prepaid insurance, $1,120; credit insurance expense, $1,120.

14. A business enterprise pays weekly salaries of $5,000 on Friday for a 5-day week ending on that day. The adjusting entry necessary at the end of the fiscal period ending on Tuesday is: (a) debit salaries payable, $2,000; credit salaries expense, $2,000; (b) debit salaries expense, $2,000; credit salaries payable, $2,000; (c) debit salaries expense, $2,000; credit drawings, $2,000; (d) debit drawings, $2,000; credit salaries payable, $2,000.

15. Cash of $650 received from a customer on account was recorded as a $560 debit to Accounts Receivable and a credit to Cash. The necessary correcting entry is: (*a*) debit Cash, $90; credit Accounts Receivable, $90; (*b*) debit Accounts Receivable, $90; credit Cash, $90; (*c*) debit Cash, $650; credit Accounts Receivable, $650; (*d*) debit Cash, $1,210; credit Accounts Receivable, $1,210.

Part II: Problems

1. Below are the account balances of the State-Rite Cleaning Company as of December 31, 19X5. Prepare (*a*) an income statement, (*b*) a capital statement, (*c*) a balance sheet.

Accounts Payable	$11,600	Miscellaneous Expense	$ 3,000
Cleaning Income	39,500	Notes Payable	2,800
Capital (beginning)	14,300	Rent Expense	12,600
Cash	9,300	Salaries Expense	9,200
Drawing	4,800	Supplies Expense	2,400
Equipment	19,200	Supplies	5,300
Equipment Repairs Expense	2,400		

2. For each numbered transaction below, indicate the account to be debited and the account to be credited by placing the letter representing the account in the appropriate column: Accounts Payable (*a*); Capital (*b*); Cash (*c*); Drawing (*d*); Equipment (*e*); Fees Income (*f*); Notes Payable (*g*); Rent Expense (*h*); Salaries Expense (*i*); Supplies (*j*); Supplies Expense (*k*).

		Debit	Credit
(1)	Invested cash in the firm.	(*c*)	(*b*)
(2)	Received cash for services rendered.	c	f
(3)	Paid salaries for the week.	i	c
(4)	Bought equipment on account.	e	a
(5)	Bought supplies on account.	j	a
(6)	Gave a note in settlement of the equipment on account.	a	g
(7)	Borrowed money from the bank.	c	a or g
(8)	Withdrew cash for personal use.	d	c
(9)	A count showed that approximately three-quarters of the supplies inventory had been used during the year.	k	j
(10)	Paid rent for the month.	h	c

3. The balances of the accounts of the Judith Playhouse, as of November 30, were as follows:

Judith Playhouse
Trial Balance
November 30

Cash	$10,000	
Accounts Receivable	2,100	
Supplies	600	
Equipment	12,000	
Building	9,000	
Accounts Payable		$ 6,500
Notes Payable		12,000
Judith Playhouse, Capital		15,200
	$33,700	$ 33,700

Selected transactions for the month of December were:

(a) Dec.   1 Bought new theatrical equipment for $3,000, paying half in cash and giving our note for the balance.
(b)   10 Paid $1,000 due on the notes payable.
(c)   14 Receipts for the 2-week period (admissions income) totaled $9,600.
(d)   20 Paid utilities, $150.
(e)   24 Paid $1,000 for 5-year insurance policy on the theatre.
(f)   28 Paid monthly salaries, $1,250.

Prepare all necessary entries to record the above transactions.

4. Using the following data, prepare journal entries for the month of December.

   (a) Weekly salaries of $8,000 are payable on Friday for a 5-day week. What is the adjusting entry if the fiscal period ends on Wednesday?

   (b) An insurance policy covering a 4-year period was purchased on February 1 for $1,200. What is the adjusting entry on December 31?

   (c) Office supplies of $700 were debited to Office Supplies during the month. The account has $300 worth still on hand. Prepare the adjusting entry.

5. After all income and expense accounts of the Gold Silver Company were closed at the end of the year, the expense and income summary had a debit balance of $125,000 and a credit balance of $190,000. The capital account had a credit balance of $72,000, whereas the drawing account had a debit balance of $12,000. Journalize the closing entries.

6. Selected accounts from a ledger are presented in T-account form. (a) Journalize the adjusting entries that have been posted to the account. (b) Journalize the closing entries that have been posted to the account.

Prepaid Insurance		Salaries Expense	
240	125	2,700	6,300
175		2,925	
		675	

Accumulated Depreciation		Insurance Expense	
	2,250	125	125
	400		

Salaries Payable		Depreciation Expense	
	675	400	400

Expense and Income Summary		Miscellaneous Expense	
7,115		25	290
		100	
		45	
		50	
		70	

7. Journalize the following transactions:

(a) Ronald Henderson began his dentistry practice by investing $24,000 cash, $12,000 in equipment, and $6,000 in supplies.

(b) Bought $5,000 worth of equipment, paying $1,000 and owing the balance to Halpern Company.

(c) Received $4,200 from fees for the month.

(d) Paid rent of $600.

(e) Paid salaries of $1,200.

(f) Paid half of the amount owed to Halpern Company.

(g) Withdrew $700 for personal use.

(h) Supplies on hand, $5,000.

8. Post from the journal in Problem 7 and present a trial balance.

9. Based on the information presented in Problem 8, journalize all necessary entries to close the accounts. Then post and rule them.

Answers to Examination I

Part I

1. (a); 2. (c); 3. (a); 4. (d); 5. (b); 6. (a); 7. (e); 8. (c); 9. (c); 10. (d); 11. (d); 12. (d); 13. (a); 14. (b); 15. (d)

Part II

1. (*a*)

State-Rite Cleaning Company
Income Statement
For the Period Ending December 31, 19X5

Cleaning Income		$39,500
Expenses		
Equipment Repairs Expense	$ 2,400	
Rent Expense	12,600	
Salaries Expense	9,200	
Supplies Expense	2,400	
Miscellaneous Expense	3,000	
Total Expenses		29,600
Net Income		$ 9,900

(*b*)

State-Rite Cleaning Company
Capital Statement
For the Period Ending December 31, 19X5

Capital, January 1, 19X5		$14,300
Net Income	$ 9,900	
Less: Drawing	4,800	
Increase in Capital		5,100
Capital, December 31, 19X5		$19,400

(*c*)

State-Rite Cleaning Company
Balance Sheet
December 31, 19X5

ASSETS

Cash	$ 9,300	
Supplies	5,300	
Equipment	19,200	
Total Assets		$33,800

LIABILITIES AND CAPITAL

Accounts Payable	$ 11,600	
Notes Payable	2,800	
Total Liabilities		$14,400
Capital, December 31, 19X5		19,400
Total Liabilities and Capital		$33,800

2.

	Debit	Credit
(1)	(c)	(b)
(2)	(c)	(f)
(3)	(i)	(c)
(4)	(e)	(a)
(5)	(j)	(a)
(6)	(a)	(g)
(7)	(c)	(g) or (a)
(8)	(d)	(c)
(9)	(k)	(j)
(10)	(h)	(c)

3.

(a)	Equipment	3,000	
	Cash		1,500
	Notes Payable		1,500

(b)	Notes Payable	1,000	
	Cash		1,000

(c)	Cash	9,600	
	Admissions Income		9,600

(d)	Utilities Expense	150	
	Cash		150

(e)	Prepaid Insurance	1,000	
	Cash		1,000

(f)	Salaries Expense	1,250	
	Cash		1,250

4.

(a) Salaries Expense   4,800

       Salaries Payable   4,800

    $[3 \times (8,000 \div 5) = 4,800]$

(b) Insurance Expense   275

       Prepaid Insurance   275

    $(1,200 \div 4 = 300;$

    $\frac{11}{12} \times 300 = 275)$

(c)	Supplies Expense		400	
	Supplies			400

5.

Expense and Income Summary		65,000	
Capital			65,000

Capital		12,000	
Drawing			12,000

6.

(a)	Insurance Expense		125	
	Prepaid Insurance			125

	Depreciation Expense		400	
	Accumulated Depreciation			400

	Salaries Expense		675	
	Salaries Payable			675

(b)	Income Summary		7,115	
	Salaries Expense			6,300
	Depreciation Expense			400
	Insurance Expense			125
	Miscellaneous Expense			290

7.

(a)	Cash		24,000	
	Supplies		6,000	
	Equipment		12,000	
	Henderson, Capital			42,000

(b)	Equipment		5,000	
	Cash			1,000
	Accounts Payable—Halpern			4,000

(c)	Cash		4,200	
	Fees Income			4,200

(d)	Rent Expense		600	
	Cash			600

(e)	Salaries Expense		1,200	
	Cash			1,200

(f)	Accounts Payable		2,000	
	Cash			2,000

| | (g) | Drawing | | 700 | |
| | | Cash | | | 700 |

| | (h) | Supplies Expense | | 1,000 | |
| | | Supplies | | | 1,000 |

8.

Cash				Accounts Payable				Fees Income			
(a)	24,000	1,000	(b)	(f)	2,000	4,000	(b)			4,200	(c)
(c)	4,200	600	(d)								
		1,200	(e)	**Capital**				**Rent Expense**			
		2,000	(f)			42,000	(a)	(d)	600		
		700	(g)								

Supplies				Drawing				Salaries Expense		
(a)	6,000	1,000	(h)	(g)	700			(e)	1,200	

Equipment					Supplies Expense		
(a)	12,000				(h)	1,000	
(b)	5,000						

Trial Balance

Cash	$22,700	
Supplies	5,000	
Equipment	17,000	
Accounts Payable		$ 2,000
Capital		42,000
Drawing	700	
Fees Income		4,200
Rent Expense	600	
Salaries Expense	1,200	
Supplies Expense	1,000	
	$48,200	$48,200

9.

| | (i) | Fees Income | 4,200 | |
| | | Expense and Income Summary | | 4,200 |

	(j)	Expense and Income Summary	2,800	
		Rent Expense		600
		Salaries Expense		1,200
		Supplies Expense		1,000

| | (k) | Expense and Income Summary | 1,400 | |
| | | Capital | | 1,400 |

| | (l) | Capital | 700 | |
| | | Drawing | | 700 |

	Capital		
(l)	700	42,000	(a)
		1,400	(k)

	Fees Income		
(i)	4,200	4,200	(i)

	Drawing		
(g)	700	700	(l)

	Rent Expense		
(d)	600	600	(j)

Expense and Income Summary

(j)	2,800	4,200	(i)
(k)	1,400		
	4,200	4,200	

	Salaries Expense		
(e)	1,200	1,200	(j)

	Supplies Expense		
(h)	1,000	1,000	(j)

Chapter 6

Repetitive Transactions—The Sales and the Purchases Journals

6.1 INTRODUCTION

In the previous chapters, each transaction was recorded by first placing an entry in the general journal and then posting the entry to the related accounts in the general ledger. This system, however, is both time-consuming and wasteful. It is much simpler and more efficient to group together those transactions that are repetitive, such as sales, purchases, cash receipts, and cash payments, and place each of them in a special journal.

Many types of transactions may require the use of special journals, for example, receipt or payment of cash and purchase or sale of goods or services.

The number and design of the special journals will vary, depending on the needs of a particular business. The special journals used in a typical firm are as follows:

Name of Special Journal	Abbreviation	Type of Transaction
Cash receipts journal	CR	All cash received
Cash disbursements journal	CD	All cash paid out
Purchases journal	P	All purchases on account
Sales journal	S	All sales on account

In addition to these four special journals, a general journal (J) is used for recording transactions that do not fit into any of the four types above. The general journal is also used for the recording of adjusting and closing entries at the end of the accounting period.

6.2 SALES JOURNAL

Only sales on account are recorded in the sales journal; cash sales are recorded in the cash receipts journal (page 145).

EXAMPLE 1

Sales on account are made during the month as follows: on February 1 to A. Anderson for $200, on February 2 to B. Butler for $350, on February 12 to C. Chase for $125, and on February 24 to D. Davis and Co. for $400. The procedure to record these sales is as follows:

1. Record the sales on account in the sales journal.

2. At the end of the month only, add the amount column and post the total amount, $1,075, to the general ledger by debiting Accounts Receivable (account number 12) and by crediting Sales Income (account number 41) for $1,075 each.

3. Place a posting reference in the sales journal by recording the account number 12 for Accounts Receivable, and the account number 41 for Sales Income, under the total.

4. In the general ledger, place the source of the entry S-1 in each account.

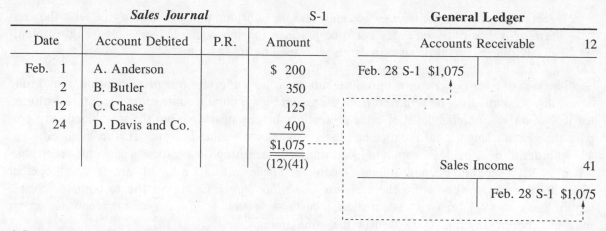

Advantages of Special Journals

1. *Reduces detailed recording.* As demonstrated in the transactions above, each sales transaction is recorded on a single line, with all details included on that line: date, customer's name, and amount.

2. *Reduces posting.* There is only *one* posting made to Accounts Receivable and *one* posting to Sales Income, regardless of the number of transactions.

3. *Permits better division of labor.* If there are several journals, more than one bookkeeper can work on the books at the same time.

6.3 SPECIAL LEDGERS (Subsidiary Ledgers)

Further simplification of the general ledger is brought about by the use of subsidiary ledgers. In particular, for those businesses that sell goods on credit and that find it necessary to maintain a separate account for each customer and each creditor, the use of a special accounts receivable ledger eliminates the need to make multiple entries in the general ledger.

The advantages of special or subsidiary ledgers are similar to the advantages of special journals. These are:

1. *Reduces ledger detail.* Most of the information will be in the subsidiary ledger, and the general ledger will be reserved chiefly for summary or total figures. Therefore, it will be easier to prepare the financial statements.

2. *Permits better division of labor.* Here again, each special or subsidiary ledger may be handled by a different person. Therefore, one person may work on the general ledger accounts while another person may work simultaneously on the subsidiary ledger.

3. *Permits a different sequence of accounts.* In the general ledger, it is desirable to have the accounts in the same sequence as in the balance sheet and income statement. As a further aid, it is desirable to use numbers to locate and reference the accounts, as explained in Section 2.5. However, in connection with accounts receivable, which involves names of customers or companies, it is preferable to have the accounts in alphabetical sequence.

4. *Permits better internal control.* Better control is maintained if a person other than the person responsible for the general ledger is responsible for the subsidiary ledger. For example, the accounts receivable or customers' ledger trial balance should agree with the balance of the accounts receivable account in the general ledger. The general ledger

account acts as a controlling account, and the subsidiary ledger must agree with the control. No unauthorized entry could be made in the subsidiary ledger, as it would immediately put that record out of balance with the control account.

The idea of *control accounts,* introduced above, is an important one in accounting. Any group of similar accounts may be removed from the general ledger and a controlling account substituted for it. Not only is another level of error protection thereby provided, but the time needed to prepare the general ledger trial balance and the financial statements becomes further reduced.

In order to be capable of supplying information concerning the business's accounts receivable, a firm needs a separate account for each customer. These customer accounts are grouped together in a subsidiary ledger known as the *accounts receivable ledger.* Each time the accounts receivable (control account) is increased or decreased, a customer's account in the accounts receivable ledger must also be increased or decreased by the same amount.

The customers' accounts are usually kept in alphabetical order and include, besides outstanding balances, information such as address, phone number, credit terms, and other pertinent items.

EXAMPLE 2

The procedure for special ledgers is as follows:

1. After the sale is entered, the amount of the sale is immediately posted as a debit to the customer's account in the subsidiary accounts receivable ledger.

2. In the sales journal, a record of the posting is made in the posting reference column by placing a check mark (✔) before the customer's name.

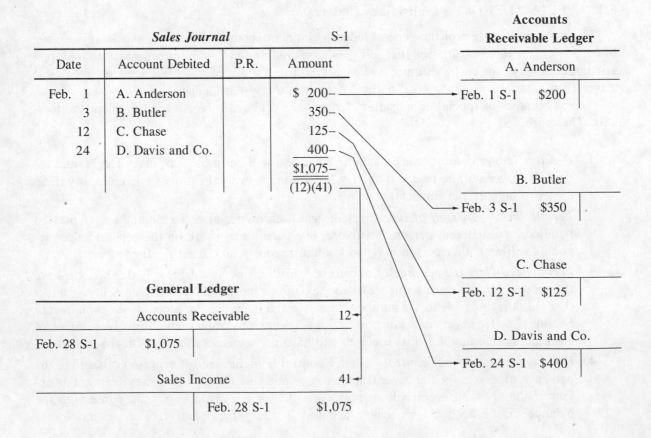

Proving That the Accounts Receivable Subsidiary Ledger Is Equal to the Control

After all individual transactions are posted to the subsidiary ledger and the totals in the sales journal are posted to the general ledger, the bookkeeper is ready to check the accuracy of the work.

EXAMPLE 3

The checking procedure is as follows:

1. At the end of the month, the bookkeeper prepares a list of all open accounts in the accounts receivable ledger.

2. The total due from customers is compared with the balance in the accounts receivable account in the general ledger. If the schedule and the control account agree, the bookkeeper has proved the accuracy of the recording.

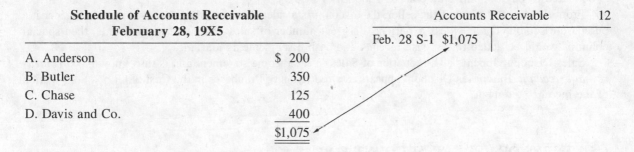

Schedule of Accounts Receivable February 28, 19X5	
A. Anderson	$ 200
B. Butler	350
C. Chase	125
D. Davis and Co.	400
	$1,075

Accounts Receivable   12

Feb. 28 S-1 $1,075

6.4 SALES RETURNS AND DISCOUNTS

If, during the year, many transactions occur in which customers return goods bought on account, a special journal known as the *sales returns journal* would be used. However, where sales returns are infrequent, the general journal is sufficient.

The entry to record return of sales on account in the general journal would be:

			J-1
	P.R.	Debit	Credit
Sales Returns	42	800	
Accounts Receivable, Lawton Company	12		800

The accounts receivable account, which is credited, is posted both in the accounts receivable controlling account and in the accounts receivable ledger, under Lawton Company.

Accounts Receivable Ledger   **General Ledger**

Lawton Company		Accounts Receivable 12		Sales Returns 42
Bal. 1,900	J-1 800	Bal. 1,900 | J-1 800	J-1 800	

If the sales returns involve the payment of cash, it would appear in the cash disbursements journal. Sales Returns appears in the income statement as a reduction of Sales Income.

To induce a buyer to make payment before the amount is due, the seller may allow the buyer to deduct a certain percentage of the bill. If payment is due within a stated number of days after the date of invoice, the number of days will usually be preceded by the letter "n," signifying net. For example, bills due in 30 days would be indicated by n/30.

A 2 percent discount offered if payment is made within 10 days would be indicated by 2/10. If the buyer has a choice of either paying the amount less 2 percent within the 10-day period or paying the entire bill within 30 days, the terms would be written as 2/10, n/30.

EXAMPLE 4

A sales invoice totaling $1,000 and dated January 2 has discount terms of 2/10, n/30. If the purchaser pays on or before January 12 (10 days after the date of purchase), he or she may deduct $20 ($1,000 × 2%) from the bill and pay only $980. If the purchaser chooses not to pay within the discount period, he or she is obligated to pay the entire amount of $1,000 by February 1.

From the point of view of the seller, the discount is a sales discount; the purchaser would consider it a purchase discount. If a business experiences a great number of sales and purchase discounts, then special columns would be added to the cash receipts and cash disbursements journals.

Sales Discount appears as a reduction of Sales in the income statement and is thus known as a *contra-revenue account.* Purchases Discount appears as a reduction of Purchases in the Cost of Goods Sold section of the income statement.

6.5   TYPES OF LEDGER ACCOUNT FORMS

The T account has been used for most illustrations of accounts thus far. The disadvantage of the T account is that it requires totaling the debit and the credit columns in order to find the balance. As it is necessary to have the balance of a customer's or creditor's account available at any given moment, an alternative form of the ledger, the *three-column account,* may be used. The advantage of this form is that an extra column, "Balance," is provided, so that the amount the customer owes, or the creditor is owed, is always shown. As each transaction is recorded, the balance is updated. Below is an illustration of an accounts receivable ledger account using this form.

M. Gersten

Date	P.R.	Debit	Credit	Balance
Jan. 2	S-1	650		650
4	S-1	409		1,059
8	J-1		500	559

6.6   PURCHASES AS A COST

Before any firm can sell merchandise (see Sales Journal), it must purchase goods to be resold. Purchasing goods for resale is synonymous with incurring an expense. Cost accounts are similar to expense accounts, because both decrease the owners' capital and both are temporary. In order to record the cost of all goods bought during an accounting period, a new account, Purchases, must be established. It is important to note that expenses are necessary in order to operate a business, but costs are incurred in order to acquire goods for resale. A full description of purchases appears in Chapter 9.

6.7 TRADE DISCOUNTS

Manufacturers and wholesalers publish catalogs in order to describe their products and list their retail prices. Usually, they offer deductions from these list prices to dealers who buy in large quantities. These deductions are known as *trade discounts.* By offering these discounts, a business can *adjust* a price at which it is willing to bill its goods without changing the list price in the catalog.

EXAMPLE 5

The Carrie Corporation wants to continue advertising its stereo radio at a list price of $150. However, the radio is offered to dealers at a trade discount of 30 percent, which amounts to $45. Therefore, the dealer pays only $105 for the set.

Assume that the Carrie Corporation wants to continue advertising its radio at a list price of $150, but because of higher costs, an increase to dealers has to be made. The corporation will issue a new price list on which the trade discount will be reduced from 30 percent to 25 percent, and so they will not have to issue a completely new catalog just to change the price of a few items.

EXAMPLE 6

A trade discount can also be increased so as to offer older goods to dealers at a lower cost. If a new type of stereo radio were to come out at $200, the Carrie Corporation might increase its trade discount to 40 percent on older models in order to encourage dealers to purchase them.

Note that trade discounts are not recorded in the accounting records, as they are used only to determine the *net* purchase price. For accounting purposes, the amount recorded would be the price that must be paid to the seller (retail price minus the trade discount). For example, if the older models were to retail for $150, less a new trade discount of 40 percent, the entry to record the purchase on account would be:

	Dr.	Cr.
Purchases	90	
Accounts Payable		90
($150 − $60 discount)		

6.8 PURCHASE CONTROL

Some procedures for proper merchandising control affect the purchase of items for resale.

1. When items are needed for resale, a *purchase requisition* is made and sent to the purchasing department.
2. The purchasing department prepares a *purchase order,* after checking all conditions of the purchase. This order consists of the price, quantity, and description of the goods to be ordered. It may also show information regarding payment terms and costs of transportation (freight).
3. When the goods are received, a *purchase invoice* is enclosed, showing the amount of the goods shipped and their related costs. This document provides the basis for recording the purchase.
4. Before paying the invoice, the accounts payable department should verify the contents of the shipment of goods received and the correctness of the purchase order to ensure that what was ordered was received.

6.9 PURCHASE INVOICES

In most businesses, purchases are made regularly and are evidenced by purchase invoices to creditors. A purchase invoice is the source document that supplies the information for recording goods on account. Such information would include:

1. Seller's name and address
2. Date of purchase and invoice number
3. Method of shipment
4. Terms of the purchase transaction
5. Type and quantity of goods shipped
6. Cost of goods billed

Where there are many transactions for purchases of merchandise for resale, for supplies or equipment, the labor-saving features of a special purchases journal should be utilized.

6.10 PURCHASES JOURNAL

The basic principles that apply to the sales journal also apply to the purchases journal. However, a single-column purchases journal is too limited to be practicable, as businesses do not usually restrict their credit purchases only to merchandise bought for resale. Various kinds of goods (office and store supplies, equipment, and so on) are bought on a charge basis. Therefore, the purchases journal can be expanded with special columns to record those accounts that are frequently affected by credit purchase transactions.

The following illustrative problem demonstrates the use of the purchases journal.

EXAMPLE 7

Jan. 4   Purchased merchandise on account from Agin Corp., $1,000.
     6   Purchased supplies on account from Baker Corp., $500.
     8   Purchased equipment from Connely Company on account, $9,000.
    15   Purchased land from J. Donald on account, $11,000.
    21   Purchased additional supplies from Baker Corp. on account, $200.
    28   Purchased additional merchandise from Agin Corp. on account, $2000.

Purchases Journal   P-1   **(1)**

Date	Account Credited	P.R.	Acct. Pay. Cr.	Purchases Dr.	Supplies Dr.	Sundry Accounts Dr.	P.R.	Amt.
Jan. 4	**(2)** Agin Corp.	✔	1,000	1,000				
6	Baker Corp.	✔	500		500			
8	Connely Company	✔	9,000			Equipment	18	9,000
15	Davis Company	✔	11,000			Land	17	11,000
21	Baker Corp.	✔	200		200	**(4)**		
28	Agin Corp.	✔	2,000	2,000				
			23,700	3,000	700			20,000
			(21)	(51)	(14)			(✔)

(3)

Notes:

(1) P-1 denotes the page number (1) of the purchases journal.

(2) The individual amounts will be posted as credits to their respective accounts in the accounts payable subsidiary ledger. The check marks in the purchases journal indicate such postings.

(3) Accounts Payable, Purchases, and Supplies are posted to the respective accounts in the general ledger as totals only.

(4) The sundry amount of $20,000 is not posted as a total; instead, the individual amounts are posted, as many different accounts may be affected each month.

General Ledger

Supplies 14		Accounts Payable 21
Jan. 31 P-1 700		P-1 Jan. 31 23,700

Land 17
Jan. 15 P-1   11,000

Equipment 18		Purchases 51
Jan. 8 P-1 9,000		Jan. 31 P-1 3,000

6.11   SUBSIDIARY ACCOUNTS PAYABLE LEDGER

Early in this chapter, a new subsidiary ledger, called Accounts Receivable, was created for all a company's customers (sales on account). A firm that purchases on account (accounts payable) would do the same thing, because the credit balance in Accounts Payable represents the total amount owed by the company for purchases on account.

Because the account shows only the total liability to all sellers, the need for a subsidiary record for each creditor in a separate ledger is apparent.

Posting to the Subsidiary Ledger

During the month, each individual credit entry is posted from the purchases journal to the creditor's account in the subsidiary ledger. A check mark is placed in the posting reference column in the purchases journal to show that the amount has been posted. The check mark is used because the individual creditors' accounts are not numbered.

1. When a purchase on account is made, the invoice becomes the basis for the credit to the creditor's ledger account.

2. When a payment is made, the account is debited.

3. Any credit balance in a subsidiary account represents an unpaid balance owed to that particular firm.

No postings are made to the general ledger until the end of the month, when all the amounts are accumulated into one total. It is at this time that the total amount of all purchases for the month, as well as other debits, including supplies, equipment, land, and so on, are posted to the respective accounts and then credited to the accounts payable controlling account in the general ledger.

The total of all the credit amounts posted to the accounts payable ledger must equal the total credit to the controlling account in the general ledger. When the postings from the purchases journal are completed for the month, the ledgers should balance.

In order to prove that the subsidiary ledger is in agreement with the controlling account of the general ledger, a schedule of accounts payable is prepared. This schedule is the total of all the balances of each of the credit accounts. Their total must equal that of the controlling accounts payable.

EXAMPLE 8

Using the information in Example 7, the accounts payable ledger after postings would appear as follows:

Accounts Payable Subsidiary Ledger

Agin Corp.		Baker Corp.	
	Jan. 4 P-1 1,000		Jan. 6 P-1 500
	28 P-1 2,000		21 P-1 200

Connely Company		R. Davis Company	
	Jan. 8 P-1 9,000		Jan. 15 P-1 11,000

To prove that the accounts payable ledger is in balance, the total owed to the four companies must agree with the balance in the accounts payable control account.

Schedule of Accounts Payable

Agin Corp.	$ 3,000		
Baker Corp.	700		
Connely Company	9,000	Accounts Payable	21
R. Davis Company	11,000		
Total	$23,700	P-1	23,700

6.12   RETURN OF MERCHANDISE

At times, a business ordering goods might find that purchases were received damaged or not meeting certain specifications. Regardless of the reason, these goods would be returned to the seller and are known as *returns*. An *allowance* would be granted by which the seller gives the purchaser either a refund or a credit adjustment (known as a credit memorandum). Instead of crediting the account Purchases for the return, correct accounting procedures would set up a new account, *Purchases Returns and Allowances*. This contra account provides a separate record of the cost reduction and allows management to exercise better control of its merchandise purchases. Since Purchases Returns and Allowances is a contra account, its normal balance will be a credit (the opposite of the debit balance of Purchases). The balance of the Purchases Returns and Allowances account appears on the income statement as a reduction of Purchases. The difference is called Net Purchases.

EXAMPLE 9

Purchases	$10,000	
Less: Returns and Allowances	3,000	
Net Purchases		$7,000

EXAMPLE 10

If there were a Purchase Discount of $1,000 in Example 9, the net purchases would appear as:

Purchases		$10,000
Less: Returns	$3,000	
Discounts	1,000	4,000
Net Purchases		$ 6,000

6.13 PURCHASE DISCOUNTS

To induce a buyer to make payment before the amount is due, the seller may allow the buyer to deduct a certain percentage from the total. If payment is due within a stated number of days after the date of invoice, the number of days will usually be preceded by the letter "n," signifying net. For example, bills due in 30 days would be indicated by n/30. A 2 percent discount offered if payment is made within 10 days would be indicated by 2/10. If the buyer has a choice of either paying the amount less 2 percent within the 10-day period or paying the entire bill within 30 days, the terms would be written as 2/10, n/30.

If the buyer chooses to pay within the discount period, a new contra (against) account, Purchase Discount, would be created and would appear as a reduction of Purchases in the cost of goods sold section of the income statement.

EXAMPLE 11

A purchase invoice of $900 on March 4 has discount terms of 2/10 n/30. If payment is made on March 12, the two entries needed to record the above information are as follows:

Mar. 4	Purchases	900	
	Accounts Payable		900
Mar. 12	Accounts Payable	900	
	Purchase Discounts		18*
	Cash		882

*(900 × 2%)

Although in most cases the cash discount period is computed from the invoice or purchase date, the date may also be computed from either the date of receipt of the goods (ROG) or starting with the end of the month (EOM).

ROG is used primarily when there is a significant gap between the date of the purchase and the delivery date. This eliminates the necessity for the buyer to pay for goods before receiving them in order to get a discount.

. EOM is used primarily as a convenience, with traditional end-of-month billing practices followed by most companies.

If a firm has many purchase returns, a *purchase returns journal* should be used. However, for illustrative purposes, entries for the return of purchases (bought on account) are made here in the general journal:

	P.R.	Debit	Credit
			J-1
Accounts Payable, H. Chen	21/✔	420	
Purchase Returns	52		420

The debit portion of the accounts payable is posted to the accounts payable account in the general ledger and also to the accounts payable subsidiary ledger. Because the controlling account and the customer's account are both debited, a diagonal line is needed in the posting reference column to show both postings. For items involving a return for cash, the cash receipts journal is used (see Chapter 7).

Accounts Payable Ledger   **General Ledger**

H. Chen   Accounts Payable   21   Purchase Returns   52

J-1	420	Bal.	800		J-1	420	Bal.	800				J-1	420

Summary

1. When transactions that are repetitive in nature are grouped together, they are placed in a _____ journal.

2. The abbreviation for the sales journal is _____ .

3. All sales _____ are recorded in the sales journal.

4. The sales journal helps reduce _____ and _____ .

5. The _____ ledger is used to maintain a separate account for each customer.

6. The account in the general ledger that, after posting, shows the total amount of dollars owed and agrees with the totals in the subsidiary ledger is termed the _____ account.

7. The extra column in a three-column T account shows the _____ of the account.

8. The list of accounts of individual customers, whose total equals the one figure in the accounts receivable controlling account, is known as the _____ .

9. The account used to show the amount of goods returned is _____ .

10. Infrequent returned sales would be recorded in the _____ journal.

11. Deductions from list or retail price offered by manufacturers or wholesalers are known as _____ .

12. A trade discount of 40 percent on an old-model TV retailing at $500 would result in a cost to the purchaser of _____ .

13. The evidence of a purchase is accomplished by a _____ .

14. The purchase journal can be expanded with _____ columns to record those accounts frequently affected by credit purchase transactions.

15. The abbreviation and notation for the fifth page of the purchases journal would be _____ .

16. The Sundry amount in the purchases journal is not posted as a _____ . Rather the _____ accounts are posted.

17. Postings to the general ledger are made _____ , whereas subsidiary accounts are posted _____ .

18. In order to prove the subsidiary ledger in agreement with the controlling account of the general ledger, a _____ is prepared.

19. If there are many returns, a special journal termed a _____ journal is used.

20. It is common to divide the ledger for a large firm into three separate ledgers, known as the _____ , _____ , and _____ ledgers.

Answers: 1. special; 2. S; 3. on account; 4. detailed recording, posting; 5. accounts receivable; 6. controlling; 7. balance; 8. schedule of accounts receivable; 9. sales returns; 10. general; 11. trade discounts; 12. $300; 13. purchase invoice; 14. special; 15. P-5; 16. total, individual; 17. at the end of the month, immediately; 18. schedule of accounts payable; 19. purchase returns; 20. general, accounts receivable, accounts payable.

Solved Problems

6.1   For each of the following transactions, indicate with a check mark the journal in which it should be recorded.

(*a*)   Sale of merchandise to B. Orzech on account, $400

(*b*)   Sale of merchandise to M. Snyder for cash, $150

(*c*)   Cash refunded to M. Snyder for goods returned

(*d*)   B. Orzech returned part of the goods sold for credit, $100

	Sales Journal	General Journal	Cash Journal
(a)			
(b)			
(c)			
(d)			

SOLUTION

	Sales Journal	General Journal	Cash Journal
(a)	✔		
(b)			✔
(c)			✔
(d)		✔	

6.2 Which of the transactions in Problem 6.1 should be posted to the subsidiary ledger?

SOLUTION

Transactions (a) and (d), because sales were on account. Transactions (b) and (c) involved cash, thus creating no accounts receivable.

Accounts Receivable	12		B. Orzech	
(a) 400	100 (d)		(a) 400	100 (d)

Sales Income	41
	400 (a)

Sales Returns	42
(d) 100	

6.3 Record the following transactions in the sales journal:

Jan. 1 Sold merchandise on account to Lombardi Company, $550.
     4 Sold merchandise on account to Gerard Company, $650.
    18 Sold merchandise on account to Harke Company, $300.
    29 Sold additional merchandise to Harke Company, $100.

Sales Journal			S-1
Date	Account Debited	P.R.	Amount

SOLUTION

Sales Journal			S-1
Date	Account Debited	P.R.	Amount
Jan. 1	Lombardi Company	✔	550
4	Gerard Company	✔	650
18	Harke Company	✔	300
29	Harke Company	✔	100
			1,600

6.4 Post the customers' accounts to the accounts receivable subsidiary ledger and prepare a schedule of accounts receivable.

Lombardi Company

Gerard Company

Harke Company

Schedule of Accounts Receivable	
Lombardi Company	
Gerard Company	
Harke Company	

SOLUTION

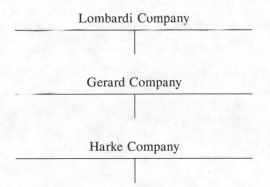

Lombardi Company

Jan 1 S-1   550

Gerard Company

Jan. 4 S-1   650

Harke Company

Jan. 18 S-1   300
20 S-1   100

Schedule of Accounts Receivable	
Lombardi Company	550
Gerard Company	650
Harke Company	400
	1,600

6.5   For Problem 6.3, make the entries needed to record the sales for the month.

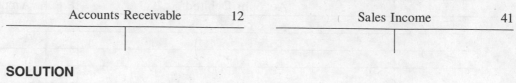

Accounts Receivable	12		Sales Income	41

SOLUTION

Accounts Receivable	12		Sales Income	41
Jan. 31 S-1 1,600			Jan. 31 S-1 1,600	

6.6   Based on the following sales journal, post each transaction to its respective accounts receivable account.

Sales Journal   S-4

Date	Account Debited	P.R.	Amount
Jan. 5	J. Gallagher	✓	350
7	R. Glatt	✓	600
9	L. Harmin	✓	450
15	J. Gallagher	✓	250
20	R. Glatt	✓	500
26	R. Glatt	✓	100

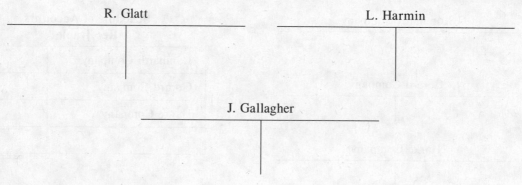

R. Glatt			L. Harmin	

J. Gallagher	

SOLUTION

R. Glatt			L. Harmin	
Jan. 7 S-4 600			Jan. 9 S-4 450	
20 S-4 500				
26 S-4 100				

J. Gallagher	
Jan. 5 S-4 350	
15 S-4 250	

6.7   Based on the information in Problem 6.6, post the necessary accounts in the general ledger.

Accounts Receivable	12		Sales Income	41

SOLUTION

Accounts Receivable	12		Sales Income	41
Jan. 31 S-4 2,250			Jan. 31 S-4 2,250	

Note: $2,250 is the total of all transactions involving the sale of goods on account.

6.8 Vitman Company was established in December of the current year. Its sales of merchandise on account and related returns and allowances during the remainder of the month are described below.

Dec. 15 Sold merchandise on account to Acme Co., $850.

   19 Sold merchandise on account to Balt Corp., $800.

   20 Sold merchandise on account to Conway, Inc., $1,200.

   22 Issued Credit Memorandum for $40 to Balt Corp. for merchandise returned.

   24 Sold merchandise on account to Davy Company, $1,650.

   25 Sold additional merchandise on account to Balt Corp., $900.

   26 Issued Credit Memorandum for $25 to Acme Co. for merchandise returned.

   27 Sold additional merchandise on account to Conway, Inc., $1,600.

Record the transactions for December in the sales journal and general journal below.

Sales Journal   S-6

Date	Account Debited	P.R.	Amount

General Journal   J-8

Date	Description	P.R.	Dr.	Cr.

SOLUTION

Sales Journal   S-6

Date	Account Debited	P.R.	Amount
Dec. 15	Acme Co.		850
19	Balt Corp.		800
20	Conway, Inc.		1,200
24	Davy Company		1,650
25	Balt Corp.		900
27	Conway, Inc.		1,600
			7,000

General Journal   J-8

Date	Description	P.R.	Dr.	Cr.
Dec. 22	Sales Returns		40	
	Accounts Receivable–Balt Corp.			40
26	Sales Returns		25	
	Accounts Receivable–Acme Co.			25

6.9 Based on the information in Problem 6.8, post to the customers' accounts.

Acme Co.   Conway, Inc.

Balt Corp.   Davy Company

SOLUTION

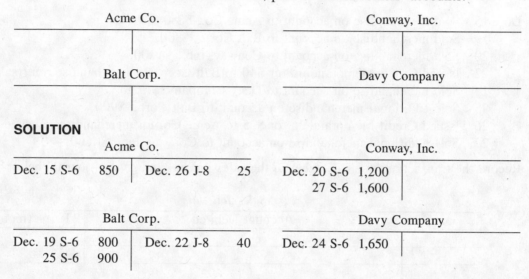

Acme Co.
Dec. 15 S-6 850 | Dec. 26 J-8 25

Conway, Inc.
Dec. 20 S-6 1,200
27 S-6 1,600

Balt Corp.
Dec. 19 S-6 800 | Dec. 22 J-8 40
25 S-6 900

Davy Company
Dec. 24 S-6 1,650

6.10 Prepare a schedule of accounts receivable based on the information in Problem 6.9.

Schedule of Accounts Receivable

Acme Co.	
Balt Corp.	
Conway, Inc.	
Davy Company	

SOLUTION

Schedule of Accounts Receivable

Acme Co.	$ 825
Balt Corp.	1,660
Conway, Inc.	2,800
Davy Company	1,650
	$6,935

6.11 Post the general journal and the sales journal to the three accounts below using the data supplied in Problem 6.8. What is the sum of the balances of the accounts in the subsidiary ledger (Problem 6.10)? What is the balance of the controlling account?

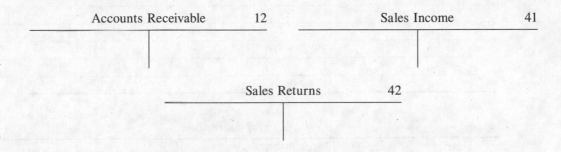

Accounts Receivable	12		Sales Income	41

Sales Returns	42

SOLUTION

Accounts Receivable		12		Sales Income		41
Dec. 31 S-6 7,000	Dec. 22 J-8 40				Dec. 31 S-6 7,000	
	26 J-8 25					

Sales Returns		42
Dec. 22 J-8 40		
26 J-8 25		

The balance in the subsidiary ledger, $6,935, is the same as the balance in the accounts receivable account (control), $6,935.

6.12 Stillman Company was established in March of the current year. Their sales and related accounts for the month of March are listed below:

Mar. 2   Sold 25 lobsters to Conrad Hotel @ $7.50 each on account—total sale $187.50.

7   Sold 40 pounds of shrimp to Green Hotel @ $11.00 per pound on account—total sale $440.00.

9   Sold 60 pounds of lox to Winston Hotel @ $9.00 per pound on account—total sale $540.00.

12   Sold 110 pounds of bluefish to Conrad Hotel @ $4.50 per pound on account—total sale $495.00.

17   Issued credit memorandum for $25.00 to Conrad Hotel for merchandise returned.

21   Sold 90 lobsters to Green Hotel @ $7.00 each on account—total sale $630.00.

25   Issued credit memorandum to Green Hotel for 12 lobsters returned @ $7.00 each ($84.00).

27   Sold 175 lobsters to Hill Top Hotel @ $7.50 each on account—total sale, $1,312.50.

Record the above transactions in the sales journal and general journal below.

Sales Journal   S-10

Date	Account Debited	P.R.	Amount

General Journal   J-4

Date	Description	P.R.	Dr.	Cr.

SOLUTION

Sales Journal   S-10

Date	Account Debited	P.R.	Amount
Mar. 2	Conrad Hotel		187.50
7	Green Hotel		440.00
9	Winston Hotel		540.00
12	Conrad Hotel		495.00
21	Green Hotel		630.00
27	Hill Top Hotel		1,312.50
			3,605.00

General Journal   J-4

Date	Description	P.R.	Dr.	Cr.
Mar. 17	Sales Returns		25	
	Accounts Rec./Conrad Hotel			25
25	Sales Returns		84	
	Accounts Rec./Green Hotel			84

From the information above, post to customers' accounts.

6.13 Post the subsidiary accounts, the general journal, and sales journal to the accounts below using the data from Problem 6.12.

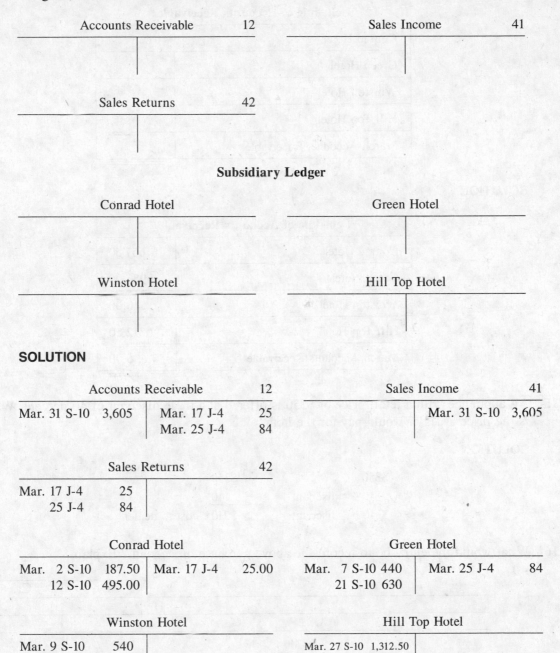

| Accounts Receivable 12 |
| Sales Income 41 |

| Sales Returns 42 |

Subsidiary Ledger

| Conrad Hotel |
| Green Hotel |

| Winston Hotel |
| Hill Top Hotel |

SOLUTION

Accounts Receivable   12

| Mar. 31 S-10 | 3,605 | Mar. 17 J-4 | 25 |
| | | Mar. 25 J-4 | 84 |

Sales Income   41

| | Mar. 31 S-10 | 3,605 |

Sales Returns   42

| Mar. 17 J-4 | 25 | |
| 25 J-4 | 84 | |

Conrad Hotel

| Mar. 2 S-10 | 187.50 | Mar. 17 J-4 | 25.00 |
| 12 S-10 | 495.00 | | |

Green Hotel

| Mar. 7 S-10 | 440 | Mar. 25 J-4 | 84 |
| 21 S-10 | 630 | | |

Winston Hotel

| Mar. 9 S-10 | 540 | |

Hill Top Hotel

| Mar. 27 S-10 | 1,312.50 | |

6.14 Prepare a schedule of accounts receivable from the information provided on the previous page.

Schedule of Accounts Receivable

Conrad Hotel	
Green Hotel	
Winston Hotel	
Hill Top Hotel	
March Accounts Receivable	

SOLUTION

Schedule of Accounts Receivable

Conrad Hotel	$ 657.50
Green Hotel	986.00
Winston Hotel	540.00
Hill Top Hotel	1,312.50
March Accounts Receivable	$3,496.00

6.15 An appliance with a retail price of $350 is offered at a trade discount of 40 percent. What is the price a dealer would pay for the item?

SOLUTION

$350		$350	
40%	discount	− 140	
$140	discount	$210	cost to dealer

6.16 What would the entry be to record the above purchase on account? Explain.

	Dr.	Cr.

SOLUTION

	Dr.	Cr.
Purchases	210	
Accounts Payable		210

Trade discounts are not recorded in the accounting records, as they are used only to determine the net purchase price. The amount recorded is the price *paid* to the seller.

6.17 Record the following transactions in the purchases journal:

Apr. 2 Purchased merchandise on account from Kane Company, $450.
      5 Purchased supplies on account from Lane Supply House, $180.
     20 Purchased merchandise on account from Hanson Company, $400.
     24 Purchased additional supplies on account from Lane Supply House, $50.
     29 Purchased equipment on account from Olin Equipment, $1,600.

Purchases Journal   P-1

Date	Account Credited	P.R.	Acct. Pay. Cr.	Purch. Dr.	Supp. Dr.	Sundry		
						Acct. Dr.	P.R.	Amount

SOLUTION

Purchases Journal   P-1

Date	Account Credited	P.R.	Acct. Pay. Cr.	Purch. Dr.	Supp. Dr.	Sundry		
						Acct. Dr.	P.R.	Amount
Apr. 2	Kane Company		450	450				
5	Lane Supply House		180		180			
20	Hanson Company		400	400				
24	Lane Supply House		50		50			
29	Olin Equipment		1,600			Equipment		1,600
			2,680	850	230			1,600

6.18 Post the information from Problem 6.17 into the accounts payable subsidiary ledger and prepare a schedule of accounts payable.

Kane Company

Lane Supply House

Hanson Company

Olin Equipment

Schedule of Accounts Payable

Kane Company	
Lane Supply House	
Hanson Company	
Olin Equipment	

SOLUTION

Kane Company

	Apr. 2 P-1 450

Lane Supply House

	Apr. 5 P-1 180
	24 P-1 50

Hanson Company

	Apr. 20 P-1 400

Olin Equipment

	Apr. 29 P-1 1,600

Schedule of Accounts Payable

Kane Company	$ 450
Lane Supply House	230
Hanson Company	400
Olin Equipment	1,600
	$2,680

6.19 Post the purchases journal totals from Problem 6.17 to the accounts in the general ledger.

General Ledger

Supplies	14	Accounts Payable	21

Equipment	17	Purchases	51

SOLUTION

General Ledger

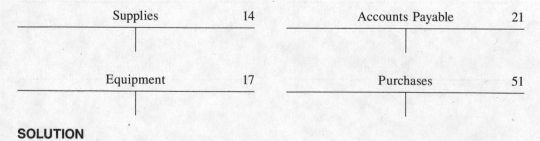

Supplies	14	Accounts Payable	21
Apr. 30 P-1 230			Apr. 30 P-1 2,680

Equipment	17		Purchases	51
Apr. 29 P-1 1,600			Apr. 30 P-1 850	

6.20 Record the following selected transactions in the purchase returns journal:

Mar. 4 Returned $300 in merchandise to Alton Co. for credit.
    8 Received credit memorandum of $150 from Baltic Corp. for defective merchandise.
   12 Received credit memorandum of $180 from Calton Co. for goods returned.

Purchase Returns			PR-1
Date	Account Dr.	P.R.	Amount

SOLUTION

Purchase Returns			PR-1
Date	Account Dr.	P.R.	Amount
Mar. 4	Alton Company		300
8	Baltic Corporation		150
12	Calton Company		180
			630

6.21 Based on the information in Problem 6.20, post to the subsidiary ledger accounts and then to the general ledger.

Subsidiary Ledger   **General Ledger**

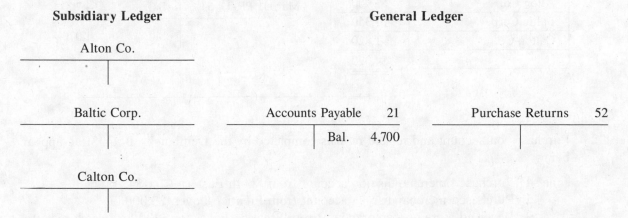

Alton Co.

Baltic Corp.

Accounts Payable	21		Purchase Returns	52
	Bal. 4,700			

Calton Co.

SOLUTION

Subsidiary Ledger	General Ledger

Alton Co.

Mar. 4 PR-1	300	Bal.	1,200

Baltic Corp.				**Accounts Payable** 21				**Purchase Returns** 52		
Mar. 8 PR-1	150	Bal.	1,500	Mar.31 PR-1 630	Bal.	4,700			Mar.31 PR-1 630

Calton Co.

Mar. 12 PR-1	180	Bal.	2,000

6.22   Prepare a schedule of accounts payable and compare it to the control account.

Schedule of Accounts Payable		Accounts Payable 21	
Alton Co.			
Baltic Corp.		Bal.	4,700
Calton Co.			

SOLUTION

Schedule of Accounts Payable		Accounts Payable 21		
Alton Co.	$ 900	Mar. 31 PR-1 630	Bal.	4,700
Baltic Corp.	1,350			
Calton Co.	1,820		Bal.	4,070
	$4,070			

6.23   Purchases on account and related returns completed by the Dembofsky Book Store appear below.

June 4 Purchased merchandise on account from South Eastern Co., $4,200.
    5 Purchased merchandise on account from Prentice-Foyer, $3,000.
    9 Received a credit memorandum from Prentice-Foyer for $200 for overshipment.
    10 Purchased office supplies from Kristt Supply, $800.
    18 Received a credit memorandum from South Eastern for goods returned, $300.
    24 Purchased office equipment from Robinson Furniture on account, $2,900.
    26 Purchased additional office supplies on account from Kristt Supply, $400.
    29 Received a credit memorandum from Kristt Supply for defective goods, $100.
    30 Purchased store supplies on account from H. Marc, $260.

Record the transactions for June in the purchases and purchase returns journals.

Purchases Journal   P-1

Date	Account Credited	P.R.	Acct. Pay. Cr.	Purch. Dr.	Off. Supp. Dr.	Sundry		
						Acct. Dr.	P.R.	Amount

Purchase Returns   PR-1

Date	Account Debited	P.R.	Amount

SOLUTION

Purchases Journal   P-1

Date	Account Credited	P.R.	Acct. Pay. Cr.	Purch. Dr.	Off. Supp. Dr.	Sundry		
						Acct. Dr.	P.R.	Amt.
June 4	South Eastern Co.		4,200	4,200				
5	Prentice-Foyer		3,000	3,000				
10	Kristt Supply		800		800			
24	Robinson Furniture		2,900			Off. Equip.	18	2,900
26	Kristt Supply		400		400			
30	H. Marc		260			Store Supp.	13	260
			11,560	7,200	1200			3,160
			(21)	(51)	(12)			(✓)

Purchase Returns   PR-1

Date	Account Debited	P.R.	Amount
June 9	Prentice-Foyer		200
18	South Eastern		300
29	Kristt Supply		100
			600
			(21/52)

6.24 Post each of the accounts from Problem 6.23 into the accounts payable subsidiary ledger and prepare a schedule of accounts payable.

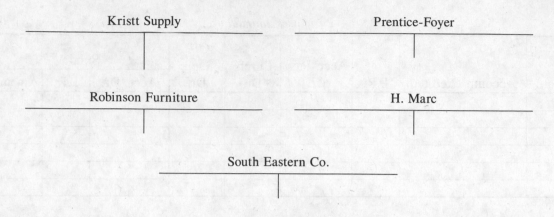

Schedule of Accounts Payable

Kristt Supply	
H. Marc	
Prentice-Foyer	
Robinson Furniture	
South Eastern Co.	

SOLUTION

Kristt Supply				Prentice-Foyer			
June 29 PR-1	100	June 10 P-1	800	June 9 PR-1	200	June 5 P-1	3,000
		26 P-1	400				

Robinson Furniture				H. Marc			
		June 24 P-1	2,900			June 30 P-1	260

South Eastern Co.			
June 18 PR-1	300	June 4 P-1	4,200

Schedule of Accounts Payable

Kristt Supply	$ 1,100
H. Marc	260
Prentice-Foyer	2,800
Robinson Furniture	2,900
South Eastern Co.	3,900
	$10,960

6.25 Post the purchases journal and purchase returns journals from Problem 6.23 to the accounts in the general ledger.

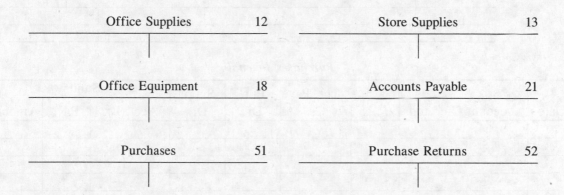

Office Supplies	12		Store Supplies	13

Office Equipment	18		Accounts Payable	21

Purchases	51		Purchase Returns	52

SOLUTION

Office Supplies	12		Store Supplies	13
June 30 P-1 1,200			June 30 P-1 260	

Office Equipment	18		Accounts Payable	21
June 30 P-1 2,900			June 30 PR-1 600	June 30 P-1 11,560

Purchases	51		Purchase Returns	52
June 30 P-1 7,200				June 30 PR-1 600

Note: Balance of Accounts Payable controlling account and total of Schedule of Accounts Payable are the same.

6.26 The Johnston Company transactions involving purchases and sales for the month of January are presented below. All purchases and sales are made on account.

Jan. 3   Sold merchandise to Acme Supply Company, $440.
   5   Purchased merchandise from Balfour Corp., $7,200.
  10   Sold merchandise to Mennon Company, $345.
  10   Sold merchandise to Blant Company, $2,400.
  14   Purchased $750 worth of equipment from Wyde Equipment.
  17   Purchased office supplies from Gold Supply, $850.
  21   Purchased merchandise from Caldon Company, $6,240.
  28   Returned damage merchandise purchased from Balfour Corp., receiving credit of $300.
  30   Issued credit of $60 to Acme Supply Company for defective goods returned to us.

Record the transactions in the sales, purchases, and general journals.

Sales Journal

S-1

Date	Account Debited	P.R.	Amount

Purchases Journal

P-1

Date	Account Credited	P.R.	Acct. Pay. Cr.	Pur. Dr.	Supp. Dr.	Sundry Acct. Dr.	P.R.	Amount

General Journal

J-1

Date	Description	P.R.	Debit	Credit

SOLUTION

Sales Journal

S-1

Date	Account Debited	P.R.	Amount
Jan. 3	Acme Supply Company	✔	440
10	Mennon Company	✔	345
10	Blant Company	✔	2,400
			3,185

Purchases Journal

P-1

Date	Account Cr.	P.R.	Acct. Pay. Cr.	Pur. Dr.	Supp. Dr.	Sundry Acct. Dr.	P.R.	Amount
Jan. 5	Balfour Corp.	✔	7,200	7,200				
14	Wyde Equipment		750			Equipment		750
17	Gold Supply		850		850			
21	Caldon Company	✔	6,240	6,240				
			15,040	13,440	850			750

General Journal

J-1

Date	Description	P.R.	Debit	Credit
Jan. 28	Accounts Payable, Balfour Corp.		300	
	Purchase Returns			300
30	Sales Returns		60	
	Accounts Receivable,			60
	Acme Supply Company			

Chapter 7

The Cash Journal

7.1 INTRODUCTION

We have observed that the use of the sales journal and the purchases journal enable us to carry out the journalizing and posting processes more efficiently. These special journals save space by permitting the recording of an entry on one line and the posting of *total* columns rather than individual figures. This is also true of the cash receipts journal and the cash disbursements journal.

7.2 CASH RECEIPTS JOURNAL

All receipts (cash and checks) received by a business are recorded daily in either a *cash receipts* or a *combination cash journal*. For control purposes, the cash handling and recording processes are separated. In addition, whenever feasible, receipts are deposited intact (without cash disbursements being made from them) daily. The most common sources of cash receipts are cash sales and collections on account.

The steps for recording and posting the cash receipts journal are described below and illustrated in Example 1.

1. Record the cash receipts in the cash receipts journal, *debiting* Cash for the amount received (Cash column) and *crediting* the appropriate column. Indicate in the Account Credited space:

    (*a*) The customer's name (subsidiary account) for collections on account.

    (*b*) An explanation (cash sale) for cash sales.

    (*c*) The title of the item involved in the Sundry account.

2. After recording collections on account, post *by date* to the appropriate subsidiary ledger (customer's) account.

    (*a*) In the customer's account, record the amount *credited* and indicate the source of the entry (Cr.) in the Posting Reference column.

    (*b*) Put a (✔) in the Posting Reference column of the journal to indicate that a posting has been completed.

3. At the *end* of the month, total all the columns of the journal and check to be sure that all the columns balance before posting. If they do balance, put a double line under the column totals.

4. Post the column totals (except the Sundry Credit column) to the appropriate general ledger account.

    (*a*) In the appropriate general ledger account, record the amount *debited* or *credited* and indicate the source of the entry (Cr.) in the Posting Reference column.

    (*b*) Place the account number of the account posted to *under* the column totals, to indicate that a posting has been completed.

    (*c*) Each item in the Sundry account is posted individually to the general ledger. The total of the Sundry account is not posted.

EXAMPLE 1

Centennial Company had the following receipts in March:

Mar. 2 Received $250 for a return of defective merchandise.
    4 Cash sale of flags for $350.
    9 Collected $50 on account from A. Anderson.
   14 Collected $350 on account from B. Butler.
   22 Cash sale of Bumper stickers, $200.
   29 Collected $100 on account from C. Chase.

Cash Receipts Journal   CR-1

Date	Account Credited	P.R.	Cash Debit	Sales Discount Debit	Accounts Receivable Credit	Sales Income Credit	Sundry Credit
Mar. 2	Purchase Returns	52	250				250
4	Cash Sales	✔	350			350	
9	A. Anderson	✔	50		50		
14	B. Butler	✔	350		350		
22	Cash Sales	✔	200			200	
29	C. Chase	✔	100		100		
			1,300		500	550	250
			(11)		(14)	(41)	(✔)

General Ledger

Cash		11
Bal.	10,000	
Mar. 31 CR-1	1,300	

Sales Income		41
	Mar. 31 CR-1	550

Accounts Receivable		14
Bal.	1,075	Mar. 31 CR-1 500

Purchase Returns		52
	Mar. 2 CR-1	250

Accounts Receivable Ledger

A. Anderson		
Bal.	200	Mar. 9 CR-1 50

C. Chase		
Bal.	125	Mar. 29 CR-1 100

B. Butler		
Bal.	350	Mar. 14 CR-1 350

7.3   CASH DISBURSEMENTS JOURNAL

The cash disbursements journal is used to record all transactions that reduce cash. These transactions may arise from payments to creditors, from cash purchases (of supplies, equipment, or merchandise), from the payment of expenses (salary, rent, insurance, and so on), as well as from personal withdrawals.

The procedure for recording and posting the cash disbursements journal parallels that of the cash receipts journal:

1.   A check is written each time a payment is made; the check numbers provide a convenient reference, and they help in controlling cash and in reconciling the bank account.

2.   The cash credit column is posted in total to the general ledger at the end of the month.

3.   Debits to Accounts Payable represent cash paid to creditors. These individual amounts will be posted to the creditors' accounts in the accounts payable subsidiary ledger. At the end of the month, the total of the accounts payable column is posted to the general ledger.

4.   The Sundry column is used to record debits for any account that cannot be entered in the other special columns. These would include purchases of equipment, inventory, payment of expenses, and cash withdrawals. Each item is posted separately to the general ledger. The total of the Sundry column is not posted.

EXAMPLE 2

Cash Disbursements Journal   CD-1

Date	Description	P.R.	Check No.	Cash Cr.	Acct. Pay. Dr.	Sundry Dr.
Mar. 2	Agin Corp.	✔	1	600	600	
8	Rent Expense	53	2	220		220
15	Salaries Expense	54	3	1,900		1,900
18	Baker Corp.	✔	4	700	700	
21	Purchases	51	5	1,600		1,600
24	Salaries Expense	54	6	1,900		1,900
				6,920	1,300	5,620
				(11)	(21)	(✔)

General Ledger

Cash	11
	Mar. 28 CD-1 6,920

Rent Expense	53
Mar. 8 CD-1 220	

Accounts Payable	21
Mar. 28 CD-1 1,300	Bal. 23,700

Salaries Expense	54
Mar. 15 CD-1 1,900	
24 CD-1 1,900	

Purchases	51
Mar. 21 CD-1 1,600	

Accounts Payable Subsidiary Ledger

Agin Corp.	
Mar. 2 CD-1 600	Bal. 3,000*

Baker Corp.	
Mar. 18 CD-1 700	Bal. 700*

Connely Company	
	Bal. 9,000*

Davis Company	
	Bal. 11,000*

*From Section 6.11, Example 8.

7.4 COMBINATION CASH JOURNAL

Some companies, primarily for convenience, prefer to record all cash transactions (receipts and disbursements) in one journal. This combination cash journal uses basically the same account columns as the cash receipts and cash disbursements journals, but with a different arrangement of accounts.

This journal makes it easier to keep track on a day-to-day basis of changes in the Cash account, since the debit and credit to Cash are adjacent to one another.

EXAMPLE 3

The combination cash journal below is constructed from the same entries involved in the cash receipts journal (Example 1) and the cash disbursements journal (Example 2).

Combination Cash Journal

Cash Dr.	Cash Cr.	Ck. No.	Date	Account	P.R.	Sundry Dr.	Sundry Cr.	Acct. Pay. Dr.	Acct. Rec. Cr.	Sales Income Cr.
250			Mar. 2	Purchase Returns	52		250			
	600	1	2	Agin Corp.	✔			600		
350			4	Cash Sales	✔					350
	220	2	8	Rent Expense	53	220				
50			9	A. Anderson	✔				50	
350			14	B. Butler	✔				350	
	1,900	3	15	Salaries Expense	54	1,900				
	700	4	18	Baker Corp.	✔			700		
	1,600	5	21	Purchases	51	1,600				
200			22	Cash Sales	✔					200
	1,900	6	24	Salaries Expense	54	1,900				
100			29	C. Chase	✔				100	
1,300	6,920					5,620	250	1,300	500	550
(11)	(11)					(✔)	(✔)	(21)	(14)	(41)

Summary

1. Receipts of a firm include _____ and _____ .

2. For cash control purposes, cash handling and _____ must be separated.

3. The _____ journal is used to record all transactions that reduce cost.

4. The cash column in the cash receipts journal is _____ , whereas the same column in the cash payments journal is _____ whenever cash is received or disbursed.

5. In order to record a cash disbursement, a _____ must be written and assigned a number.

6. _____ to Accounts Payable represent cash paid to creditors.

7. Accounts Payable is to the cash disbursements journal as _____ is to the cash receipts journal.

8. Sales Discounts and Purchase Discounts appear in the _____ statement as reductions of Sales and of Purchases, respectively.

9. Terms of 2/10, n/30 on a $800 purchase of March 6 paid within the discount period would provide a discount of _____ and a net cost of _____ .

10. The _____ journal contains all records of cash transactions (receipts and disbursements).

Answers: 1. cash, checks; 2. recording; 3. cash disbursements; 4. debited, credited; 5. check; 6. Debits; 7. Accounts Receivable; 8. income; 9. $16, $784; 10. combination cash

Solved Problems

7.1 A sales invoice totaling $3,000 and dated January 14 has discount terms of 2/10, n/30. If it is paid by January 23, what would be the entry (in general journal form) to record this transaction?

SOLUTION

Cash	2,940	
Sales Discount	60	
Accounts Receivable		3,000

7.2   The cash receipts journal below utilizes a special column for sales discounts. Record the following cash transactions in the journal:

May   2   Received a check for $588 from A. Banks in settlement of his $600 April invoice.
     12   Received $686 in settlement of the April invoice of $700 from J. Johnson.
     26   Received a check for $495 in settlement of B. Simpson's April account of $500.

Cash Receipts Journal   CR-1

Date	Account Cr.	P.R.	Cash Dr.	Sales Disc. Dr.	Acct. Rec. Cr.	Sundry Cr.

SOLUTION

Cash Receipts Journal   CR-1

Date	Account Cr.	P.R.	Cash Dr.	Sales Disc. Dr.	Acct. Rec. Cr.	Sundry Cr.
Mar 2	A. Banks		588	12	600	
12	J. Johnson		686	14	700	
26	B. Simpson		495	5	500	
			1,769	31	1,800	

7.3   The cash disbursements journal below utilizes the special column Purchases Discount. Record the cash transactions into the cash disbursements journal.

June   2   Paid J. Thompson $490 in settlement of our April invoice for $500, Check 24.
     10   Sent a check to B. Rang, $297, in settlement of the May invoice of $300, Check 25.
     21   Paid A. Johnson $588 in settlement of the $600 invoice of last month, Check 26.

Cash Disbursements Journal   CD-1

Date	Check No.	Account Dr.	P.R.	Cash Cr.	Purchases Disc. Cr.	Acct. Pay. Dr.	Sundry Dr.

SOLUTION

Cash Disbursements Journal   CD-1

Date	Check No.	Account Dr.	P.R.	Cash Cr.	Purchases Disc. Cr.	Acct. Pay. Dr.	Sundry Dr.
June 2	24	J. Thompson		490	10	500	
10	25	B. Rang		297	3	300	
21	26	A. Johnson		588	12	600	
				1,375	25	1,400	

7.4 Record the following transactions in the cash receipts journal:

Mar. 2 Received $600 from J. Kappala in full settlement of her account.
   10 Received $615 from B. Elder in full settlement of his account.
   14 Cash sales for a 2-week period, $4,400.
   28 Sold $200 of office supplies (not a merchandise item) to Smith Company as a courtesy.
   30 Owner made additional investment, $1,500.
   30 Cash sales for the last 2 weeks, $2,600.

Cash Receipts Journal   CR-1

Date	Account Credited	P.R.	Cash Dr.	Acct. Rec. Cr.	Sales Income Cr.	Sundry Cr.

SOLUTION

Cash Receipts Journal   CR-1

Date	Account Credited	P.R.	Cash Dr.	Acct. Rec. Cr.	Sales Income Cr.	Sundry Cr.
Mar 2	J. Kappala	✔	600	600		
10	B. Elder	✔	615	615		
14	Cash Sales	✔	4,400		4,400	
28	Office Supplies	15	200			200
30	Capital	31	1,500			1,500
30	Cash Sales	✔	2,600		2,600	
			9,915	1,215	7,000	1,700

7.5 Post the information from Problem 7.4 into the accounts receivable subsidiary ledger.

Accounts Receivable Ledger

J. Kappala			B. Elder		
Bal.	600		Bal.	615	

SOLUTION

Accounts Receivable Ledger

J. Kappala				B. Elder			
Bal.	600	Mar. 2 CR-1	600	Bal.	615	Mar. 10 CR-1	615

7.6 Post the cash receipts journal totals from Problem 7.4 to the accounts in the general ledger.

General Ledger

Cash		11	Capital		31
Bal.	10,000			Bal.	6,500

Accounts Receivable		12	Sales Income		41
Bal.	3,000				

Office Supplies		15
Bal.	3,500	

SOLUTION

General Ledger

Cash		11	Capital		31
Bal.	10,000			Bal.	6,500
Mar. 31 CR-1	9,915			Mar. 30 CR-1	1,500

Accounts Receivable		12	Sales Income		41
Bal.	3,000	Mar. 31 CR-1 1,215			Mar. 31 CR-1 7,000

Office Supplies		15
Bal.	3,500	Mar. 28 CR-1 200

7.7 Record the following transactions in the cash disbursements journal:

Mar. 1   Paid rent for the month, $320 (Check #16).
    7   Paid J. Becker $615 for his February invoice (Check #17).
  10   Bought store supplies for cash, $110 (Check #18).
  15   Paid salaries for the 2-week period, $685 (Check #19).
  23   Paid B. Cone for February invoice, $600 (Check #20).
  30   Paid salaries for the second half of the month, $714 (Check #21).

Cash Disbursements Journal   CD-1

Date	Check No.	Account Dr.	P.R.	Cash Cr.	Acct. Pay. Dr.	Sundry Dr.

SOLUTION

Cash Disbursements Journal   CD-1

Date	Check No.	Account Dr.	P.R.	Cash Cr.	Acct. Pay. Dr.	Sundry Dr.
Mar. 1	16	Rent Expense		320		320
7	17	J. Becker	✔	615	615	
10	18	Store Supplies		110		110
15	19	Salaries Expense		685		685
23	20	B. Cone	✔	600	600	
30	21	Salaries Expense		714		714
				3,044	1,215	1,829

7.8 Post the information from Problem 7.7 into the accounts payable subsidiary ledger.

Accounts Payable Ledger

J. Becker		B. Cone	
	Bal. 615		Bal. 600

SOLUTION

Accounts Payable Ledger

J. Becker		B. Cone	
Mar. 7 CD-1 615	Bal. 615	Mar. 23 CD-1 600	Bal. 600

7.9   Post the cash disbursements journal from Problem 7.7 to the accounts in the general ledger.

General Ledger

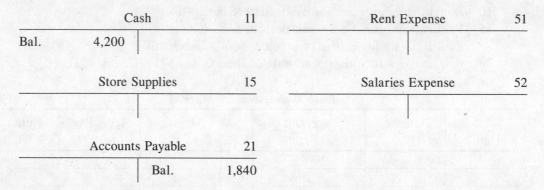

Cash	11
Bal. 4,200	

Store Supplies	15

Accounts Payable	21
	Bal. 1,840

Rent Expense	51

Salaries Expense	52

SOLUTION

General Ledger

Cash	11
Bal. 4,200	Mar. 31 CD-1 3,044

Store Supplies	15
Mar. 10 CD-1 110	

Accounts Payable	21
Mar. 31 CD-1 1,215	Bal. 1,840

Rent Expense	51
Mar. 1 CD-1 320	

Salaries Expense	52
Mar. 15 CD-1 685	
30 CD-1 714	

7.10   All transactions affecting the cash account of Park Company for the month of January 19X5 are presented below:

Jan. 1   Received cash from Alden Company for the balance due on their account, $1,600, less 2 percent discount.

      5   Received payment from Walk Company on account, $1,550.

      8   Paid rent for the month, $650, Check #165.

      10   Purchased supplies for cash, $614, Check #166.

      14   Cash sales for the first half of the month, $5,280.

      15   Paid biweekly salaries, $1,600, Check #167.

      19   Received $406 in settlement of a $400 note receivable plus interest.

      19   Received payment from J. Cork of $500, less 1 percent discount.

      20   Paid B. Simmons $686 in settlement of our $700 invoice, Check #168.

      24   Paid $450 on account to L. Hann, Check #169.

      27   Paid H. Hiram $800, less 2 percent, on account, Check #170.

      30   Paid biweekly salaries, $1,680, Check #171.

Record the above transactions in both the cash receipts and the cash disbursements journals.

Cash Receipts Journal   CR-1

Date	Account Cr.	P.R.	Cash Dr.	Sales Disc. Dr.	Sales Income Cr.	Acct. Rec. Cr.	Sundry Cr.

Cash Disbursements Journal   CD-1

Date	Check No.	Account Dr.	P.R.	Cash Cr.	Pur. Disc. Cr.	Acct. Pay. Dr.	Sundry Dr.

SOLUTION

Cash Receipts Journal   CR-1

Date	Account Cr.	P.R.	Cash Dr.	Sales Disc. Dr.	Sales Income Cr.	Acct. Rec. Cr.	Sundry Cr.
Jan. 1	Alden Co.		1,568	32		1,600	
5	Walk Co.		1,550			1,550	
14	Cash Sales		5,280		5,280		
19	Notes Rec.						400
19	Interest Inc.		406				6
19	J. Cork		495	5		500	
			9,299	37	5,280	3,650	406

Cash Disbursements Journal   CD-1

Date	Check No.	Account Dr.	P.R.	Cash Cr.	Pur. Disc. Cr.	Acct. Pay. Dr.	Sundry Dr.
Jan. 8	165	Rent Expense		650			650
10	166	Supplies		614			614
15	167	Salaries Exp.		1,600			1,600
20	168	B. Simmons		686	14	700	
24	169	L. Hann		450		450	
27	170	H. Hiram		784	16	800	
30	171	Salaries Exp.		1,680			1,680
				6,464	30	1,950	4,544

Comprehensive Review Problem: Repetitive Transactions

1.   William Drew began business on March 1, 19X5. The transactions completed by the Drew Company for the month of March are listed below. Record these transactions, using the various journals provided.

Mar.	1	Deposited $14,000 in a bank account for the operation of Drew Company
	2	Paid rent for the month, $600, Check #1
	4	Purchased equipment on account from Andon Equipment, $10,000
	7	Purchased merchandise on account from Baily Company, $1,200
	7	Cash sales for the week, $1,650
	10	Issued Check #2 for $150, for store supplies
	11	Sold merchandise on account to Manny Company, $600
	12	Sold merchandise on account to Nant Company, $350
	14	Paid biweekly salaries of $740, Check #3
	14	Cash sales for the week, $1,800
	16	Purchased merchandise on account from Cotin Company, $1,100
	17	Issued Check #4 to Baily Company for March 7 purchase, less 2%
	18	Bought $250 worth of store supplies from Salio Supply House on account
	19	Returned defective merchandise of $200 to Cotin Company and received credit
	19	Sold merchandise on account to Olin Company, $645
	21	Issued Check #5 to Andon Equipment for $500, in part payment of equipment purchase
	22	Received check from Nant Company in settlement of their March 12 purchase, less 2% discount
	22	Purchased merchandise from Canny Corporation for cash, $750, Check #6
	23	Cash sales for the week, $1,845
	24	Purchased merchandise on account from Daily Corporation, $850
	25	Sold merchandise on account to Pallit Corporation, $740
	26	Purchased additional supplies, $325, from Salio Supply House on account
	27	Received check from Manny Company in settlement of their account, less 1% discount
	30	Cash sales for the week, $1,920
	30	Received $300 on account from Olin Company
	31	Paid biweekly salaries, $810, Check #7

General Journal   J-1

Date	Description	P.R.	Debit	Credit

Cash Receipts Journal   CR-1

Date	Account Credited	P.R.	Cash Dr.	Sales Disc. Dr.	Acct. Rec. Cr.	Sales Income Cr.	Sundry Cr.

Cash Disbursements Journal   CD-1

Date	Check No.	Account Debited	P.R.	Cash Cr.	Pur. Disc. Cr.	Acct. Pay. Dr.	Sundry Dr.

Purchases Journal   P-1

Date	Account Credited	P.R.	Acct. Pay. Cr.	Pur. Dr.	Store Supp. Dr.	Office Supp. Dr.	Sundry Acct. Dr.		
							Acct.	P.R.	Amount

Sales Journal   S-1

Date	Account Debited	P.R.	Accounts Receivable Dr. Sales Cr.	Amount

SOLUTION

General Journal   J-1

Date	Description	P.R.	Dr.	Cr.
Mar. 19	Accounts Payable, Cotin Co.	21 ✔	200	
	Purchase Returns	52		200
	Defective goods			

Cash Receipts Journal   CR-1

Date	Account Credited	P.R.	Cash Dr.	Sales Disc. Dr.	Acct. Rec. Cr.	Sales Income Cr.	Sundry Cr.
Mar. 1	Drew Company, Capital	31	14,000				14,000
7	Cash Sales	✔	1,650			1,650	
14	Cash Sales	✔	1,800			1,800	
22	Nant Company	✔	343	7	350		
23	Cash Sales	✔	1,845			1,845	
27	Manny Company	✔	594	6	600		
30	Cash Sales	✔	1,920			1,920	
30	Olin Company	✔	300		300		
			22,452	13	1,250	7,215	14,000
			(11)	(42)	(12)	(41)	(✔)

Cash Disbursements Journal   CD-1

Date	Check No.	Account Dr.	P.R.	Cash Cr.	Pur. Disc. Cr.	Acct. Pay. Dr.	Sundry Dr.
Mar. 2	1	Rent Expense	54	600			600
10	2	Store Supplies	14	150			150
14	3	Salaries Expense	55	740			740
17	4	Baily Company	✔	1,176	24	1,200	
21	5	Andon Equipment	✔	500		500	
22	6	Purchases	51	750			750
31	7	Salaries Expense	55	810			810
				4,726	24	1,700	3,050
				(11)	(53)	(21)	(✔)

Purchases Journal   P-1

Date	Account Cr.	P.R.	Acct. Pay. Cr.	Pur. Dr.	Store Supp. Dr.	Office Supp. Dr.	Sundry Acct. Dr. Acct.	P.R.	Amount
Mar. 4	Andon Equipment	✔	10,000				Equip.	19	10,000
7	Baily Company	✔	1,200	1,200					
16	Cotin Company	✔	1,100	1,100					
18	Salio Supply House	✔	250		250				
24	Daily Corporation	✔	850	850					
26	Salio Supply House	✔	325		325				
			13,725	3,150	575				10,000
			(21)	(51)	(14)				(✔)

Sales Journal   S-1

Date	Account Debited	P.R.	Amount
Mar. 11	Manny Company	✔	600
12	Nant Company	✔	350
19	Olin Company	✔	645
25	Pallit Corporation	✔	740
			2,335
			(12)(41)

2. Based on the work in part 1, post all transactions to the appropriate accounts in the general ledger, the accounts receivable ledger, and the accounts payable ledger.

General Ledger

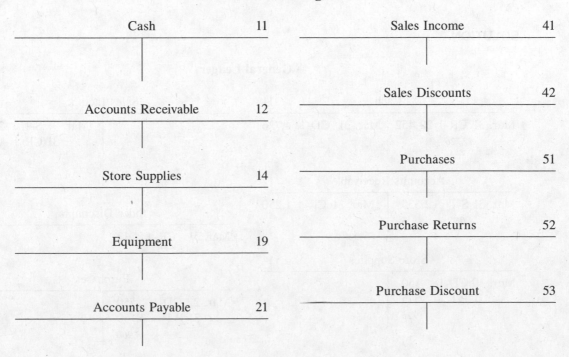

| Cash | 11 | Sales Income | 41 |

| Accounts Receivable | 12 | Sales Discounts | 42 |

| Store Supplies | 14 | Purchases | 51 |

| Equipment | 19 | Purchase Returns | 52 |

| Accounts Payable | 21 | Purchase Discount | 53 |

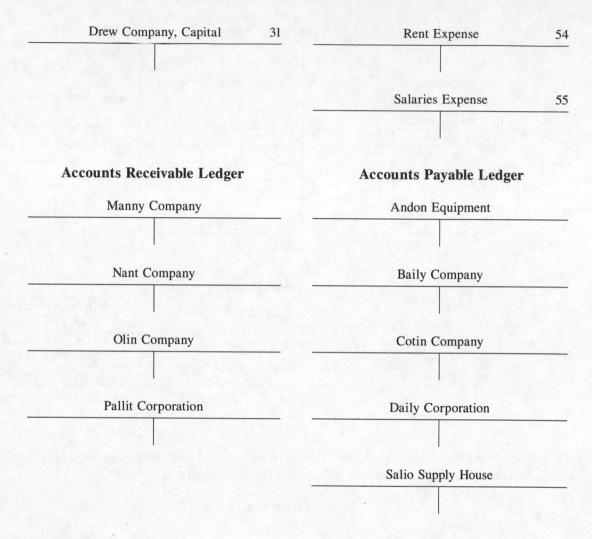

Drew Company, Capital	31		Rent Expense	54

		Salaries Expense	55

Accounts Receivable Ledger

Manny Company

Nant Company

Olin Company

Pallit Corporation

Accounts Payable Ledger

Andon Equipment

Baily Company

Cotin Company

Daily Corporation

Salio Supply House

SOLUTION

General Ledger

	Cash	11			Sales Income	41
Mar. 31 CR-1	22,452	Mar. 31 CD-1 4,726			Mar. 31 S-1	2,335
17,726					31 CR-1	7,215
						9,550

	Accounts Receivable	12
Mar. 31 S-1	2,335	Mar. 31 CR-1 1,250
1,085		

	Sales Discounts	42
Mar. 31 CR-1	13	

	Store Supplies	14
Mar. 10 CD-1	150	
31 P-1	575	
725		

	Purchases	51
Mar. 22 CD-1	750	
31 P-1	3,150	
3,900		

Equipment		19
Mar. 4 P-1 10,000		

Purchase Returns		52
	Mar. 19 J-1	200

Accounts Payable		21
Mar. 19 J-1 200	Mar. 31 P-1	13,725
31 CD-1 1,700	*11,825*	

Purchase Discount		53
	Mar. 31 CD-1	24

Drew Company, Capital		31
	Mar. 1 CR-1	14,000

Rent Expense		54
Mar. 2 CD-1 600		

Salaries Expense		55
Mar. 14 CD-1 740		
31 CD-1 810		
1,550		

Accounts Receivable Ledger

Manny Company

Mar. 11 S-1 <u>600</u>	Mar. 27 CR-1 <u>600</u>

Nant Company

Mar. 12 S-1 <u>350</u>	Mar. 22 CR-1 <u>350</u>

Olin Company

Mar. 19 S-1 645	Mar. 30 CR-1 300
345	

Pallit Corporation

Mar. 25 S-1 740	

Accounts Payable Ledger

Andon Equipment

Mar. 21 CD-1 500	Mar. 4 P-1 10,000
	9,500

Baily Company

Mar. 17 CD-1 <u>1,200</u>	Mar. 7 P-1 <u>1,200</u>

Cotin Company

Mar. 19 J-1 200	Mar. 16 P-1 1,100
	900

Daily Corporation

	Mar. 24 P-1 850

Salio Supply House

	Mar. 18 P-1 250
	26 P-1 325
	575

3. Based on the information in parts 1 and 2, prepare a schedule of accounts receivable, a schedule of accounts payable, and a trial balance.

Drew Company	
Schedule of Accounts Receivable	
March 31, 19X5	
Olin Company	
Pallit Corporation	

Drew Company
Schedule of Accounts Payable
March 31, 19X5

Andon Equipment	
Cotin Company	
Daily Corporation	
Salio Supply House	

Drew Company
Trial Balance
March 31, 19X5

Cash		
Accounts Receivable		
Store Supplies		
Equipment		
Accounts Payable		
Drew Company, Capital		
Sales		
Sales Discount		
Purchases		
Purchase Returns		
Purchase Discount		
Rent Expense		
Salaries Expense		

SOLUTION

Drew Company
Schedule of Accounts Receivable
March 31, 19X5

Olin Company	$ 345
Pallit Corporation	740
	$ 1,085

Drew Company
Schedule of Accounts Payable
March 31, 19X5

Andon Equipment	$ 9,500
Cotin Company	900
Daily Corporation	850
Salio Supply House	575
	$11,825

Drew Company Trial Balance March 31, 19X5		
Cash	$ 17,726	
Accounts Receivable	1,085	
Store Supplies	725	
Equipment	10,000	
Accounts Payable		$11,825
Drew Company, Capital		14,000
Sales		9,550
Sales Discount	13	
Purchases	3,900	
Purchase Returns		200
Purchase Discount		24
Rent Expense	600	
Salaries Expense	1,550	
	$35,599	$35,599

Chapter 8

Summarizing and Reporting via the Worksheet

8.1 INTRODUCTION

The recording of transactions and the adjusting and closing procedures have been discussed in previous chapters. It is reasonable to expect that among the hundreds of computations and clerical tasks involved, some errors will occur, such as posting a debit as a credit. Today many financial records are maintained on the computer or on mechanical bookkeeping systems. The use of machine time to correct errors can be very costly and may provoke questions from financial managers.

One of the best ways yet developed of avoiding errors in the permanent accounting records, and also of simplifying the work at the end of the period, is to make use of an informal record called a *worksheet.*

8.2 WORKSHEET PROCEDURES FOR A SERVICE BUSINESS

We are already familiar with the types of accounts found in a service business—that is, a business in which revenue comes from services rendered—so we shall first discuss the worksheet for such a business.

The worksheet is usually prepared in pencil on a large sheet of accounting stationery called *analysis paper.* On the worksheet, the ledger accounts are adjusted, balanced, and arranged in proper form for preparing the financial statements. All procedures can be reviewed quickly, and the adjusting and closing entries can be made in the formal records with less chance of error. Moreover, with the data for the income statement and balance sheet already proved out on the worksheet, these statements can be prepared more quickly.

For a typical service business, we may suppose the worksheet to have eight money columns; namely, a debit and a credit column for four groups of figures:

1. Trial balance
2. Adjustments
3. Income statement
4. Balance sheet

A ten-column worksheet also is used, consisting of (1) trial balance, (2) adjustments, (3) adjusted trial balance, (4) income statement, and (5) balance sheet. The adjusted trial balance columns simplify the extension to the financial statement columns, but, for the illustrations in this chapter, the eight-column worksheet will be used.

The steps in completing the worksheet are then:

1. Enter the trial balance figures from the ledger.
2. Enter the adjustments.
3. Extend the adjusted trial balance and the adjustment figures to either the income statement or balance sheet columns.
4. Total the income statement columns and the balance sheet columns.
5. Enter the net income or net loss.

EXAMPLE 1

From the following trial balance and adjustment information, prepare an eight-column worksheet.

T. Dembofsky
Trial Balance
December 31, 19X5

	Dr.	Cr.
Cash	$ 7,000	
Accounts Receivable	3,500	
Prepaid Rent	3,000	
Supplies	800	
Equipment	6,200	
Accounts Payable		$ 4,500
T. Dembofsky, Capital		12,000
Fees Income		10,000
Salaries Expense	4,600	
General Expense	1,400	
	$26,500	$26,500

Adjustment Information

(a)	Rent Expired for Year	$1,200
(b)	Supplies on Hand	200
(c)	Salaries Accrued	400

T. Dembofsky
Worksheet
December 31, 19X5

Account Title	Trial Balance Dr.	Trial Balance Cr.	Adjustments Dr.	Adjustments Cr.	Income Statement Dr.	Income Statement Cr.	Balance Sheet Dr.	Balance Sheet Cr.
Cash	7,000						7,000	
Accounts Receivable	3,500						3,500	
Prepaid Rent	3,000			(a) 1,200			1,800	
Supplies	800			(b) 600			200	
Equipment	6,200						6,200	
Accounts Payable		4,500						4,500
T. Dembofsky, Cap.		12,000						12,000
Fees Income		10,000				10,000		
Salaries Expense	4,600		(c) 400		5,000			
General Expense	1,400				1,400			
	26,500	26,500						
Rent Expense			(a) 1,200		1,200			
Supplies Expense			(b) 600		600			

(continued)
T. Dembofsky
Worksheet
December 31, 19X5

Account Title	Trial Balance		Adjustments		Income Statement		Balance Sheet	
	Dr.	Cr.	Dr.	Cr.	Dr.	Cr.	Dr.	Cr.
Salaries Payable				(c) 400				400
			2,200	2,200	8,200	10,000	18,700	16,900
Net Income					1,800			1,800
					10,000	10,000	18,700	18,700

Use the following procedures:

1. **Enter the trial balance figures.** The balance of each general ledger account is entered in the appropriate trial balance column of the worksheet. The balances summarize all the transactions for December before any adjusting entries have been applied.

2. **Enter the adjustments.** After the trial balance figures have been entered and the totals are in agreement, the adjusting entries should be entered in the second pair of columns. The related debits and credits are keyed by letters so that they may be rechecked quickly for any errors. The letters should be in proper sequence, beginning with the accounts at the top of the page.

(a) *Rent.* Rent may be paid in advance, at which time the debit would be to Prepaid Rent (an asset). As it expires, the Prepaid Rent account will be reduced, as it must reflect only what has been prepaid. The entry to record the expired rent is:

Rent Expense	1,200	
Prepaid Rent		1,200

The account name, Rent Expense, should be written in at the bottom of the worksheet.

(b) *Supplies.* This firm may have purchased $800 worth of supplies to last for a few years. Only the cost of the supplies used during each year is considered as an operating expense for that period; the unused portion is deferred to future periods. For this reason, the purchase of supplies is debited to an asset account and adjusted at the end of the year. Because supplies of $200 were still on hand at the close of the period, it is understood that $600 had been used and should be charged to the expense.

Supplies Expense	600	
Supplies		600

The account Supplies Expense should be written in at the bottom of the worksheet.

(c) *Salaries.* The salaries amount in the trial balance column should include only the payments that have been recorded and paid during the month. The portion that was *earned* in December but paid in the following year, because the weekly pay period ended in January, should not be included. Therefore an adjusting entry is needed to reflect the $400 earned but not yet paid.

Salaries Expense	400	
Salaries Payable		400

The account title Salaries Payable should also be written in on the worksheet.

3. ***Extend the trial balance figures and the adjustment figures to either the income statement or balance sheet columns.***   The process of extending the balances horizontally should begin with the account at the top of the sheet. The revenue and expense accounts should be extended to the income statement columns; the assets, liabilities, and capital to the balance sheet columns. Each figure is extended to only one of the columns. After the adjusted trial balance column totals have been proved out, then the income statement columns and the balance sheet columns should also prove out.

4. ***Total the income statement columns and the balance sheet columns.***   The difference between the debit and credit totals in both sets of columns should be the same amount, which represents net income or net loss for the period.

5. ***Enter the net income or net loss.***   In this example, the credit column total in the income statement is $10,000, the debit column total is $8,200. The credit column, or income side, is the larger, representing a net income of $1,800 for the month. Since net income increases capital, the net income figure should go on the credit side of the balance sheet. The balance sheet credit column total of $16,900 plus net income of $1,800 totals $18,700, which equals the debit column total. Since both the income statement columns and balance sheet columns are in agreement, it is a simple matter to prepare the formal income statement and balance sheet.

   If there had been a loss, the debit or expense column in the income statement would have been the larger, and the loss amount would have been entered in the credit column in order to balance the two columns. As a loss would decrease the capital, it would be entered in the balance sheet debit column.

Summary

1. Because the worksheet is an informal statement, it is prepared in _____ .

2. The balances that appear in the first two columns of the worksheet originate from the _____ .

3. All changes in accounts appear in the _____ columns of the worksheet.

4. If the total of the debit column of the income statement in the worksheet is larger than the total of the credit column of the income statement, the balance is said to be a _____ for the period.

Answers: 1. pencil; 2. ledger; 3. adjustment; 4. net loss

Solved Problems

8.1   Joe Hurt owns and operates Rent-a-Wreck Company, a used car rental business. On the following page is a trial balance before the month-end adjustments.

Trial Balance

	Dr.	Cr.
Cash	$ 1,940	
Accounts Receivable	1,575	
Supplies	1,740	
Prepaid Rent	2,900	
Equipment	16,500	
Accounts Payable		$ 1,000
Joe Hurt, Capital		21,650
Joe Hurt, Drawing	2,500	
Rental Income		7,125
Salaries Expense	1,800	
Utilities Expense	540	
Miscellaneous Expense	280	
	$29,775	$29,775

Listed below are the month-end adjustments:

(a) Inventory of supplies at end of month, $975
(b) Rent for the month, $900
(c) Depreciation expense for month, $500
(d) Salaries payable, $200

Prepare an adjusted trial balance and make the necessary adjusting entries.

Account Title	Trial Balance		Trial Balance Adjustments		Adjusted Trial Balance	
	Dr.	Cr.	Dr.	Cr.	Dr.	Cr.

Adjusting entries:

(a) _____
    _____

(b) _____
    _____

(c) _____
    _____

(d) _____
    _____

SOLUTION

Account Title	Trial Balance		Trial Balance Adjustments		Adjusted Trial Balance	
	Dr.	Cr.	Dr.	Cr.	Dr.	Cr.
Cash	1,940				1,940	
Accounts Receivable	1,575				1,575	
Supplies	1,740			(a) 765	975	
Prepaid Rent	2,900			(b) 900	2,000	
Equipment	16,500				16,500	
Accounts Payable		1,000				1,000
J. Hurt, Capital		21,650				21,650
J. Hurt, Drawing	2,500				2,500	
Rental Income		7,125				7,125
Salaries Expense	1,800		(d) 200		2,000	
Utilities Expense	540				540	
Miscellaneous Expense	280				280	
	29,775	29,775				
Supplies Expense			(a) 765		765	
Rent Expense			(b) 900		900	
Depreciation Expense			(c) 500		500	
Accumulated Depreciation				(c) 500		500
Salaries Payable				(d) 200		200
Total Adjustments			2,365	2,365		
Total Adjusted Trial Balance					30,475	30,475

Adjusting Entries:

(a)	Supplies Expense	765	
	Supplies		765
(b)	Rent Expense	900	
	Prepaid Rent		900
(c)	Depreciation Expense	500	
	Accumulated Depreciation		500
(d)	Salaries Expense	200	
	Salaries Payable		200

8.2 From the partial view of the worksheet below, determine the net income or loss.

Income Statement		Balance Sheet	
Dr.	Cr.	Dr.	Cr.
19,500	36,200	54,200	37,500

SOLUTION

36,200	(total credits of income statement)
− 19,500	(total debits of income statement)
16,700	(net income)

	Income Statement		Balance Sheet	
	Dr.	Cr.	Dr.	Cr.
	19,500	36,200	54,200	37,500
Net Income	16,700			16,700
	36,200	36,200	54,200	54,200

8.3 The following selected accounts are taken from the ledger of C. Gold. Place check marks in the appropriate columns to which the accounts will be extended in the worksheet.

Title	Income Statement		Balance Sheet	
	Dr.	Cr.	Dr.	Cr.
(1) Cash				
(2) Accounts Receivable				
(3) Accounts Payable				
(4) C. Gold, Drawing				
(5) C. Gold, Capital				
(6) Fees Income				
(7) Depreciation Expense				
(8) Salaries Payable				

SOLUTION

Title	Income Statement		Balance Sheet	
	Dr.	Cr.	Dr.	Cr.
(1) Cash			✔	
(2) Accounts Receivable			✔	
(3) Accounts Payable				✔
(4) C. Gold, Drawing			✔	
(5) C. Gold, Capital				✔
(6) Fees Income		✔		
(7) Depreciation Expense	✔			
(8) Salaries Payable				✔

8.4 From the following trial balances and adjustments information, prepare an eight-column worksheet.

W. Gurney Company
Trial Balance
December 31, 19X5

Account Title	Trial Balance		Adjustments		Income Statement		Balance Sheet	
	Dr.	Cr.	Dr.	Cr.	Dr.	Cr.	Dr.	Cr.
Cash	8,000							
Accounts Receivable	3,500							
Prepaid Rent	3,000							
Supplies	800							
Equipment	6,200							
Accounts Payable		5,500						
W. Gurney, Capital		12,000						
Fees Income		10,000						
Salaries Expense	4,600							
General Expense	1,400							
	27,500	27,500						

(continued)
W. Gurney Company
Trial Balance
December 31, 19X5

Account Title	Trial Balance Dr.	Cr.	Adjustments Dr.	Cr.	Income Statement Dr.	Cr.	Balance Sheet Dr.	Cr.

Adjustments:

(*a*) Rent expired for year, $1,000

(*b*) Supplies on hand, $300

(*c*) Salaries accrued, $400

SOLUTION

W. Gurney Company
Worksheet
December 31, 19X5

Account Title	Trial Balance Dr.	Cr.	Adjustments Dr.	Cr.	Income Statement Dr.	Cr.	Balance Sheet Dr.	Cr.
Cash	8,000						8,000	
Accounts Receivable	3,500						3,500	
Prepaid Rent	3,000			(*a*)1,000			2,000	
Supplies	800			(*b*) 500			300	
Equipment	6,200						6,200	
Accounts Payable		5,500						5,500
W. Gurney, Capital		12,000						12,000
Fees Income		10,000				10,000		
Salaries Expense	4,600		(*c*) 400		5,000			
General Expense	1,400				1,400			
	27,500	27,500						
Rent Expense			(*a*) 1,000		1,000			
Supplies Expense			(*b*) 500		500			
Salaries Payable				(*c*) 400				400
			1,900	1,900	7,900	10,000	20,000	17,900
Net Income					2,100			2,100
					10,000	10,000	20,000	20,000

8.5   From the information in Problem 8.4, prepare all adjusting and closing entries.

Adjusting Entries

(a)		
(b)		
(c)		

Closing Entries

(a)		
(b)		
(c)		

SOLUTION

Adjusting Entries

(a)	Rent Expense	1,000	
	Prepaid Rent		1,000
(b)	Supplies Expense	500	
	Supplies		500
(c)	Salaries Expense	400	
	Salaries Payable		400

Closing Entries

(a)	Fees Income	10,000	
	Expense and Income Summary		10,000
(b)	Expense and Income Summary	7,900	
	Salaries Expense		5,000
	General Expense		1,400
	Rent Expense		1,000
	Supplies Expense		500
(c)	Expense and Income Summary	2,100	
	W. Gurney, Capital		2,100

8.6   From the data of Problem 8.4, prepare the income statement and balance sheet.

W. Gurney Company
Income Statement
For the Period Ending December 31, 19X5

Fees Income		
Expenses:		
Salaries Expense		
Rent Expense		
Supplies Expense		
General Expense		
Total Expenses		
Net Income		

W. Gurney Company
Balance Sheet
December 31, 19X5

ASSETS		LIABILITIES AND CAPITAL		
Current Assets:		Liabilities:		
Cash		Accounts Payable		
Accounts Receivable		Salaries Payable		
Prepaid Rent		Total Liabilities		
Supplies		Capital:		
Total Current Assets		Capital, Jan. 1, 19X5		
Fixed Assets:		Add: Net Income		
Equipment		Capital, Dec. 31, 19X5		
Total Assets		Total Liabilities and Capital		

SOLUTION

W. Gurney Company
Income Statement
For the Period Ending December 31, 19X5

Fees Income		$10,000
Expenses:		
Salaries Expense	$5,000	
Rent Expense	1,000	
Supplies Expense	500	
General Expense	1,400	
Total Expenses		7,900
Net Income		$ 2,100

W. Gurney Company
Balance Sheet
December 31, 19X5

ASSETS		LIABILITIES AND CAPITAL		
Current Assets:		Liabilities:		
Cash	$ 8,000	Accounts Payable		$ 5,500
Accounts Receivable	3,500	Salaries Payable		400
Prepaid Rent	2,000	Total Liabilities		$ 5,900
Supplies	300	Capital:		
Total Current Assets	$13,800	Capital, Jan. 1, 19X5	$12,000	
Fixed Assets:		Add: Net Income	2,100	
Equipment	6,200	Capital, Dec. 31, 19X5		14,100
Total Assets	$20,000	Total Liabilities and Capital		$20,000

Examination II

Part I: Multiple Choice

1. The type of transaction that would appear in the sales journal would be (*a*) sale of merchandise for cash; (*b*) sale of equipment for cash; (*c*) sale of equipment in exchange for a note; (*d*) sale of merchandise on account; (*e*) none of the above.

2. The receipt of cash arising from a sales transaction would be recorded in (*a*) the cash receipts journal; (*b*) the cash payments journal; (*c*) the sales journal; (*d*) the purchases journal; (*e*) none of the above.

3. The classification and normal balance of the sales discount account would be (*a*) expense, debit; (*b*) revenue, credit; (*c*) contra revenue, debit; (*d*) asset, debit; (*e*) none of the above.

4. If an item retailing for $1,000, subject to a trade discount of 25 percent, is paid for within the sales discount period, terms 2/10, n/30, the amount of the check received would be (*a*) $1,000; (*b*) $750; (*c*) $740; (*d*) $735; (*e*) none of the above.

5. Each time an entry is recorded in the purchases journal, the credit would be entered in the (*a*) purchase column; (*b*) accounts payable column; (*c*) supply column; (*d*) accounts receivable column; (*e*) none of the above.

6. Which of the following items would be recorded in the purchases journal? (*a*) supplies purchased on accounts; (*b*) equipment purchased on account; (*c*) merchandise purchased on account; (*d*) all of the above; (*e*) none of the above.

7. The controlling account in the general ledger that summarizes the debits and credits to the individual accounts in the customers' ledger is entitled (*a*) Accounts Receivable; (*b*) Accounts Payable; (*c*) Sales; (*d*) Purchases; (*e*) none of the above.

8. The item that reflects the payment of cash is known as a(n) (*a*) check; (*b*) invoice; (*c*) voucher; (*d*) draft; (*e*) none of the above.

9. Infrequent sales returns would appear in which journal? (*a*) sales; (*b*) sales returns; (*c*) general; (*d*) cash receipts; (*e*) cash payments.

10. The combined cash journal would be used for (*a*) all cash received during the month; (*b*) all payments made in cash during the month; (*c*) any item that has to do with either income or outgo of cash; (*d*) all of the above; (*e*) none of the above.

Part II: Problems

1. In the following table, indicate in which of the five journals each transaction is to be recorded.

176

	Cash Payments	Cash Receipts	Sales Income	Purchases	General
(a) Sale of merchandise for cash					
(b) Sale of merchandise on account					
(c) Cash refunded to a customer					
(d) Receipt of cash from a customer in settlement of an account					
(e) Purchase of merchandise for cash					
(f) Purchase of merchandise on account					
(g) Payment of salaries					
(h) Note payable sent to a creditor in settlement of an account					
(i) Payment of interest on the mortgage					
(j) Received a note in settlement of a customer's account					

2. S. Perk began business on March 1, 19X5. The transactions completed by the company for the month of March 19X5 are listed below. Record these transactions using a general journal, cash receipts journal, cash disbursements journal, purchases journal, and sales journal.

March 1　Deposited $18,000 in a bank account for the operation of Perkowski Company.
2　Paid rent for the month, $800, Check #1.
4　Purchased equipment on account from Anton Equipment, $5,000.
7　Purchased merchandise on account from Bail Company, $1,000.
7　Cash sales for the week, $2,000.
10　Issued Check #2 of $150 for store supplies.
11　Sold merchandise on account to Manny Company, $700.
12　Sold merchandise on account to Nanny Company, $350.
14　Paid biweekly salaries of $840. Check #3.
14　Cash sales for the week, $1,800.
16　Purchased merchandise on account from Cotin Company, $1,000.
17　Issued Check #4 to Bail Company for Mar. 7 purchase, less 2 percent.
18　Bought $250 worth of store supplies from Salid Supply House on account.
19　Returned defective merchandise of $200 to Cotin Company and received credit.
19　Sold merchandise on account to Polin Company, $645.
21　Issued Check #5 of $600 to Anton Equipment in part payment of equipment purchase.
22　Received check from Nanny Company in settlement of their Mar. 12 purchase, less 2 percent discount.
22　Purchased merchandise from Fredie Corporation for cash, $750, Check #6.
23　Cash sales for the week, $1,845.
24　Purchased merchandise on account from Daily Corporation, $850.

25   Sold merchandise on account to Sunco Corporation, $740.
26   Cash sales for the week, $1,920.
27   Paid biweekly salaries, $800, Check #7.

General Journal   J-1

Date	Description	P.R.	Debit	Credit

Cash Receipts Journal   CR-1

Date	Account Cr.	P.R.	Cash Dr.	Sales Disc. Dr.	Acct. Rec. Cr.	Sales Income Cr.	Sundry Cr.

Cash Disbursements Journal   CD-1

Date	Check No.	Account Dr.	P.R.	Cash Cr.	Pur. Disc. Cr.	Acct. Pay. Dr.	Sundry Dr.

Purchases Journal   P-1

Date	Account Cr.	P.R.	Acct. Pay. Cr.	Pur. Dr.	Store Supp. Dr.	Sundry		
						Acct. Dr.	P.R.	Amt.

Sales Journal   S-1

Date	Account Debited	P.R.	Accounts Receivable Dr. / Sales Income Cr.

3. Using the information in parts 1 and 2, post all transactions to the appropriate accounts in the general ledger, the accounts receivable ledger, and the accounts payable ledger.

General Ledger

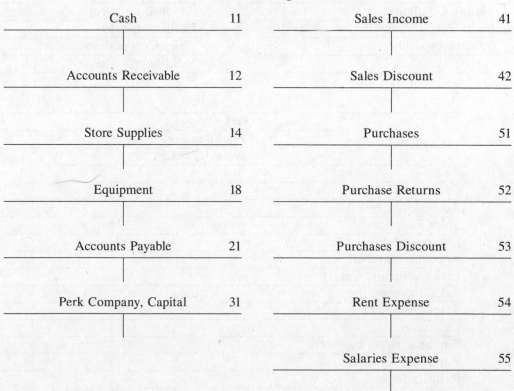

| Cash | 11 | Sales Income | 41 |

| Accounts Receivable | 12 | Sales Discount | 42 |

| Store Supplies | 14 | Purchases | 51 |

| Equipment | 18 | Purchase Returns | 52 |

| Accounts Payable | 21 | Purchases Discount | 53 |

| Perk Company, Capital | 31 | Rent Expense | 54 |

| | | Salaries Expense | 55 |

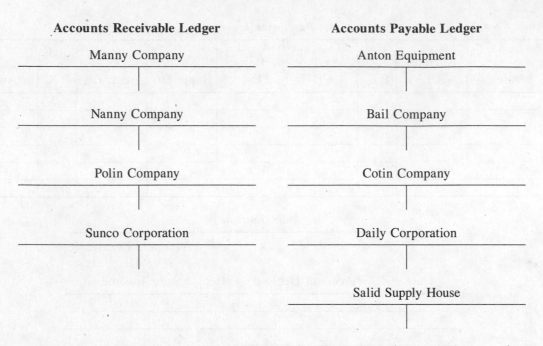

Accounts Receivable Ledger	Accounts Payable Ledger
Manny Company	Anton Equipment
Nanny Company	Bail Company
Polin Company	Cotin Company
Sunco Corporation	Daily Corporation
	Salid Supply House

4. Based on the information above, prepare (*a*) a schedule of accounts receivable; (*b*) a schedule of accounts payable; (*c*) a trial balance.

(*a*)

Perk Company
Schedule of Accounts Receivable
March 31, 19X5

Manny Company	
Polin Corporation	
Sunco Corporation	

(*b*)

Perk Company
Schedule of Accounts Payable
March 31, 19X5

Anton Equipment	
Cotin Company	
Daily Corporation	
Salid Supply House	

(*c*)

Perk Company
Trial Balance
March 31, 19X5

Cash		
Accounts Receivable		
Store Supplies		
Equipment		
Accounts Payable		
Perk Company, Capital		
Sales Income		
Sales Discount		
Purchases		
Purchase Returns		
Purchases Discount		
Rent Expense		
Salaries Expense		

5. Hy Sharp owns the Real Sharp Knife Shop. Hy completed a trial balance sheet and has asked you, his accountant, to complete his year-end financial statements. Upon examining his books, you discover the following adjusting entries that must be made to complete the worksheet for the year-end financial statements. Complete the worksheet.

(*a*) Insurance expired, $2,100

(*b*) Mortgage payment made on last day of year but not recorded, paid with check (cash), $2,400

(*c*) Supplies on hand at year-end, $5,900

(*d*) Salaries owed at year-end, $1,950

(*e*) Depreciation for the year, $7,100

(*f*) Rent expired on storage building, $3,200

Account Title	Trial Balance Dr.	Trial Balance Cr.	Adjustments Dr.	Adjustments Cr.	Income Statement Dr.	Income Statement Cr	Balance Sheet Dr.	Balance Sheet Cr.
Cash	12,600							
Accounts Receivable	16,900							
Prepaid Rent	9,600							
Prepaid Insurance	7,400							
Supplies	14,100							
Equipment	42,900							
Accounts Payable		1,100						
Notes Payable		1,200						
Mortgage Notes Pay.		24,500						
Hy Sharp, Capital		17,200						
Hy Sharp, Drawing	16,200							
Sales Income		104,150						
Salaries Expense	26,500							
Utilities Expense	1,950							
	148,150	148,150						

Answers to Examination II

Part I

1. (*d*); **2.** (*a*); **3.** (*c*); **4.** (*d*); **5.** (*b*); **6.** (*d*); **7.** (*a*); **8.** (*a*); **9.** (*c*); **10.** (*d*)

Part II

1.

	Cash Payments	Cash Receipts	Sales Income	Purchases	General
(*a*)		✔			
(*b*)			✔		
(*c*)	✔				
(*d*)		✔			
(*e*)	✔				
(*f*)				✔	
(*g*)	✔				
(*h*)					✔
(*i*)	✔				
(*j*)					✔

2.

General Journal   J-1

Date	Description	P.R.	Debit	Credit
Mar. 19	Accounts Payable-Cotin Co.	21/✔	200	
	Purchase Returns	52		200
	Defective goods			

Cash Receipts Journal   CR-1

Date	Account Cr.	P.R.	Cash Dr.	Sales Disc. Dr.	Acct. Rec. Cr.	Sales Income Cr.	Sundry Cr.
Mar. 1	Perk Co., Capital	31	18,000				18,000
7	Cash Sales	✔	2,000			2,000	
14	Cash Sales	✔	1,800			1,800	
22	Nanny Company	✔	343	7	350		
23	Cash Sales	✔	1,845			1,845	
30	Cash Sales	✔	1,920			1,920	
			25,908	7	350	7,565	18,000
			(11)	(42)	(12)	(41)	(✔)

Cash Disbursements Journal   CD-1

Date	Check No.	Account Dr.	P.R.	Cash Cr.	Pur. Disc. Cr.	Acct. Pay. Dr.	Sundry Dr.
Mar. 2	1	Rent Expense	54	800			800
10	2	Store Supplies	14	150			150
14	3	Salaries Expense	55	840			840
17	4	Bail Company	✔	980	20	1,000	
21	5	Anton	✔	600		600	
22	6	Purchases	51	750			750
31	7	Salaries Expense	55	800			800
				4,920	20	1,600	3,340
				(11)	(53)	(21)	(✔)

Purchases Journal   P-1

Date	Account Cr.	P.R.	Acct. Pay. Cr.	Pur. Dr.	Store Supp. Dr.	Sundry Acct. Dr.	Sundry P.R.	Sundry Amt.
Mar. 4	Anton Equip.	✔	5,000			Equip.	18	5,000
7	Bail Company	✔	1,000	1,000				
16	Cotin Company	✔	1,000	1,000				
18	Salid House	✔	250		250			
24	Daily Corp.	✔	850	850				
			8,100	2,850	250			5,000
			(21)	(51)	(14)			(✔)

Sales Journal   S-1

Date	Account Debited	P.R.	Accounts Receivable Dr. Sales Income Cr.
Mar. 11	Manny Company	✔	700
12	Nanny Company	✔	350
19	Polin Company	✔	645
25	Sunco Corp.	✔	740
			2,435
			(12)(41)

3.   **General Ledger**

Cash 11	Sales Income 41
Mar. 31 CR-1 25,908 | Mar. 31 CD-1 4,920	| Mar. 31 S-1 2,435
20,988	| 31 CR-1 7,565
	| *10,000*

Accounts Receivable 12	Sales Discount 42
Mar. 31 S-1 2,435 | Mar. 31 CR-1 350	Mar. 31 CR-1 7 |
2,085	

General Ledger *(continued)*

Store Supplies		14
Mar. 10 CD-1	150	
31 P-1	250	
	400	

Purchases		51
Mar. 22 CD-1	750	
31 P-1	2,850	
	3,600	

Equipment		18
Mar. 4 P-1	5,000	

Purchase Returns		52
	Mar. 19 J-1	200

Accounts Payable			21
Mar. 19 J-1	200	Mar. 31 P-1	8,100
31 CD-1	1,600		*6,300*
	1,800		

Purchases Discount		53
	Mar. 31 CD-1	20

Perk Company, Capital		31
	Mar. 31 CR-1	18,000

Rent Expense		54
Mar. 2 CD-1	800	

Salaries Expense		55
Mar. 14 CD-1	840	
31 CD-1	800	
	1,640	

Accounts Receivable Ledger

Manny Company

Mar. 11	S-1	700		

Nanny Company

Mar. 12	S-1	350	Mar. 22	CR-1	350

Polin Company

Mar. 19	S-1	645		

Sunco Corporation

Mar. 25	S-1	740		

Accounts Payable Ledger

Anton Equipment

Mar. 21	CD-1	600	Mar. 4	P-1	5,000

Bail Company

Mar. 17	CD-1	1,000	Mar. 7	P-1	1,000

Cotin Company

Mar. 14	J-1	200	Mar. 16	P-1	1,000

Daily Corporation

			Mar. 24	P-1	850

Salid Supply House

			Mar. 18	P-1	250

4. *(a)*

Perk Company	
Schedule of Accounts Receivable	
March 31, 19X5	
Manny Company	700
Polin Company	645
Sunco Corporation	740
	2,085

(b)

Perk Company	
Schedule of Accounts Payable	
March 31, 19X5	
Anton Equipment	4,400
Cotin Company	800
Daily Corporation	850
Salid Supply House	250
	6,300

(c)

Perk Company		
Trial Balance		
March 31, 19X5		
Cash	20,988	
Accounts Receivable	2,085	
Store Supplies	400	
Equipment	5,000	
Accounts Payable		6,300
Perk Company, Capital		18,000
Sales Income		10,000
Sales Discount	7	
Purchases	3,600	
Purchase Returns		200
Purchases Discount		20
Rent Expense	800	
Salaries Expense	1,640	
	34,520	34,520

5.

Account Title	Trial Balance Dr.	Trial Balance Cr.	Adjustments Dr.	Adjustments Cr.	Income Statement Dr.	Income Statement Cr.	Balance Sheet Dr.	Balance Sheet Cr.
Cash	12,600			(b) 2,400			10,200	
Accounts Rec.	16,900						16,900	
Prepaid Rent	9,600			(f) 3,200			6,400	
Prepaid Insurance	7,400			(a) 2,100			5,300	
Supplies	14,100			(c) 8,200			5,900	
Equipment	42,900						42,900	
Accounts Payable		1,100						1,100
Notes Payable		1,200						1,200
Mortgage Notes Pay.		24,500	(b) 2,400					22,100
Hy Sharp, Capital		17,200						17,200
Hy Sharp, Drawing	16,200						16,200	
Sales Income		104,150				104,150		
Salaries Expense	26,500		(d) 1,950		28,450			
Utilities Expense	1,950				1,950			
	148,150	148,150						
Insurance Expense			(a) 2,100		2,100			
Supplies Expense			(c) 8,200		8,200			
Salaries Payable				(d) 1,950				1,950
Depreciation Expense			(e) 7,100		7,100			
Accum. Depreciation				(e) 7,100				7,100
Rent Expense			(f) 3,200		3,200			
			24,950	24,950	51,000	104,150	103,800	50,650
Net Income					53,150			53,150
					104,150	104,150	103,800	103,800

Chapter 9

The Merchandising Company

9.1 INTRODUCTION

There are three types of business enterprises that make up the business society:

(1) *Service.* Companies and individuals that yield a service to the consumer, such as lawyers, physicians, airlines, entertainment, etc.

(2) *Manufacturing.* Companies that convert raw materials into finished products, such as housing construction companies and lumber mills.

(3) *Merchandising.* Companies that engage in buying and selling finished goods, such as department stores and retail establishments.

This chapter examines the third type, merchandising companies.

9.2 PURCHASES

When the periodic inventory system is used to account for inventory, purchases of merchandise during the period are not debited to the Merchandise Inventory account (see Physical and Perpetual Inventory, Chapter 10), but rather are debited to a separate account known as Purchases. This account includes only merchandise bought for resale. Other types of purchases (machinery, furniture, trucks, etc.) that are to be used in the business, rather than sold, are debited to the particular asset account involved and appear in the balance sheet.

EXAMPLE 1

(*a*) Bought merchandise for resale, $6,000.

Purchases	6,000	
Cash		6,000

(*b*) Bought a truck costing $22,000 for delivery purposes.

Truck	22,000	
Cash		22,000

Note: While Truck ($22,000) is entered on the balance sheet as an asset, the account purchases appears in the cost of goods sold section of the income statement.

9.3 ADJUSTING ENTRY PROCEDURES

Merchandising (trading) businesses are those whose income derives largely from buying and selling goods rather than from rendering services.

Inventory represents the value of goods on hand at either the beginning or the end of the accounting period. The beginning balance is the same amount as the ending balance of the previous period. Generally, not all purchases of merchandise are sold in the same period, so unsold merchandise must be counted and priced, and its total recorded in the ledger as Ending Inventory. The amount of this inventory is shown as an asset in the balance sheet. The amount of goods sold during the period is shown as cost of goods sold in the income statement. (See Section 9.6.)

EXAMPLE 2

Assume that the January 1 (beginning) inventory is $2,700 and the December 31 (ending) inventory is $2,900. Two entries are required to show the replacement of the old inventory by the new inventory:

Entry 1:	Expense and Income Summary	2,700	
	Merchandise Inventory		2,700
Entry 2:	Merchandise Inventory	2,900	
	Expense and Income Summary		2,900

The effect on Merchandise Inventory and the Expense and Income Summary account balance is as follows:

Merchandise Inventory				Expense and Income Summary			
Jan. 1	2,700	Dec. 31	2,700	Dec. 31	2,700	Dec. 31	2,900
Dec. 31	2,900						

9.4 WORKSHEET PROCEDURES

As discussed in Chapter 8, the worksheet is usually prepared in pencil on a multicolumn sheet of accounting stationery called analysis paper. On the worksheet, the ledger accounts are adjusted, balanced, and arranged in proper form for preparing the financial statements. All procedures can be reviewed quickly, and the adjusting and closing entries can be made in the formal records with less chance of error. Moreover, with the data for the income statement and balance sheet already proved out on the worksheet, these statements can be prepared more readily.

For a typical merchandise business, we may suppose the worksheet to have eight money columns, namely: a debit and a credit column for each of four groups of figures: (1) trial balance, (2) adjustments, (3) income statement, and (4) balance sheet. The steps in completing the worksheet are, then, similar to those for a service business:

1. ***Enter the trial balance figures.***   The balance of each general ledger account is entered in the appropriate trial balance column of the worksheet. The balances summarize all the transactions for the period before any adjusting entries have been applied.

2. ***Enter the adjustments.***   After the trial balance figures have been entered and the totals are in agreement, the adjusting entries should be entered in the second pair of columns. The related debits and credits are keyed by letters so that they may be rechecked quickly for any errors. The letters should be in proper sequence, beginning with the accounts at the top of the page. For the purpose of this chapter, only the adjusting entry for Merchandise Inventory will be considered, although entries for prepaid expenses, accrued salaries, depreciation, and unearned income are normally found in the adjusting columns.

3. ***Extend the trial balance figures and the adjustment figures to either the income statement or balance sheet columns.***   The process of extending the balance horizontally should begin with the account at the top of the sheet. The revenue and expense accounts should be extended to the income statement columns; the assets, liabilities, and capital to the balance sheet columns.

You will notice that both the debit and credit amounts for Expense and Income Summary are extended to the income statement. This occurs because both the debit amount adjustment ($2,700 of Beginning Inventory) and the credit amount adjustment ($2,900) of Ending Inventory) are needed to prepare the income statement. It would not be practical to net the two items, as the single figure would not yield sufficient information regarding the beginning and ending inventories.

The Beginning Inventory figure ($2,700) is extended as a debit in the Income Statement column because it will be combined with the Purchases account balance to determine the cost of goods available for sale. The Ending Inventory figure ($2,900) is a credit in the Income Statement column because it will be deducted from the goods available for sale in order to determine the cost of goods sold. The Ending Inventory is also recorded and entered as a debit in the balance sheet column because that will show the goods on hand at the end of the period, and thus an asset of the firm.

4. *Total the income statement columns and the balance sheet columns.* The difference between the debit and credit totals in both sets of columns should be the same amount, which represents net income or net loss for the period.

5. *Enter the net income or net loss.* In Example 3, below, the credit column total in the income statement is $42,700, the debit column total is $35,600. The credit column, or income side, is the larger, representing a net income of $7,100 for the month. Since net income increases capital, the net income figure should go on the credit side of the balance sheet. The balance sheet credit column total of $25,050 plus net income of $7,100 totals $32,150, which equals the debit column total. Since both the income statement columns and the balance sheet columns are in agreement, it is a simple matter to prepare the formal income statement and balance sheet.

EXAMPLE 3

From the trial balance of the J. C. Company below, you can prepare an eight-column worksheet. The Ending Merchandise Inventory (Dec. 31, 19X5) was found to be $2,900, as shown in Example 2.

J.C. Company
Trial Balance
December 31, 19X5

	Debit	Credit
Cash	$12,300	
Accounts Receivable	16,000	
Merchandise Inventory	2,700	
Supplies	450	
Prepaid Insurance	500	
Accounts Payable		$ 3,200
Notes Payable		7,100
J.C. Capital		14,750
Sales		39,800
Purchases	17,200	
Salaries Expense	11,400	
Advertising Expense	2,300	
General Expense	2,000	
	$64,850	$64,850

J.C. Company
Worksheet
Year Ended June 30, 19X5

Account Title	Trial Bal. Dr.	Trial Bal. Cr.	Adjustments Dr.	Adjustments Cr.	Income Statement Dr.	Income Statement Cr.	Bal. Sheet Dr.	Bal. Sheet Cr.
Cash	12,300						12,300	
Accounts Receivable	16,000						16,000	
Merchandise Inventory	2,700		(a) 2,900	(a) 2,700			2,900	
Supplies	450						450	
Prepaid Insurance	500						500	
Accounts Payable		3,200						3,200
Notes Payable		7,100						7,100
J. C. Capital		14,750						14,750
Sales		39,800				39,800		
Purchases	17,200				17,200			
Salaries Expense	11,400				11,400			
Advertising Expenses	2,300				2,300			
General Expenses	2,000				2,000			
	64,850	64,850						
Expense and Income Summary			(a) 2,700	(a) 2,900	2,700	2,900		
			5,600	5,600	35,600	42,700	32,150	25,050
Net Income					7,100			7,100
					42,700	42,700	32,150	32,150

9.5 CLOSING ENTRIES

The information for the month-to-month adjusting entries and the related financial statements can be obtained from the worksheet. After the income statement and balance sheet have been prepared from the worksheet for the last month in the fiscal year, a summary account—known as Expense and Income Summary—is set up. Then, by means of closing entries, each expense account is credited so as to produce a zero balance, and the total amount of the closed-out accounts is debited to Expense and Income Summary. Similarly, the individual revenue accounts are closed out by debiting, and the total amount is credited to the summary account. Thus, the new fiscal year starts with zero balances in the revenue and expense accounts, though assets, liabilities, and capital accounts are carried forward. Note that the Expense and Income Summary balance gives the net income or net loss for the old year. Finally, Expense and Income Summary is closed to the Capital account.

EXAMPLE 4

The adjusting entry for inventory and the closing entries based on the information obtained from the worksheet in Example 3 appear below.

Expense and Income Summary	2,700	
Merchandise Inventory (Jan.)		2,700
Merchandise Inventory (Dec.)	2,900	
Expense and Income Summary		2,900

| Sales | 39,800 | |
| Expense and Income Summary | | 39,800 |

Expense and Income Summary	32,900	
Purchases		17,200
Salaries Expenses		11,400
Advertising Expenses		2,300
General Expenses		2,000

| Expense and Income Summary | 7,100* | |
| J.C. Capital | | 7,100 |

The final result of the adjusting and closing entries appears below.

Merchandise Inventory		Sales		Purchases		Salaries Expense	
2,700	2,700	34,800	34,800	17,200	17,200	11,400	11,400
2,900							

Advertising Expenses		General Expenses		Expense and Income Summary		Capital	
2,300	2,300	2,000	2,000	2,700	2,900		14,750
				32,900	39,800		
				35,600	42,700		
				7,100*			7,100*
				42,700	42,700		21,850

*This represents the net income figure.

9.6   FINANCIAL STATEMENT TREATMENT

The Income Statement

The classified income statement sets out the amount of each function and enables management, stockholders, analysts, and others to study the changes in function costs over successive accounting periods. There are three functional classifications of the income statement.

(1) *Revenue.*   Revenue includes gross income from the sale of products or services. It may be designated as sales, income from fees, and so on, to indicate gross income. The gross amount is reduced by sales returns and by sales discounts to arrive at net sales.

(2) *Cost of goods sold.*   The inventory of a merchandising business consists of goods on hand at the beginning of the accounting period and those on hand at the end of the accounting period. The beginning inventory appears in the income statement (Cost of Goods Sold section, also known as COGS) and is added to purchases to arrive at the cost of goods available for sale. Ending inventory is deducted from the cost of goods available for sale to arrive at cost of goods sold.

EXAMPLE 5 (from Example 3)

Beginning Inventory	$ 2,700
Add: Purchases	17,200
Cost of Merchandise Available for Sale	$19,900
Less: Ending Inventory	2,900
Cost of Goods Sold	$17,000

(3) ***Operating expenses.*** Operating expenses includes all expenses or resources consumed in obtaining revenue. Operating expenses are further divided into two groups. Selling expenses are those related to the promotion and sale of the company's product or service. Generally, one individual is held accountable for this function, and his or her performance is measured by the results in increasing sales and maintaining selling expenses at an established level. General and administrative expenses are those related to the overall activities of the business, such as the salaries of the president and other officers. When preparing income statements, list expenses from highest to lowest except Miscellaneous, which is always last, no matter how large the amount may be.

EXAMPLE 6

J.C. Company
Income Statement
Year Ended June 30, 19X5

Sales		$39,800
Cost of Goods Sold:		
Inventory (Beginning)	$ 2,700	
Purchases	17,200	
Goods Available for Sale	$19,900	
Less: Inventory (Ending)	2,900	
Cost of Goods Sold		17,000
		$22,800
Operating Expenses:		
Salaries Expenses	$11,400	
Advertising Expenses	2,300	
General Expenses	2,000	
Total Operating Expenses		15,700
Net Profit		$ 7,100

J.C. Company
Balance Sheet
Year Ended June 30, 19X5

Assets:

Cash		$12,300
Accounts Receivable		16,000
Merchandise Inventory (Ending)		2,900
Supplies		450
Prepaid Insurance		500
Total Assets		$32,150

Liabilities:

Accounts Payable	$ 3,200	
Notes Payable	7,100	
Total Liabilities		$10,300

Capital:

Capital (Beginning)	$14,750	
Add: Net Income	7,100	
Total Capital		21,850*
Total Liabilities and Capital		$32,150

*A separate capital statement could be used instead of the data presented in the Capital section.

9.7 SUMMARY

Under the periodic inventory method of inventory calculation (see Chapter 10), all purchases are recorded in the Purchases account. At the end of the accounting period, the firm takes a physical count of all inventory that is on hand. The cost of the inventory includes the net purchase price (Purchases less both Purchases Returns and Allowances and Purchase Discounts) plus any cost of transportation (Freight-In). The total cost of purchases is then added to Beginning Inventory to get cost of goods available for sale. The cost of the Ending Inventory (that which has not been sold as of the end of the period) is then subtracted from the cost of goods available for sale to get cost of goods sold (the cost of the inventory that was sold during the period). The cost of goods sold is then subtracted from Sales to get gross profit, which is then reduced by operating expenses to determine net income.

Summary

1. Merchandise Inventory (ending) appears as an _____ in the _____ (financial statement).

2. Merchandise Inventory is adjusted through the _____ account.

3. The worksheet is prepared on a multicolumn sheet of accounting stationery known as _____ .

4. The number of columns normally used for worksheet presentation is _____ .

5. The only account figure that appears on both the income statement and the balance sheet is _____ .

6. The beginning balance of Merchandise Inventory would be the same amount as the ending balance of the _____ period.

7. Worksheets are not considered formal statements, and therefore can be prepared in _____ .

8. The net income that comes from the data in the worksheet would carry a _____ balance.

9. Each of the revenue, and each of the expense account balances is closed into the _____ account by means of _____ .

10. The accounts with zero balance at the beginning of the year would be those involving _____ and _____ .

Answers: 1. asset, balance sheet; 2. Expense and Income Summary; 3. analysis paper; 4. eight; 5. Merchandise Inventory; 6. preceding; 7. pencil; 8. credit; 9. Expense and Income Summary, closing entries; 10. income, expenses

Solved Problems

9.1   The Mills Company purchased merchandise costing $150,000. What is the cost of goods sold under each assumption below?

	Beginning Inventory	Ending Inventory
(a)	100,000	60,000
(b)	75,000	50,000
(c)	50,000	30,000
(d)	0	10,000

SOLUTION

Beginning Inventory + Purchases − Ending Inventory = Cost of Goods Sold

(a)	100,000	150,000	60,000	190,000
(b)	75,000	150,000	50,000	175,000
(c)	50,000	150,000	30,000	170,000
(d)	0	150,000	10,000	140,000

9.2 For each situation below, determine the missing figures.

	Beginning Inventory	Purchases During Period	Ending Inventory	Cost of Goods Sold
(a)	$18,000	$40,000	——	$35,000
(b)	——	41,000	$15,000	42,000
(c)	21,000	37,000	20,000	——
(d)	27,000	——	25,000	38,000

SOLUTION

(a) $23,000; (b) $16,000; (c) $38,000; (d) $36,000

9.3 Compute the cost of goods sold from the following information: Beginning Inventory, $30,000; Purchases, $70,000; Purchase Returns, $3,000; Transportation-In, $1,000; Ending Inventory, $34,000. (Transportation-In is to be added to the cost.)

SOLUTION

Beginning Inventory		$30,000
Purchases	$70,000	
Less: Purchase Returns	3,000	
Net Purchases	$67,000	
Add: Transportation-In	1,000	68,000
Goods Available for Sale		$98,000
Less: Ending Inventory		34,000
Cost of Goods Sold		$64,000

9.4 Prepare an income statement based on the following data.

(a) Merchandise inventory, Jan. 1, 19X5, $30,000

(b) Merchandise inventory, Dec. 31, 19X5, $24,000

(c) Purchases, $66,000

(d) Sales income, $103,000

(e) Purchase returns, $2,000

(f) Total selling expenses, $15,500

(g) Total general expenses, $12,400

(h) Sales returns, $3,000

Income Statement

SOLUTION

Income Statement

Sales Income		$103,000
Less: Sales Returns		3,000
Net Sales		$100,000
Cost of Goods Sold:		
Merchandise Inventory, Jan. 1	$30,000	
Purchases	$66,000	
Less: Purchase Returns	2,000	64,000
Goods Available for Sale		$94,000
Less: Merchandise Inventory, Dec. 31		24,000
Cost of Goods Sold		70,000
Gross Profit		$ 30,000
Expenses:		
Total Selling Expenses	$15,500	
Total General Expenses	12,400	
Total Expenses		27,900
Net Profit		$ 2,100

9.5   Journalize the following data:

(a)   Merchandise inventory, January 1, $31,800; December 31, $38,500.

(b)   Prepaid insurance before adjustment, $1,540. It was found that $460 had expired during the year.

(c)   Office supplies physically counted on December 31 were worth $120. The original balance of Supplies was $750.

(d)   Office salaries for a 5-day week ending on Friday average $2,500. The last payday was on Friday, December 27.

(a)

(b)

(c)

(d)

SOLUTION

		Dr.	Cr.
(a)	Expense and Income Summary	31,800	
	Merchandise Inventory		31,800
	Merchandise Inventory	38,500	
	Expense and Income Summary		38,500
(b)	Insurance Expense	460	
	Prepaid Insurance		460
(c)	Office Supplies Expense	630	
	Office Supplies		630
(d)	Office Salaries Expense	1,000	
	Salaries Payable (December 30 and 31)		1,000

9.6   A section of a worksheet is presented below. Enter the adjustment required for Inventory, if it is assumed that Ending Inventory was $39,000.

Title	Trial Balance		Adjustments	
	Dr.	Cr.	Dr.	Cr.
Merchandise Inventory	32,400			
Expense and Income Summary				

SOLUTION

Title	Trial Balance Dr.	Trial Balance Cr.	Adjustments Dr.	Adjustments Cr.
Merchandise Inventory	32,400		39,000	32,400
Expense and Income Summary		.	32,400	39,000

9.7 Using the information in Problem 9.6, extend the accounts in the worksheet. What classification does the Inventory of $39,000 represent?

Title	Income Statement Dr.	Income Statement Cr.	Balance Sheet Dr.	Balance Sheet Cr.
Merchandise Inventory				
Expense and Income Summary				

SOLUTION

Title	Income Statement Dr.	Income Statement Cr.	Balance Sheet Dr.	Balance Sheet Cr.
Merchandise Inventory			39,000	
Expense and Income Summary	32,400	39,000		

Merchandise inventory of $39,000 represents the value of the goods on hand and is classified as a current asset.

9.8 John Bright runs Bright Light, a light fixture store. John has completed his trial balance for the fiscal year just ended and has asked you, his accountant, to complete the worksheet and make any adjustments necessary. Below are the necessary adjustments that you have discovered.

(*a*) Merchandise inventory on December 31, $27,400

(*b*) Office supplies on hand on December 31, $850

(*c*) Rent expired during the year, $3,000

(*d*) Depreciation expense (building), $3,250

(*e*) Depreciation expense (equipment), $2,500

(*f*) Salaries accrued, $1,150

(*g*) Insurance expired, $2,000

Complete the worksheet and show the necessary adjusting entries as of the end of the fiscal year, December 31, 19X5.

Account Title	Trial Balance		Adjustments		Income Statement		Balance Sheet	
	Dr.	Cr.	Dr.	Cr.	Dr.	Cr.	Dr.	Cr.
Cash	14,000							
Accounts Receivable	14,500							
Prepaid Rent	4,200							
Merchandise Inventory	21,700							
Office Supplies	1,950							
Prepaid Insurance	3,650							
Building	65,000							
Acc. Deprec.—Build.		32,500						
Equipment	28,500							
Acc. Deprec.—Equip.		9,000						
Accounts Payable		4,250						
John Bright, Capital		46,800						
John Bright, Drawing	16,900							
Exp. & Inc. Summary								
Sales Income		137,400						
Salaries Expense	41,700							
Advertising Expense	8,400							
Utilities Expense	8,700							
Miscellaneous Expense	750							
	229,950	229,950						
Office Supplies Expense								
Rent Expense								
Insurance Expense								
Deprec. Exp.—Build.								
Deprec. Exp.—Equip.								
Salaries Payable								
Net Income								

Adjusting Entries

(a)	Dec. 31			
	•			
(b)	31			
(c)	31			
(d)	31			

Adjusting Entries (continued)

(e)	31			
(f)	31			
(g)	31			

SOLUTION

Account Title	Trial Balance Dr.	Trial Balance Cr.	Adjustments Dr.	Adjustments Cr.	Income Statement Dr.	Income Statement Cr.	Balance Sheet Dr.	Balance Sheet Cr.
Cash	14,000						14,000	
Accounts Receivable	14,500						14,500	
Prepaid Rent	4,200			(d) 3,000			1,200	
Merchandise Inventory	21,700		(b) 27,400	(a) 21,700			27,400	
Office Supplies	1,950			(c) 1,100			850	
Prepaid Insurance	3,650			(e) 2,000			1,650	
Building	65,000						65,000	
Acc. Deprec.—Build.		32,500		(f) 3,250				35,750
Equipment	28,500						28,500	
Acc. Deprec.—Equip.		9,000		(g) 2,500				11,500
Accounts Payable		4,250						4,250
John Bright, Capital		46,800						46,800
John Bright, Drawing	16,900						16,900	
Exp. & Inc. Summary			(a) 21,700	(b) 27,400	21,700	27,400		
Sales Income		137,400				137,400		
Salaries Expense	41,700		(h) 1,150		42,850			
Advertising Expense	8,400				8,400			
Utilities Expense	8,700				8,700			
Miscellaneous Expense	750				750			
	229,950	229,950						
Office Supplies Expense			(c) 1,100		1,100			
Rent Expense			(d) 3,000		3,000			
Insurance Expense			(e) 2,000		2,000			
Deprec. Exp.—Build.			(f) 3,250		3,250			
Deprec. Exp.—Equip.			(g) 2,500		2,500			
Salaries Payable				(h) 1,150				1,150
			62,100	62,100	94,250	164,800	170,000	99,450
Net Income					70,550			70,550
					164,800	164,800	170,000	170,000

Adjusting Entries

(a)	Dec. 31	Expense and Income Summary	21,700	
		Merchandise Inventory		21,700
(b)	31	Merchandise Inventory	27,400	
		Expense and Income Summary		27,400
(c)	31	Office Supplies Expense	1,100	
		Office Supplies		1,100
(d)	31	Rent Expense	3,000	
		Prepaid Rent		3,000
(e)	31	Depreciation Expense	3,250	
		Depreciation Expense	2,500	
		Accumulated Depreciation—Building		3,250
		Accumulated Depreciation—Equipment		2,500
(f)	31	Salaries Expense	1,150	
		Salaries Payable		1,150
(g)	31	Insurance Expense	2,000	
		Prepaid Insurance		2,000

9.9 From the information in the following T accounts, prepare the necessary closing entries for December 31.

Cash		Accounts Receivable		Supplies Expense	
8,175		1,750		1,250	

Wages Expense		T. Tom, Capital		T. Tom, Drawing	
19,200			37,500	11,950	

Rent Expense		Fuel Expense		Insurance Expense	
3,175		1,325		4,750	

Equipment		Miscellaneous Expense		Sales Income	
75,090		235			89,400

Closing Entries

(a)			
(b)			
(c)			
(d)			

SOLUTION

Closing Entries

(a)	Sales Income	89,400	
	Expense and Income Summary		89,400
(b)	Expense and Income Summary	29,935	
	Wages Expense		19,200
	Insurance Expense		4,750
	Rent Expense		3,175
	Fuel Expense		1,325
	Supplies Expense		1,250
	Miscellaneous Expense		235
(c)	Expense and Income Summary	59,465	
	T. Tom, Capital		59,465
(d)	T. Tom, Capital	11,950	
	T. Tom, Drawing		11,950

9.10 From the trial balance of the Manell Sales Company, as of December 31, which follows, prepare an eight-column worksheet, using the following additional information for year-end adjustments: (a) merchandise inventory on December 31, $42,000; (b) supplies on hand, December 31, $4,000; (c) insurance expired during this year, $2,000; (d) depreciation for the current year, $800; (e) salaries accrued on December 31, $400.

Mannell Sales Company
Trial Balance

Cash	$ 15,000	
Accounts Receivable	6,500	
Merchandise Inventory	38,100	
Supplies	4,200	
Prepaid Insurance	8,000	
Equipment	15,100	
Accumulated Depreciation		$ 4,400
Accounts Payable		11,200
Manell, Capital		37,000
Manell, Drawing	2,400	
Sales Income		98,200
Purchases	42,100	
Purchase Returns		300
Salaries Expense	11,200	
Rent Expense	4,500	
Misc. General Expense	4,000	
	$151,100	$151,100

Manell Sales Company
Worksheet

Account Title	Trial Balance		Adjustments		Income Statement		Balance Sheet	
	Dr.	Cr.	Dr.	Cr.	Dr.	Cr.	Dr.	Cr.

SOLUTION

Manell Sales Company
Worksheet

Account Title	Trial Balance Dr.	Trial Balance Cr.	Adjustments Dr.	Adjustments Cr.	Income Statement Dr.	Income Statement Cr.	Balance Sheet Dr.	Balance Sheet Cr.
Cash	15,000						15,000	
Accounts Receivable	6,500						6,500	
Merchandise Inventory	38,100		(a) 42,000	(a) 38,100			42,000	
Supplies	4,200			(b) 200			4,000	
Prepaid Insurance	8,000			(c) 2,000			6,000	
Equipment	15,100						15,100	
Accumulated Deprec.		4,400		(d) 800				5,200
Accounts Payable		11,200						11,200
Manell, Capital		37,000						37,000
Manell, Drawing	2,400						2,400	
Sales Income		98,200				98,200		
Purchases	42,100				42,100			
Purchase Returns		300				300		
Salaries Expense	11,200		(e) 400		11,600			
Rent Expense	4,500				4,500			
Misc. Gen. Expense	4,000				4,000			
	151,100	151,100						
Exp. and Inc. Sum.			(a) 38,100	(a) 42,000	38,100	42,000		
Supplies Expense			(b) 200		200			
Insurance Expense			(c) 2,000		2,000			
Depreciation Expense			(d) 800		800			
Salaries Payable				(e) 400				400
			83,500	83,500	103,300	140,500	91,000	53,800
Net Income					37,200			37,200
					140,500	140,500	91,000	91,000

9.11 From the information in Problem 9.10, prepare all necessary adjusting and closing entries.

Adjusting Entries

(a)

(b)

Adjusting Entries (continued)

(c)			
(d)			
(e)			

Closing Entries

(a)			
(b)			
(c)			
(d)			

SOLUTION

Adjusting Entries

(a)	Expense and Income Summary	38,100	
	Merchandise Inventory		38,100
	Merchandise Inventory	42,000	
	Expense and Income Summary		42,000
(b)	Supplies Expense	200	
	Supplies		200
(c)	Insurance Expense	2,000	
	Prepaid Insurance		2,000
(d)	Depreciation Expense	800	
	Accumulated Depreciation		800
(e)	Salaries Expense	400	
	Salaries Payable		400

Closing Entries

(a)	Sales Income	98,200	
	Purchase Returns	300	
	Expense and Income Summary		98,500
(b)	Expense and Income Summary	65,200	
	Purchases		42,100
	Salaries Expense		11,600
	Rent Expense		4,500
	Misc. General Expense		4,000
	Supplies Expense		200
	Insurance Expense		2,000
	Depreciation Expense		800
(c)	Expense and Income Summary	37,200	
	Manell, Capital		37,200
(d)	Manell, Capital	2,400	
	Manell, Drawing		2,400

9.12 From the information in Problem 9.10, prepare all financial statements.

Manell Sales Company		
Income Statement		
For the Period Ending December 31, 19X5		

Manell Sales Company
Capital Statement
For the Period Ending December 31, 19X5

Manell Sales Company
Balance Sheet
December 31, 19X5

SOLUTION

Manell Sales Company
Income Statement
For the Period Ending December 31, 19X5

Sales Income		$98,200
Cost of Goods Sold:		
Merchandise Inventory, Jan. 1	$38,100	
Purchases	$42,100	
Less: Purchase Returns	300	41,800
Goods Available for Sale		$79,900
Less: Merchandise Inventory, Dec. 31		42,000
Cost of Goods Sold		37,900
		$60,300
Operating Expenses:		
Salaries Expense	$11,600	
Rent Expense	4,500	
Insurance Expense	2,000	
Depreciation Expense	800	
Supplies Expense	200	
Misc. General Expense	4,000	
Total Expenses		23,100
Net Income		$37,200

Manell Sales Company
Capital Statement
For the Period Ending December 31, 19X5

Capital, January 1, 19X5		$37,000
Net Income	$37,200	
Less: Drawing	2,400	
Increase in Capital		34,800
Capital, December 31, 19X5		$71,800

Manell Sales Company		
Balance Sheet		
December 31, 19X5		
ASSETS		
Current Assets:		
Cash	$15,000	
Accounts Receivable	6,500	
Merchandise Inventory	42,000	
Supplies	4,000	
Prepaid Insurance	6,000	
Total Current Assets		$73,500
Fixed Assets:		
Equipment	$15,100	
Less: Accumulated Depreciation	5,200	9,900
Total Assets		$83,400
LIABILITIES AND CAPITAL		
Current Liabilities:		
Accounts Payable	$11,200	
Salaries Payable	400	
Total Current Liabilities		$11,600
Capital, December 31, 19X5		71,800
Total Liabilities and Capital		$83,400

Comprehensive Review Problem: The Merchandising Worksheet

1.   The accounts and their balances in the M. Rothfield Company ledger on December 31, 19X5, the end of the fiscal year, are as follows:

Cash	$ 4,600
Accounts Receivable	6,900
Merchandise Inventory	28,300
Supplies	750
Prepaid Rent	1,800
Equipment	16,000
Accumulated Depreciation, Equip.	1,900
Accounts Payable	6,110
M. Rothfield, Capital	35,300
Sales	128,000
Purchases	91,000
Advertising Expense	3,200
Salaries Expense	16,600
Miscellaneous Expense	2,160

Prepare an eight-column worksheet with the following adjustment: Merchandise Inventory as of December 31, $33,400.

Account Title	Trial Balance Dr.	Trial Balance Cr.	Adjustments Dr.	Adjustments Cr.	Income Statement Dr.	Income Statement Cr.	Balance Sheet Dr.	Balance Sheet Cr.
Cash	4,600							
Accounts Receivable	6,900							
Merchandise Inventory	28,300							
Supplies	750							
Prepaid Rent	1,800							
Equipment	16,000							
Accumulated Depreciation		1,900						
Accounts Payable		6,110						
Rothfield, Capital		35,300						
Sales		128,000						
Purchases	91,000							
Advertising Expense	3,200							
Salaries Expense	16,600							
Miscellaneous Expense	2,160							
	171,310	171,310						

SOLUTION

Account Title	Trial Balance Dr.	Trial Balance Cr.	Adjustments Dr.	Adjustments Cr.	Income Statement Dr.	Income Statement Cr.	Balance Sheet Dr.	Balance Sheet Cr.
Cash	4,600						4,600	
Accounts Receivable	6,900						6,900	
Merchandise Inventory	28,300		(a) 33,400	(a) 28,300			33,400	
Supplies	750						750	
Prepaid Rent	1,800						1,800	
Equipment	16,000						16,000	
Accumulated Depreciation		1,900						1,900
Accounts Payable		6,110						6,110
Rothfield, Capital		35,300						35,300
Sales		128,000				128,000		
Purchases	91,000				91,000			
Advertising Expense	3,200				3,200			
Salaries Expense	16,600				16,600			
Miscellaneous Expense	2,160				2,160			
	171,310	171,310						
Exp. & Inc. Summary			(a) 28,300	(a) 33,400	28,300	33,400		
			61,700	61,700	141,260	161,400	63,450	43,310
Net Income					20,140			20,140
					161,400	161,400	63,450	63,450

2.   Based on the information in part 1, prepare the adjusting entries, the closing entries, and the income statement.

Adjusting Entries		

Closing Entries		

Expense & Income Summary

M. Rothfield Company		
Income Statement		
December 31, 19X5		

SOLUTION

Adjusting Entries		
Expense & Income Summary	28,300	
Merchandise Inventory		28,300
Merchandise Inventory	33,400	
Expense & Income Summary		33,400
Closing Entries		
Sales	128,000	
Expense & Income Summary		128,000
Expense & Income Summary	112,460	
Purchases		91,000
Advertising Expense		3,200
Salaries Expense		16,600
Miscellaneous Expense		2,160
Expense & Income Summary	20,140*	
Capital		20,140

Income Summary

28,300	33,400
112,960	128,000
141,260	161,400
20,140*	
161,400	161,400

M. Rothfield Company
Income Statement
December 31, 19X5

Sales		$128,000
Cost of Goods Sold		
Merchandise Inventory, January 1, 19X5	$ 28,300	
Purchases	91,000	
Goods Available for Sale	$119,300	
Merchandise Inventory, December 31, 19X5	33,400	
Cost of Goods Sold		85,900
Gross Profit		$ 42,100
Expenses		
Advertising Expense	$ 3,200	
Salaries Expense	16,600	
Miscellaneous Expense	2,160	
Total Expenses		21,960
Net Income		$ 20,140

Chapter 10

Costing Merchandise Inventory

10.1 INTRODUCTION

In a merchandising business, inventory is merchandise that is held for resale. As such, it will ordinarily be converted into cash in less than a year and is thus a current asset. In a manufacturing business, there will usually be inventories of raw materials and goods in process in addition to an inventory of finished goods. Since we have discussed the Merchandise Inventory account as it relates to the worksheet (Chapter 9), let us now examine how the merchandise inventory amount is calculated.

10.2 DETERMINING INVENTORY: PHYSICAL COUNT

Under the *periodic method*, inventory is physically counted at regular intervals (annually, quarterly, or monthly). When this system is used, credits are made to the Inventory account or to Purchases, not as each sale is made, but rather in total at the end of the inventory period.

To approach the problem of inventory measurement, in order to assign the business cost to each item, three methods of valuation (FIFO, LIFO, and weighted average) have been developed and approved by GAAP (General Accepted Accounting Practices). To compare these three methods, the same data (Chart 1) will be used in all of the following inventory examples.

Chart 1

Date	Type	Units	Unit Cost	Totals
Jan. 1	Inventory	100	$ 6	$ 600
Mar. 10	Purchase	150	$ 8	1,200
June 6	Purchase	200	$ 9	1,800
Oct. 4	Purchase	250	$10	2,500
Available for sale		700		$6,100

It will be assumed that a physical count of inventory on the last day of the accounting period (December 31) showed 320 units on hand. Therefore, 380 units (700 − 320) were sold during the year.

Costing Inventory: First-In, First-Out (FIFO)

The first-in, first-out (FIFO) method of costing inventory assumes that goods are sold in the order in which they were purchased. Therefore, the goods that were bought first (first-in) are the first goods to be sold (first-out), and the goods that remain on hand (ending inventory) are assumed to be made up of the latest costs. Therefore, for income determination, earlier costs are matched with revenue and the most recent costs are used for balance sheet valuation.

This method is consistent with the actual flow of costs, since merchandisers attempt to sell their old stock first. (Perishable items and high-fashion items are examples.) FIFO is the most widely used inventory method of those that will be discussed.

EXAMPLE 1

Under FIFO, those goods left at the end of the period are considered to be those received last. Therefore, the 320 units on hand on December 31 would be costed as follows:

Most recent purchase (Oct. 4)	250 units @ $10 =	$2,500
Next most recent purchase (June 6)	70 units @ $ 9 =	630
Ending inventory	320 units	$3,130

The latest cost of the inventory consists of 250 units at $10. However, since the ending inventory consists of 320 units, we must refer to the next most recent purchase of 70 units at $9. Therefore, you could say that the process for determining the cost of the units on hand involves working backward through the purchases until there is a sufficient quantity to cover the ending inventory count. Thus the ending inventory under the FIFO method would be valued and recorded at $3,130.

EXAMPLE 2

The cost of goods sold can be determined by subtracting the value of the ending inventory from the total value of the inventory available for sale ($6,100 − $3,130 = $2,970). Since 320 units remain as ending inventory, the number of units sold is 380 (700 − 320).

This can also be computed as

100 units of inventory (Jan. 1)	@ $6 =	$ 600
150 units purchased (Mar. 10)	@ $8 =	1,200
130 units purchased (June 6)	@ $9 =	1,170
380	Total cost of goods sold	$2,970

It should be noted that as a method of assigning costs, FIFO may be used regardless of the actual physical flow of merchandise. Indeed, we might say that FIFO really stands for first-price-in, first-price-out. In a period of rising prices—inflation—the FIFO method will yield the largest inventory value, thus resulting in a larger net income. This situation occurs because this method assigns an inventory cost based on the most recent, higher costs. Conversely, the FIFO method would produce a smaller cost of goods sold, because the earlier, lower costs are assigned to the cost of goods sold. Because FIFO results in the most recent charges to inventory, the value of the ending inventory is closer to its replacement cost than under any other method.

EXAMPLE 3

Two years of determining the value of the same number of units in the inventory are shown below.

(a) First year, 19X4 (rising costs):

Inventory	10 units @ $5 =	$ 50
First purchase	10 units @ 6 =	60
Second purchase	10 units @ 7 =	70
Third purchase	10 units @ 8 =	80
	40 units	$260

If 10 units are on hand, the value under FIFO would be computed as

Third purchase	10 units @ $8 =	$80.

Thus, the ending inventory of 10 units is $80.

The cost of goods sold would be calculated as $260 − $80 = $160.

(b)   Second year, 19X5 (falling costs):

Inventory	10 units @ $8 =	$ 80
First purchase	10 units @ 7 =	70
Second purchase	10 units @ 6 =	60
Third purchase	10 units @ 5 =	50
	40 units	$260

If 10 units are on hand, the value under FIFO would be computed as

Third purchase   10 units @ $5 = $50.

Thus, the ending inventory of 10 units is $50.

The cost of goods sold would be calculated as $260 − $50 = $210.

Note that even though there are 10 units left in both years, under FIFO, the year 19X4 produces a higher ending inventory in a rising market, thus producing a higher net income. This is because the cost of goods sold is lower in a rising market ($260 − 80 = $160) than in a declining market ($260 − $50 = $210). Thus the lower the cost, the higher the profit.

Costing Inventory: Last-In, First-Out (LIFO)

The last-in, first-out (LIFO) method of costing inventory assumes that the most recently purchased items are the first ones sold and the remaining inventory consists of the earliest items purchased. In other words, the goods are sold in the reverse order in which they are bought. Unlike FIFO, the LIFO method specifies that the cost of inventory on hand (ending inventory) is determined by working forward from the beginning inventory through purchases until sufficient units are obtained to cover the ending inventory. This is the opposite of the FIFO system.

Remember that FIFO assumes costs flow in the order in which they are incurred, while LIFO assumes that costs flow in the reverse order form that in which they are incurred.

EXAMPLE 4

Under LIFO, the inventory at the end of the period is considered to be merchandise purchased in the first part of the period. What is the cost of the 320 units on hand? (See Chart 1.)

Earliest purchase (Jan. 1)	100 units @ $6 =	$ 600
Next purchase (Mar. 10)	150 units @ $8 =	1,200
Next purchase (June 6)	70 units @ $9 =	630
Ending inventory	320 units	$2,430

Thus, ending inventory under the LIFO method would be valued at $2,430.

EXAMPLE 5

The cost of goods sold is determined (from Example 4) by subtracting the value of the ending inventory from the total value of the inventory available for sale ($6,100 − $2,430 = $3,670). This cost may also be computed as

Oct. 4	250 units @ $10 =	$2,500
June 6	130 units @ $ 9 =	1,170
Cost of goods sold	380 units	$3,670

A disadvantage of the LIFO method is that it does not represent the actual physical movement of goods in the business, as most businesses do not move out their most recent purchases. Yet firms favor this method because it does match the most recent costs against current revenue, thereby keeping earnings from being greatly distorted by any fluctuating increases or decreases in prices. Yet it sometimes allows too much maneuvering by managers to change net income. For example, if prices are rising rapidly and a company wishes to pay less taxes (lower net income) for that year, management can buy large amounts of inventory near the end of that period. These higher inventory costs, because of rising prices, under LIFO immediately become an expense (cost of goods sold), and thus result in the financial statement showing a lower net income. Conversely, if the firm is having a bad year, management may want to increase net income to garner favor with stockholders. This can be done by delaying any large purchase of high-cost inventory until the following period by keeping the purchase out of the Cost of Goods Sold section for the current year, and thus avoiding any decrease in net income.

In a rising price market, certain tax advantages are gained through LIFO because it yields a lower profit because of its higher cost of goods sold.

EXAMPLE 6

Use Chart 1.

	FIFO		LIFO	
Sales (assumed)		$20,000		$20,000
Cost of Goods Sold:				
Goods Available for Sale	$6,100		$6,100	
Less: Ending Inventory	3,130		2,430	
Cost of Goods Sold		2,970		3,670
Gross Profit		$17,030		$16,330

As Example 6 shows, LIFO produces (in a rising price market) (1) a lower ending inventory, (2) a higher cost of goods sold, and (3) a lower gross profit. FIFO will produce the opposite.

The IRS will permit companies to use LIFO for tax purposes only if they use LIFO for financial reporting purposes. Thus, if a business uses LIFO for tax purposes, it must also report inventory and income on the same valuation basis in its financial statements, but it is allowed to report an alternative inventory amount in the notes to the financial statements. This is permitted because it affords true financial analysis in comparing, on a similar basis, one business with another. It should be noted that a business cannot change its inventory valuation method any time it chooses. Once a method has been adopted, the business should use the same procedure from one period to the next. If management feels a need to change, permission must be granted by the IRS. The business must then follow specific authoritative guides that detail how the changes should be treated on financial statements.

Costing Inventory: Average Cost Valuation

The average cost valuation system, also known as weighted average, is based on the average cost of inventory during the period and takes into consideration the quantity and the price of the inventory items by assigning the same amount of cost to identical items. In other words, it spreads the total dollar cost of the goods available for sale equally among all the units.

The ending inventory is determined by the following procedure:

1. The cost of the total number of units available for sale (beginning inventory plus purchases) is divided by the total units available for sale.
2. The number of units in the ending inventory is multiplied by this weighted average figure.

EXAMPLE 7

Referring to the data in Chart 1, the cost of the 320 units on hand would be calculated as follows:

1. $6,100 ÷ 700 units = $8.71 unit cost.
2. $8.71 × 320 units on hand = $2,787* ending inventory.

---

*Rounded to the nearest dollar.

EXAMPLE 8

The cost of goods sold is then calculated by subtracting the value of the ending inventory from the total value of the inventory available for sale ($6,100 − $2,787 = $3,313).

Because there were 700 units available for sale and 320 units on hand at the end of the period, the number of units sold was determined as 700 − 320 = 380 units. Therefore, another method of computation to determine the cost of goods sold would be $8.71 × 380 units (cost of goods sold) = $3,310.*

---

*Rounded to the nearest dollar.

The average cost method is best used by firms that buy large amounts of goods that are similar in nature and stored in a common place. Grain, gasoline, and coal are good examples of products that could logically be costed under weighted average.

There are some limitations that should be noted in this valuation procedure. Unit cost cannot be related to any physical purchase and does not represent any price changes. In those industries that are greatly affected by price and style change, this method will not yield specific cost determination. Also, the time needed to assemble the data is greater under this method than for FIFO or LIFO, if there are many purchases of a variety of different items bought.

Comparison of Inventory Methods

The three methods of inventory valuation discussed are based on an assumption as to the flow of costs. The FIFO method is based on the assumption that costs flow in the order in which they were incurred; the LIFO method assumes that costs flow in the reverse order from that in which they were incurred; and weighted average assumes that costs should be assigned to the merchandise inventory based on an average cost per unit. Note that if the cost of all purchases remains the same, all three methods of inventory valuation will yield identical results. As you will realize, prices never stay constant, so each of these three methods will result in a different cost for ending inventory. Remember that the ending figure is subtracted from the cost of goods available for sale to arrive at the cost of goods sold (COGS). Therefore, the net income or loss will vary according to the inventory method chosen. Also, the ending inventory on the balance sheet will vary with each method.

In Example 9 below, we compare the results of the FIFO, LIFO, and weighted average methods, with regard to both ending inventory and cost of goods sold. Since the two amounts are related through the equation

$$\text{Goods available for sale} - \text{Ending inventory} = \text{Cost of goods sold}$$

it is seen that if ending inventory is *overstated,* cost of goods sold will be *understated* and net profit *overstated.* On the other hand, if inventory is *understated,* then cost of goods sold will be *overstated* and net profit *understated.* Clearly, the method chosen for inventory computation can have a marked effect on the profit of the firm. There is no *one* method that is best for all firms, but careful consideration of the following factors will be helpful in making the decision: (1) the effect on the income statement and balance sheet, (2) the effect on taxable income, (3) the effect on the selling price.

EXAMPLE 9

	First-In, First-Out	Last-In, First-Out	Weighted Average
Goods available for sale	$6,100	$6,100	$6,100
Ending inventory, Dec. 31	3,130	2,430	2,787
Cost of goods sold	$2,970	$3,670	$3,313

Based on Example 9, the following evaluation is considered:

FIFO

1. Yields the lowest cost of goods sold
2. Yields the highest gross profit
3. Yields the highest ending inventory

Note: During a period of inflation or rising prices, the use of FIFO will result in the yields shown above, but in a declining price economy the results will be reversed. The major criticism of this method is the tendency to maximize the effect of inflationary and deflationary trends on amounts reported as gross profit.

LIFO

1. Yields the highest cost of goods sold
2. Yields the lowest gross profit
3. Yields the lowest ending inventory

Because the costs of the most recently acquired units approximate the costs of their replacement, this method can be defended on the basis that its use more nearly matches current costs with current revenues. The major justification for LIFO is that it minimizes the effect of price trends on gross profit.

Weighted Average

1. Yields results between FIFO and LIFO for cost of goods sold
2. Yields results between FIFO and LIFO for gross profit
3. Yields results between FIFO and LIFO for ending inventory

This compromise method of inventory costing makes the effect of price trends (up or down) more stable, as all factors are averaged, both in the determination of gross profit and in determining inventory cost. For any given series of prices, the average cost will be the same, regardless of the direction or price trends.

10.3   DETERMINING INVENTORY: ESTIMATION

Although a physical inventory is taken once a year, there are occasions when the value of the inventory must be known during the year. When interim financial statements are requested (monthly, quarterly, or semiannually), an inventory amount must be estimated. If no physical count is taken, the amount of inventory must be estimated. Also, in the event of fire or any other casualty, an amount must be reported as a loss. Two of the most popular methods of estimating inventory (when no physical count is used) are the *gross profit method* and the *retail method*.

Gross Profit Method

The gross profit method rearranges the Cost of Goods Sold section of the income statement. As stated previously, the cost of goods sold formula is

$$
\begin{array}{l}
\quad \text{Inventory (beginning)} \\
+ \;\underline{\text{Net purchases}} \\
\quad \text{Goods available for sale} \\
- \;\underline{\text{Inventory (ending)}} \\
\quad \text{Cost of goods sold}
\end{array}
$$

Note that when you subtract inventory (ending) from the goods available for sale, the cost of goods sold is determined. Conversely, if you subtract the estimated cost of goods sold from the goods available for sale, the value of the inventory (ending) will result. The estimated cost of goods sold figure is arrived at by using the past year's gross profit percentage and subtracting the resulting amount from sales.

EXAMPLE 10

During the past 5 years, a company's gross profit averaged 30 percent of sales. If the sales for this interim period are $70,000, the inventory at the beginning of the period is $30,000, and the net purchases are $50,000, you would estimate the inventory (ending) under the gross profit method as follows:

Inventory (beginning)		$30,000
Add: Net Purchases		50,000
Goods Available for Sale		$80,000
Sales	$70,000	
Estimated Gross Profit (30%)*	21,000	
Less: Estimated Cost of Goods Sold		49,000
Estimated Inventory (Ending)		$31,000

---

*($70,000 × 30%)

This method of estimating ending inventory is also useful for determining casualty losses such as fires, flood, or theft, when such a calamity destroys a company's inventory. It is obvious that a dollar amount must be assigned to the inventory lost before any insurance claim can be made. Although this may appear to be an impossible task, it is possible to build up to the inventory figure. For example, the dollar amounts of all the sales, purchases, and beginning inventory can be obtained from the previous year's financial statements. Also, information can be further provided by customers, suppliers, sellers, etc.

EXAMPLE 11

A fire occurred in a retail store, and most records were destroyed. If the average gross profit rate, based on the last 3 years of operations, is 40 percent, and the net sales (according to various sales records) were $90,000, determine the ending inventory by the gross profit method of estimation. Assume that outside verification has determined that the beginning inventory was $40,000, and all purchases (net) were $76,000.

Inventory (Beginning)	$ 40,000
+ Net Purchases	76,000
Goods Available for Sale	$116,000
− Estimated Cost of Goods Sold	54,000*
Estimated Ending Inventory	$ 62,000

*Sales	$90,000	
− Gross profit estimate	36,000	($90,000 × 40%)
Cost of goods sold estimated	$54,000	

Bear in mind that the gross profit method is not intended to replace the physical inventory count but is used to estimate the inventory cost when a physical counting is not deemed possible. This method is based on the assumption that over the years the rate of gross profit has been fairly stable in the past periods under examination and will remain so in the future. Without this stability, the calculations of inventory using the gross profit method will be inaccurate and not useful in any accounting procedure. Since this method is based solely on estimation, it is not acceptable for tax purposes unless no other physical inventory method is available.

Retail Inventory Method

The retail inventory method of inventory costing is used by retail businesses, particularly department stores. Department stores usually determine gross profit monthly but take a physical inventory only on an annual basis. The retail inventory method permits a determination of inventory any time of the year and also produces a comparison of the estimated ending inventory with the physical inventory ending inventory, both at retail prices. This will help to identify any inventory shortages resulting from theft or other causes.

This method, similar to the gross profit method, is used to estimate the dollar cost of inventory (ending) when a physical count cannot be done. The procedure for determination under the retail inventory method is as follows:

1. Beginning inventory and purchases must be recorded both at cost and at selling price.
2. Total goods available for sale is then computed on both bases, cost and selling price.
3. Sales for the period are deducted from the goods available for sale at the selling price.
4. Ending inventory at the selling price is the result of step 3. This amount is then converted to ending inventory at cost by multiplying by the appropriate markup ratio.

EXAMPLE 12

		Cost	Selling Price
Step 1.	Beginning Inventory	$280,000	$400,000
	+ Net Purchases for Period	110,000	180,000
Step 2.	Goods Available for Sales	$390,000	$580,000
Step 3.	− Net Sales for Period		340,000
	Ending Inventory at Selling Price		$240,000

Step 4.   Cost to Selling Price Ratio ($390,000 ÷ $580,000) = 67%
            Ending Inventory at Cost ($240,000 × 67%) = $160,800

In Example 12, the cost percentage is 67 percent, which means that the inventory and purchases are marked up on an average of 33 percent (100 percent − 67 percent).

Certainly not all items in the goods available for sale are marked up exactly 33 percent. (There are those marked higher and those lower than 33 percent.) In other words, the retail method uses a percentage that represents an average of markup cost. Suppose that a retailer had different categories of inventory, each with different cost ratios. How would the firm use the retail method to estimate the total cost of all the inventory on hand at any time of the year? The retailer would simply apply the retail inventory method to each category separately, using its own specific cost ratio, then add the costs of the three categories to determine an estimate of the overall cost of inventory.

Summary

The major difference between the gross profit method and the retail inventory method is that the former uses the historical gross profit rates, and the latter uses the percentage markup (cost-to-selling-price ratio from the current period). In other words, the gross profit method uses past experience as a basis, while the retail inventory method uses current experience.

The gross profit method is usually less reliable, because past situations may be different than current ones. Remember that both methods are useful, because they allow the accountant to prepare financial statements more frequently without the cost of time spent on a physical count (perpetual method) each time or by the requirement to maintain perpetual inventory records.* However, the physical method does require an annual physical count, as it will disclose any loss due to theft or other shrinkage conditions and will serve as the basis for an adjustment to all inventory records and the Inventory account.

*When goods are very expensive, the perpetual method of counting each time a sale is made or goods are bought is used.

Summary

1. When inventory is physically counted at the end of an accounting period, we have the _____ method.

2. The inventory method used when units are generally of high value is the _____ method.

3. The _____ inventory method is most commonly used in retail establishments.

4. A method of inventory valuation based on the concept that the goods are sold in the order in which received is known as _____ .

5. The valuation of inventory based on the concept that the most recent costs incurred should be charged against income is known as _____ .

6. In a rising market, net income under _____ would be smaller, thus producing a smaller tax.

7. The inventory method based on the concept that the unit cost of merchandise sold is the average of all expenditures for inventory is known as _____ .

8. The gross profit method is not intended to replace the _____ inventory.

9. The gross profit method is based solely on _____ .

10. When determining ending inventory under the retail method, the ratio of cost to _____ must be used.

11. Of the two methods of estimation, the _____ is less reliable as an indicator of the inventory.

12. It can be said that the gross profit method uses _____ experience as a basis, while the retail method uses _____ experience.

Answers: 1. periodic; 2. perpetual; 3. periodic; 4. first-in, first-out (FIFO); 5. last-in, first-out (LIFO); 6. LIFO; 7. weighted average; 8. physical; 9. estimation; 10. selling price; 11. gross profit method; 12. past, current

Solved Problems

10.1 The inventory information of a product is given below:

Jan. 1	Inventory	12 units	$15
Feb. 16	Purchase	8 units	16
Mar. 4	Purchase	15 units	18
Oct. 15	Purchase	10 units	20

After taking a physical count, we find that we have 14 units on hand. Determine the ending inventory cost by the FIFO method.

SOLUTION

Most recent purchase (Oct. 15)	10 units @ $20 =	$200
Next most recent purchase (Mar. 4)	4 units @ 18 =	72
Ending inventory	14	$272

Remember that values are assigned to the inventory based on the latest cost (the most recent purchases).

10.2 Assign a value to the ending inventory under FIFO using the following cost data:

Beginning inventory	200 units @ $10 = $2,000
First purchase	300 units @ 12 = 3,600
Second purchase	300 units @ 11 = 3,300
Available for sale	800 $8,900

An inventory count at the end of the period reveals that 450 units are still on hand.

SOLUTION

Second purchase	300 units @ $11 = $3,300
First purchase	150 units @ 12 = 1,800
Ending inventory	450 $5,100

10.3 Based on the information in Problem 10.2, determine the cost of goods sold for the period.

SOLUTION

There are two methods to determine the cost of those goods sold.

(*a*)

Total goods available	$8,900
Ending inventory	5,100
Cost of goods sold	$3,800

(*b*)

Beginning inventory	200 units @ $10 = $2,000
First purchase	150 units @ 12 = 1,800
Cost of goods sold	350 units $3,800

Since there were a total of 800 units available and 450 were on hand at the end of the period, 350 units were sold (800 − 450 = 350).

10.4 Product information for item #204 is as follows:

Jan. 1	Inventory	50 units @ $10 = $ 500
Apr. 24	Purchase	30 units @ 8 = 240
July 10	Purchase	40 units @ 7 = 280
Nov. 15	Purchase	35 units @ 8 = 280
Units available		155 Total cost $1,300

By a physical count, it is estimated that 95 units are left in the ending inventory. (*a*) What is the value of the ending inventory under FIFO valuation? (*b*) Determine the cost of goods sold.

SOLUTION

(*a*)

Nov. 15	35 units @ $8 = $280
July 10	40 units @ 7 = 280
Apr. 24	20* units @ 8 = 160
Ending inventory	95 units $720

---

*A total of 95 units are on hand. Since we have 75 units (35 + 40) from the two most recent purchases, only 20 of 30 units of the April 24 purchase are needed.

(b) $1,300   Total amount of goods
    − 720   Ending inventory
    $ 580   Cost of goods sold

Alternative method:

Jan. 1	50 units @ $10 =	$500
Apr. 24	10 units @ 8 =	80
Cost of goods sold	60 units	$580

Note that since there were 155 units available and 95 units were on hand, 60 units (155 − 95) were used to determine the cost of goods sold.

10.5 Based on the following information, determine under LIFO valuation (a) ending inventory of 120 units and (b) its cost of goods sold.

Beginning inventory	100 units @ $15 =	$1,500
Apr. 30	100 units @ 17 =	1,700
Sept. 30	100 units @ 18 =	1,800
Dec. 30	100 units @ 21 =	2,100
Available for sale	400 units	$7,100

SOLUTION

(a)
Beginning inventory	100 units @ $15 =	$1,500
Apr. 30	20 units @ 17 =	340
Ending inventory	120 units	$1,840

(b)
Dec. 30	100 units @ $21 =	$2,100
Sept. 30	100 units @ 18 =	1,800
Apr. 30	80 units @ 17 =	1,360
Cost of goods sold	280 units	$5,260

Proof:	$7,100	Available units
	− 1,840	Ending inventory
	$5,260	Cost of goods sold

10.6 Based on the following information in a rising price market, determine (a) ending inventory of 260 units under LIFO and (b) the cost of goods sold.

Beginning inventory	100 units $ 5 =	$ 500
Mar. 30 Purchase	100 units 6 =	600
Sept. 30 Purchase	100 units 8 =	800
Nov. 30 Purchase	100 units 9 =	900
Dec. 30 Purchase	100 units 12 =	1,200
	500 units	$4,000

SOLUTION

(a) Beginning inventory   100 units @ $5 = $ 500
     Mar. 30 Purchase   100 units @   6 =   600
     Sept. 30 Purchase   60 units @   8 =   480
     Ending inventory   260 units $1,580

(b) The ending inventory is $1,580 and the cost of goods sold is ($4,000 − $1,580 = $2,420), computed as

           Dec. 30   100 units @ $12 = $1,200
           Nov. 30   100 units @   9 =   900
           Sept. 30   40 units @   8 =   320
           Cost of goods sold 240* $2,420

*Since there were 500 units in the total inventory, and 260 remained, 240 units had been sold.

10.7 If, in Problem 10.6, management had decided to delay the December 30 purchase until the following year (in order to show a higher profit based on a lower cost), what would be the cost of goods sold without the last December purchase?

SOLUTION

Four hundred units (the December purchase of 100 units is eliminated) were available to be sold and 260 units remained on hand. Thus the 140 units sold will be costed as follows:

           Nov. 30*   100 units @ $9 = $ 900
           Sept. 30   40 units @ 8 =   320
           Cost of goods sold 140 units $1,220

*No December purchase is considered.

Therefore, management now has a cost of $1,220 rather than $2,420 (Problem 10.6), thus meeting its objective of higher profits. This lower cost will then yield a higher profit, yet it keeps the ending inventory at the same figure.

10.8 The beginning inventory and various purchases of product Y were as follows:

           Jan.   1   Beginning inventory   8 units @ $10 = $ 80
           Apr.   4   First purchase   12 units @ 11 = 132
           July 16   Second purchase   16 units @ 12 = 192
           Aug. 25   Third purchase   15 units @ 13 = 195
           Dec. 24   Fourth purchase   18 units @ 14 = 252
           Available for sale   69 units $851

An inventory count disclosed that 30 units of product Y were on hand. (a) Determine the ending inventory under the weighted average method. (b) Determine the cost of goods sold.

SOLUTION

(a) (1) $851 ÷ 69 = $12.33   per unit
     (2) $12.33 × 30 = $370   ending inventory*

---

*Rounded to the nearest dollar.

(b) Since 69 units were available for sale and 30 of those units were on hand, 69 − 30 = 39 units
     were sold. To determine the total cost of goods sold, multiply the units sold by the average cost
     of each unit. Therefore:

$$39 \text{ units} × \$12.33 \text{ per unit} = \underline{\underline{\$481}}$$

Alternative method:

Total value of goods	$851
Ending inventory	−370
Cost of goods sold	$481

10.9 In an inflationary market, Essex Corp. bought the following items:

Jan. 1	Beginning inventory	150 units @ $2.00 =	$ 300
May 14	First purchase	300 units @ 4.00 =	1,200
Oct. 6	Second purchase	300 units @ 5.00 =	1,500
Nov. 14	Third purchase	250 units @ 6.00 =	1,500
Dec. 19	Fourth purchase	200 units @ 7.50 =	1,500
Available for sale		1,200 units	$6,000

If 225 units are left on hand, determine (a) the ending inventory in this inflationary period
under the average cost method and (b) the cost of goods sold.

SOLUTION

(a) $6,000 ÷ 1,200 units = $5 per unit
     225 units on hand × $5 per unit = $1,125 ending inventory

(b) 1,200 units − 225 units on hand = 975 units sold
     975 × $5 per unit = $4,875 cost of goods sold

     To prove that both items (a) and (b) are correct:

$1,125	Ending inventory
+4,875	Cost of goods sold
$6,000	Goods available for sale

10.10 In a deflationary market, the Elizabeth Corp. bought the following items:

Jan. 1	Beginning inventory	200 units @ $7.50 =	$1,500
May 14	First purchase	250 units @ 6.00 =	1,500
Oct. 6	Second purchase	300 units @ 5.00 =	1,500
Nov. 14	Third purchase	300 units @ 4.00 =	1,200
Dec. 19	Fourth purchase	150 units @ 2.00 =	300
Available for sale		1,200 units	$6,000

If 225 units are left on hand, determine (*a*) the ending inventory in this deflationary period under the average cost method and (*b*) the cost of goods sold.

SOLUTION

(*a*) $6,000 ÷ 1,200 units = $5 per unit
       225 units on hand × $5 per unit = $1,125 ending inventory

(*b*)   1,200 units − 225 units on hand = 975 units sold
       975 units × $5 per unit = $4,875 cost of goods sold

   Proof: $1,125 + $4,875 = $6,000   Goods available for sale

   Note that in both this problem and Problem 10.9, the ending inventory value is the same regardless of inflation (rising prices) or deflation (falling prices). This happens because we are averaging the entire accounting period. In the next problem, different values do occur, because the inventory is valued under FIFO and LIFO as well as average cost.

10.11 From the following information, determine the cost of inventory by first-in, first-out (FIFO), by last-in, first-out (LIFO), and by the weighted average cost method.

Unit Number	Inventory January 1, 19X5	March Purchases	June Purchases	September Purchases	Number of Units in Inventory December 31, 19X5
101	3 @ $480	5 @ $490	6 @ $500	5 @ $510	6
103	6 @ 208	10 @ 210	11 @ 220	7 @ 222	7
105	4 @ 200	5 @ 200	4 @ 210	2 @ 215	3
107	3 @ 225	9 @ 240	7 @ 245	4 @ 250	5
109	1 @ 295	1 @ 300	3 @ 315	—	2

Unit Number	Quantity	Cost per Unit	Total Cost
First-In, First-Out			
Total inventory			

Unit Number	Quantity	Cost per Unit	Total Cost
Last-In, First-Out			
Total inventory			

Unit Number	Quantity	Cost per Unit	Total Cost
Weighted Average Cost			
Total inventory			

SOLUTION

Unit Number	Quantity	Cost per Unit	Total Cost
First-In, First-Out			
101	5	$510	$2,550
101	1	500	500
103	7	222	1,554
105	2	215	430
105	1	210	210
107	4	250	1,000
107	1	245	245
109	2	315	630
Total inventory			$7,119

Unit Number	Quantity	Cost per Unit	Total Cost
Last-In, First-Out			
101	3	$480	$1,440
101	3	490	1,470
103	6	208	1,248
103	1	210	210
105	3	200	600
107	3	225	675
107	2	240	480
109	1	295	295
109	1	300	300
Total inventory			$6,718

Unit Number	Quantity	Cost per Unit	Total Cost
Weighted Average Cost			
101	6	$496.84	$2,981.04
103	7	215.35	1,507.45
105	3	204.67	614.01
107	5	241.30	1,206.50
109	2	308.00	616.00
Total inventory			$6,925.00

10.12 Determine the gross profit under the (a) LIFO and (b) FIFO assumptions, given the following information:

Sales	$40,000
Goods available for sale	12,000
Ending inventory (under LIFO)	6,500
Ending inventory (under FIFO)	3,500

SOLUTION

	LIFO		FIFO	
Sales		$40,000		$40,000
Cost of Goods Sold:				
Goods Available	$12,000		$12,000	
Less Ending Inventory	6,500		3,500	
Cost of Goods Sold		5,500		8,500
Gross Profit		$34,500		$31,500

Since FIFO had a lower ending inventory, its corresponding profit was lower. Also, as a proof, FIFO had a higher cost of goods sold, therefore yielding a lower gross profit.

10.13 Based on the following inventory information and other pertinent data, determine

(a) Ending inventory—36 units

(b) Cost of goods sold

(c) Gross profit

Beginning inventory	20 units @ $9 =	$180
First purchase	15 units @ 8 =	120
Second purchase	22 units @ 7 =	154
Third purchase	10 units @ 6 =	60
Available for sale	67 units	$514

	FIFO	LIFO
Sales	$10,000	$10,000
Cost of Goods Sold		
Goods Available for Sale	$514	$514
Less Ending Inventory	(a)	(a)
Cost of Goods Sold	(b)	(b)
Gross Profit	(c)	(c)

SOLUTION

In order to determine the gross profit, we must first determine the ending inventory and cost of goods sold under both the FIFO and LIFO methods.

Ending Inventory

FIFO

Third purchase	10 units @ $6 = $ 60	
Second purchase	22 units @ 7 = 154	
First purchase	4 units @ 8 = 32	
	36 units $246	(a)

LIFO

Beginning inventory	20 units @ $9 = $180	
First purchase	15 units @ 8 = 120	
Second purchase	1 units @ 7 = 7	
	36 units $307	(a)

Cost of Goods Sold*

FIFO

Beginning inventory	20 units @ $9 = $180	
First purchase	11 units @ 8 = 88	
	31 units $268	(b)

LIFO

Third purchase	10 units @ $6 = $ 60	
Second purchase	21 units @ 7 = 147	
	31 units $207	(b)

*Since there are available 67 units and 36 remain as inventory, 31 units (67 − 36) have been sold.

	FIFO		LIFO	
Sales	$10,000		$10,000	
Cost of Goods Sold				
Goods Available for Sale	$514		$514	
Less Ending Inventory	246	(a)	307	(a)
Cost of Goods Sold	268	(b)	207	(b)
Gross Profit	$ 9,732	(c)	$ 9,793	(c)

10.14 Based on data below, determine the inventory that was destroyed by fire under the gross profit method.

Beginning inventory	$20,000
Net purchases	40,000
Net sales	65,000
Gross profit average	25%

SOLUTION

Inventory (beginning)		$20,000
Add: Net purchases		40,000
Goods available for sale		$60,000
Sales	$65,000	
Estimated gross profit	16,250	(65,000 × 25%)
Less: Estimated cost of goods sold		48,750
Estimated ending inventory		$11,250

10.15 A flood destroyed most records and inventory of the Noah Company in March 19X5. After investigating outside records of various sources, the following information was obtained:

Inventory, 12/31/X4	$ 24,000
Purchases during 19X5	56,000
Purchase returns during 19X5	6,000
Net sales during 19X5	100,000
Gross profit rate:	
19X2 30%	
19X3 40%	
19X4 50%	

Determine the amount of the inventory loss to be claimed during 19X5 under the gross profit method.

SOLUTION

Inventory, 1/1/X5*		$24,000
Purchases	$ 56,000	
Less: Purchase returns	6,000	
Net purchases		50,000
Goods available for sale		$74,000
Sales	$100,000	
Estimated gross profit	40,000	(100,000 × 40%)†
Less: Estimated cost of goods sold		60,000
Estimated ending inventory, 3/31/X5		$14,000

---

*The ending inventory of 12/31/X4 becomes the beginning inventory of 1/1/X5.
†The average of 30% + 40% + 50% ÷ 3 = 40%.

10.16 Determine by the retail method the estimated cost of the December 31 inventory.

	Cost	Retail
Dec. 1 inventory	$300,000	$400,000
Dec. 1–31, purchases	110,000	180,000
Goods available for sale	$410,000	$580,000
Sales for December		340,000

SOLUTION

	Cost	Retail
Dec. 1 inventory	$300,000	$400,000
Dec. 1–31 purchases	110,000	180,000
Goods available for sale	$410,000	$580,000
Less: Sales for month		340,000
Dec. 31, inventory at retail		$240,000
Inventory at estimated cost		
($240,000 × 71%*)	$170,400	

* Cost ratio 71% ($410,000 ÷ $580,000).

10.17 Determine by the retail method the estimated cost of the ending inventory on December 31.

	Cost	Retail
Inventory, Dec. 1	$200,000	$300,000
Purchases, Dec. 1–31	105,000	190,000
Goods available for sale	$305,000	$490,000
Sales, Dec. 1–31		$400,000

SOLUTION

	Cost	Retail
Inventory, Dec. 1	$200,000	$300,000
Purchases, Dec. 1–31	105,000	190,000
Goods available for sale	$305,000	$490,000
Less: Net sales, Dec. 1–31		400,000
Inventory, Dec. 31		$ 90,000
Ratio of cost to retail ($305,000 ÷ $490,000 = 62%)		
Ending inventory at cost ($90,000 × 62%)	$55,800	

10.18 A fire destroyed the inventory of a boating store. Based on past records, it was determined that the gross profit rate averaged 45 percent, the net sales $160,000, ending inventory of the previous year $50,000, and net purchases during the year $70,000. What is the amount the boating company can claim on its damaged inventory on hand?

SOLUTION

Inventory (beginning)		$ 50,000
Net purchases		70,000
Goods available for sale		$120,000
Sales	$160,000	
Estimated gross profit	72,000	($160,000 × 45%)
Less: Estimated cost of goods sold		88,000
Estimated inventory (ending)		$ 32,000

10.19 Determine the total estimated inventory destroyed by fire under the retail inventory method for two different inventories of the Happy Department Store.

	Cost	Retail
Inventory I:	$280,000	$400,000
Net purchases	110,000	180,000
Net sales		340,000
Inventory II:	18,000	24,000
Net purchases	34,000	41,000
Net sales		37,000

SOLUTION

	Cost	Retail
Inventory I:		
Inventory (beginning)	$280,000	$400,000
Net purchases	110,000	180,000
Goods available for sale	$390,000	$580,000
Less: Sales		340,000
Inventory at retail		$240,000
Inventory at estimated cost ($240,000 × 67%*)	$160,800	

———————

*Cost ratio 67% ($390,000 ÷ $580,000).

	Cost	Retail
Inventory II:		
Inventory (beginning)	$18,000	$24,000
Net purchases	34,000	41,000
Goods available for sale	$52,000	$65,000
($52,000 ÷ $65,000 = 80% ratio)		
Less: Sales		37,000
Inventory at retail		$28,000
Inventory at estimated cost ($28,000 × 80%)	$22,400	

	Cost	Retail
Total estimated inventory at cost:		
Inventory I	$160,800	
Inventory II	22,400	
Total estimated inventory at cost	$183,200	

10.20 Determine the ending inventory under the retail inventory method using the following merchandising data for two specific inventories:

	Cost	Retail
Inventory A		
Inventory beginning	$25,000	$ 40,000
Net purchases	53,000	90,000
Net sales		110,000
Inventory B		
Inventory beginning	$14,000	$ 22,000
Net purchases	70,000	98,000
Net sales		90,000

SOLUTION

	Cost	Retail
Inventory A:		
Inventory (beginning)	$25,000	$ 40,000
+ Net purchases	53,000	90,000
Goods available for sale	$78,000	$130,000
− Net sales		110,000
Inventory (ending)		$ 20,000

Ratio of cost to retail price

$$\frac{\$78,000}{\$130,000} = 60\%$$

Ending inventory at cost ($20,000 × 60%) $12,000

	Cost	Retail
Inventory B:		
Inventory (beginning)	$14,000	$ 22,000
+ Net purchases	70,000	98,000
Goods available for sale	$84,000	$120,000
− Net sales		90,000
Ending inventory		$ 30,000

Ratio of cost to retail price

$$\frac{\$84,000}{\$120,000} = 70\%$$

Ending inventory at cost ($30,000 × 70%) $21,000

Then add:

Ending inventory (A) at cost	$12,000
Ending inventory (B) at cost	21,000
Total ending inventory at cost	$33,000

Note that the total ending inventory at retail would be $50,000 ($20,000 + $30,000).

Chapter 11

Pricing Merchandise

11.1 TRADE DISCOUNTS

When merchandise is offered for sale by manufacturers or wholesalers, a *list* or *catalog price* is set for each item. This represents the price that the ultimate consumer will pay for the item.

Rather than printing separate prices for each of the potential purchasers (wholesaler, retailer, consumer), the seller gives the various classes of buyers a separate discount sheet, detailing the discount offered to his or her class of purchaser. Thus, the trade discount is not a true discount but is considered to be an *adjustment of the price.*

The use of a list or catalog price also cuts down on printing. If the seller wishes to change the price offered to the wholesaler or retailer, a revised discount schedule, using the original list or catalog price, would be sent. The list or catalog price also provides the retailer with a suggested selling price for the item.

The price the buyer pays for the item (*net cost price*) is computed by multiplying the list or catalog price by the discount rate and then subtracting this discount from the list or catalog price.

EXAMPLE 1

A \$250 (list price) television is sold to a wholesaler at a 20 percent trade discount. The cost to the wholesaler is:

Step 1	\$250	List price
	$\times$ 20%	Trade discount percent
	\$ 50	Trade discount
Step 2	\$250	
	$-$ 50	
	\$200	Net cost price

Mathematically, this procedure may be simplified by multiplying the list or catalog price by the complement of the discount rate (the difference between the discount rate and 100 percent).

EXAMPLE 2

\$250	List price
$\times$ 80%	(100% $-$ 20%)
\$200	Net cost price

Transportation costs (if applicable) are not subject to a trade discount and would be added to the net cost price.

EXAMPLE 3

A \$250 (list price) television is sold to a wholesaler at a 20 percent trade discount. Transportation charges on the shipment total \$10. The net cost price is:

236

$250   List price
× ___80%___   (100% − 20%)
$200
Add   + ___10___   Transportation charges
$210   Net cost price including transportation

11.2 CHAIN DISCOUNTS

Rather than give varying increasing single discounts to different classes of purchasers, some companies use chain discounts. These have the advantage of appearing to be higher and emphasizing to the buyer the fact that she or he receives *more* than one discount.

When using chain discounts, there are two methods that may be used to compute the net cost price:

1. Determine a *single equivalent discount* and then proceed to compute the net cost price as illustrated earlier. This method is also useful for companies that wish to compare varying discount policies of competing companies.

    To compute an equivalent discount, *multiply* the complements of each of the discounts (100 percent − discount) together and *subtract* the result from 100 percent. For example, the single discount equivalent of 10 percent and 20 percent is computed as:

    Step 1 $(100\% − 10\%) × (100\% − 20\%)$
    Step 2 $0.90 × 0.80 = 0.72$
    Step 3   Equivalent discount $= 100\% − 72\% = 28\%$

EXAMPLE 4

A stereo set is offered to wholesalers at a list price of $600, *less* chain discounts of 25 percent and 20 percent. What is the net cost price?

1. $(100\% − 25\%) × (100\% − 20\%)$
2. $(0.75) × (0.80) = 0.60$
3. Equivalent discount $= 100\% − 60\% = 40\%$
4. Discount $= \$600 × 0.40 = \$240$
5. Net cost price $= \$600 − \$240 = \$360$

Alternative method:

1. $\$600 × 0.25 = \$150$ Price × first discount percentage
2. $\$600 − \$150 = \$450$ Price minus first discount
3. $\$450 × 0.20 = \$90$ Discounted price × second discount percentage
4. $\$450 − \$90 = \$360$ Discounted price minus second discount

2. The net cost price can be computed directly by *multiplying* the list price by the complement of each of the discounts in the series. It does not make any difference in what order the discounts are arranged.

EXAMPLE 5

Assume the same information as in Example 4:

1. $(100\% - 25\%) \times (100\% - 20\%)$
2. $(0.75) \times (0.80) = 0.60$
3. $\$600 \times 0.60 = \$360$

11.3   CASH DISCOUNTS

Cash discounts are an inducement offered to the buyer to encourage payment of a bill within a specified period of time. They tend to narrow the gap between the time of sale and the time of collection, which can become a source of cash flow difficulties for the seller.

Cash discounts are referred to as *terms* and may appear on a bill as 2/10, net 30, where

2 = the percent of the discount

10 = number of days within which the buyer must pay in order to qualify for the discount

net 30 = number of days at which payment must be made in full

EXAMPLE 6

An invoice of $300, dated March 6, has terms of 2/10, net 30. If payment is made on March 16, the net amount is:

1. $\$300 \times 2\% = \$6$ discount
2. $\$300 - \$6 = \$294$

If payment is made on March 17, the entire $300 is due.

Some companies offer a varied cash discount depending on when payment is made—for example, 2/10, 1/20, net 30. This means that the company offers a 2 percent discount if the buyer pays within 10 days; if he or she pays after 10 days, but within 20 days of purchase, he or she gets a 1 percent discount; the net amount is due within 30 days.

EXAMPLE 7

A $600 invoice dated April 6 has terms of 3/10, 2/15, net 30. If paid by April 16, the discount will be $18. If the invoice is paid after April 16, but by April 21, the discount will be $12. The entire bill of $600 must be paid by May 6.

Although in most cases the cash discount period is computed from the "invoice" or purchase date, the date may also be computed from either the date of *receipt of the goods* (ROG) or starting with the *end of the month* (EOM).

ROG is used primarily when there is a significant gap between the date of the sale and the delivery date. This eliminates the necessity for the buyer to pay for goods before receiving them in order to get a discount.

EOM is used primarily as a convenience with traditional end-of-month billing practices followed by most companies.

EXAMPLE 8

The last date on which a discount can be taken is shown below:

	Invoice Date	Goods Received	Terms	Last Day on Which Discount Can Be Taken
Invoice $500	Oct. 3	Oct. 8	2/10, n/30 ROG	Oct. 18
Invoice $700	Oct. 3	Oct. 8	2/10, n/30 EOM	Nov. 10*

*10 days after the end of month (EOM).

Trade and Cash Discounts

When both trade and cash discounts are offered, the cash discount is computed *after* the trade discount has been taken.

EXAMPLE 9

An invoice of $300, dated March 17, with a trade discount of 30 percent and terms 2/10, n/30, was paid on March 20. The amount of the payment is computed as:

$$
\begin{array}{rl}
\$300 & \text{List price} \\
\times\ \ 70\% & (100\% - 30\%) \\
\hline
\$210 & \text{Net cost} \\
\times\ \ 2\% & \text{Cash discount percent} \\
\hline
\$4.20 & \text{Cash discount}
\end{array}
$$

$210 − $4.20 − $205.80 − amount of payment

11.4 MARKUP

In order to make a profit, each company must sell its products for more than they cost. The difference between cost and selling price is referred to as *markup*.

EXAMPLE 10

A washing machine selling for $300 costs the seller $200. The markup is $100.

Percent Markup

Markup is generally expressed in terms of a percentage:

$$\text{Percent} = \frac{\text{percentage}}{\text{base}}$$

where

$$
\begin{aligned}
\text{percent} &= \text{markup percent} \\
\text{percentage} &= \text{markup} \\
\text{base} &= \text{selling price or cost}
\end{aligned}
$$

11.5   SELLING PRICE AS A BASIS: COMPUTING PERCENT MARKUP

EXAMPLE 11

A book selling for $8 cost the seller $6. What is the percent markup based on selling price?

$$\text{Percent} = \frac{\$2}{\$8} \quad (\$8 - \$6)$$
$$\text{Percent markup} = 25\%$$

Computing Cost

In order to use the percent markup to compute either the cost or the selling price, the selling price formula must be reexamined in terms of percents. It should be noted that the base is 100 percent.

EXAMPLE 12

A book selling for $8 has a markup percent of 25 percent. What is the cost?

$$25\% = \frac{x}{8}$$
$$x = 25\% \times \$8$$
$$= \$2 \text{ (markup)}$$
$$\text{Cost} = \$8 - \$2 = \$6$$

Computing Selling Price

EXAMPLE 13

A book has a markup percent of $2, which is 25 percent of the selling price. What is the selling price?

$$25\% = \frac{\$2}{x}$$
$$25\%x = \$2$$
$$x = \frac{\$2}{0.25}$$
$$x = \$8$$

11.6   COST AS A BASIS

When cost is used as a base for markup percent, it is sometimes referred to as a *markon*. It has the advantage of expressing clearly the fact that the price increase is added *directly* to its basis (cost).

Computing Percent Markup

$$\text{Percent markup} = \frac{\$ \text{ markup}}{\text{cost}}$$

EXAMPLE 14

A ball point pen that sells for $6 cost $4. What is the percent markup based on cost?

$$\text{Percent markup} = \frac{\$2}{\$4} \quad (\$6 - \$4)$$
$$= 50\%$$

EXAMPLE 15   Computing the Cost

If an item selling for $72 has a 20 percent markup on cost, what is the cost?

$$
\begin{aligned}
\text{Selling price} &= \text{cost} + \text{markup} \\
\$72 &= 100\% + 20\% \\
\$72 &= 120\% \\
\$72 \div 1.20 &= \text{Cost} \\
\$60 &= \text{Cost}
\end{aligned}
$$

Computing Selling Price

In order to compute the selling price from either the cost or the markup, you once again must look at the formula for selling price from the point of view of percents. The cost (basis) is 100 percent.

EXAMPLE 16

If a tie that costs $10 has a markup of 30 percent on cost, what is the selling price?

$$
\begin{aligned}
\text{Selling price} &= \text{cost} + \$ \text{ markup} \\
&= \$10 + (0.30)(\$10) \\
&= \$10 + \$3 \\
&= \$13
\end{aligned}
$$

11.7   MARKDOWNS

Once the price of an item has been established, there is no guarantee that this will represent the ultimate selling price. Downward adjustments of the selling price are often necessary to induce customers to buy. These are referred to as *markdowns*. The seller is in effect forced, perhaps because of overstocking or too high a selling price, to abandon the original price. Markdowns take the form of *direct price reductions*.

EXAMPLE 17

A suit listing for $150 was marked down 30 percent. What is the new selling price?

$$
\begin{aligned}
\$150 \times 30\% &= \$45 \text{ markdown} \\
\$150 - \$45 &= \$105 \text{ selling price}
\end{aligned}
$$

11.8   TURNOVER—RATIOS FOR INVENTORY

The firm's investment in inventory also has a direct effect on its working capital. Excess inventory means that funds are tied up in inventory that could be used more profitably elsewhere. Also, additional costs are being incurred for storage, insurance, and property taxes, not to mention the danger of a price decline and obsolescence of goods.

Whenever any consideration is given to pricing and profit planning, it is important to consider the *merchandise inventory turnover*. This is the number of times the average inventory is sold during a year. The turnover shows how quickly the inventory is moving. Assuming that the company maintains a reasonable inventory for its type of business, a high turnover rate (such as for a grocery store) indicates that only a relatively small profit need be added to the price of each item to maintain a high profit overall. Turnover is also a good indication of the amount of working capital that needs to be tied up in inventory at one time.

Merchandise inventory turnover can be computed from the cost of goods sold section of the income statement. It should be noted, however, that the turnover is an *annual* rate and should not be computed from interim statements.

$$\text{Merchandise inventory turnover} = \frac{\text{cost of goods sold}}{\text{average merchandise inventory}^*}$$

_____

* Beginning inventory + ending inventory ÷ 2.

EXAMPLE 18

Cost of Goods Sold:		
Merchandise Inventory, Jan. 1	$10,000	
Net Purchases	85,000	
Merchandise Available for Sale	$95,000	
Merchandise Inventory, Dec. 31	20,000	
Cost of Goods Sold		$75,000

$$\text{Merchandise inventory turnover} = \frac{\$75,000}{15,000^*} = 5$$

_____

* $10,000 (beg.) + $20,000 (end) ÷ 2.

In a retail business, such as a department store, turnover may effectively be computed either by departments or by classes of items. This can be accomplished by using the following turnover formula, which will yield approximately the same turnover rate as above:

$$\text{Merchandise inventory turnover} = \frac{\text{sales in units}}{\text{average inventory in units}^*}$$

_____

* Beginning inventory + ending inventory ÷ 2.

EXAMPLE 19

Rosedale Speciality Shop sells dresses in four colors, red, blue, white, and pink, all of which sell for the same price. What is the turnover for each color as computed from the data below? What, if any, problems does the turnover analysis reveal?

	Sales in Units	Beginning Inventory	End Inventory
Red	600	75	125
Blue	800	140	120
White	300	210	190
Pink	900	200	150

$$\text{Red turnover} = \frac{600}{100} = 6$$

$$\text{Blue turnover} = \frac{800}{130} = 6.15$$

$$\text{White turnover} = \frac{300}{200} = 1.5$$

$$\text{Pink turnover} = \frac{900}{175} = 5.14$$

The white dress should be eliminated because of its low rate of turnover.

11.9   NUMBER OF DAYS' SALES IN INVENTORY

The relationship between inventory and cost of goods sold can also be expressed as the number of days' sales in inventory. In this ratio, the inventory at the end of the year is divided by the average daily cost of goods sold. The latter figure is determined by dividing the cost of goods sold by 365. The number of days' sales in inventory provides a rough measure of the length of time required to buy, sell, and then replace the inventory.

EXAMPLE 20

The Baker Company
Turnover of Inventory

Cost of Goods Sold	$750,000
Merchandise Inventory:	
Beginning of Year	$ 84,200
End of Year	130,100
Total	$214,300
Average	$107,150
Turnover of Inventory	7.0*

*$750,000 ÷ 107,150

The average daily cost of goods sold is $750,000 ÷ 365 = $2,055.

The Baker Company
Number of Days' Sales in Inventory

	19X5
Inventory at End of Year	$130,100
Average Daily Cost of Goods Sold	2,055
Number of Days' Sales in Inventory	63.3*

*$130,100 ÷ 2,055

Summary

1. An adjustment of the retail price is known as a _____ .

2. A substitute for varying increasing single discounts to different classes of purchases is referred to as a _____ .

3. An inducement offered to the buyer to encourage payment of his or her bill within a specific period of time is called a _____ .

4. Cash discounts are referred to as _____ .

5. The "2" in 2/10, n/30 is the _____ .

6. The abbreviation ROG stands for _____ .

7. The difference between cost and selling price is referred to as _____ .

8. When cost is used as a basis for markup percent, it is sometimes known as _____ .

9. Downward adjustments of the selling price are often necessary to induce customers to buy and are referred to as _____ .

10. In order to give consideration to pricing and profit planning, it is important to consider the _____ .

Answers: 1. trade discount; 2. chain discount; 3. cash discount; 4. terms; 5. percent discount; 6. receipt of goods; 7. markup; 8. markon; 9. markdowns; 10. merchandise inventory turnover

Solved Problems

11.1   Equipment of $400 is sold to a retailer at a 25 percent trade discount. What is the retailer's cost?

SOLUTION

$400	List price	$400	
× 25%	Trade discount	− 100	
$100	Trade discount	$300	Net cost

11.2   If transportation of $20 were added to the purchase in Problem 11.1, what would the net cost be?

SOLUTION

$300
+ 20   Transportation
$320

Transportation costs are added to the net cost of the item and are not subject to trade discounts.

11.3 Determine the single equivalent discount in each of the following examples: (*a*) 20 percent, 5 percent; (*b*) 25 percent, 10 percent.

SOLUTION

(*a*) 24% (100% − 20%) × (100% − 5%) = 80% × 95% = 76%
           100% − 76% = 24%
(*b*) 32.5% (100% − 25%) × (100% − 10%) = 75% × 90% = 67.5%
           100% − 67.5% = 32.5%

11.4 Laura Edelstein bought $800 of supplies for her company, less chain discounts of 30 percent and 20 percent. (*a*) What is the single equivalent discount? (*b*) What is the net cost to the company?

SOLUTION

(*a*) (100% − 30%) × (100% − 20%) = 70% × 80% = 56%
       Single equivalent discount = 44% (100% − 56%)
(*b*) $800 × 44% = $352
       Net cost = $448 ($800 − $352)

11.5 Company A gives terms of 20 percent discounts on all items purchased. Company B gives chain discounts of 15 percent and 10 percent. If J. Snyder bought $500 of supplies, how much would he save by dealing with Company B rather than with Company A?

SOLUTION

Company A	Company B
$500 × 20% − $100 discount	(100% − 15%) × (100% − 10%)
	85% × 90% = 76.5%
	$500 × 23.5% = $117.50 discount

$117.50   Company B
− 100.00   Company A
$ 17.50   Savings

11.6 Determine the last day allowable for a company to take advantage of the full discount.

	Term	Date of Order	Date of Delivery
(*a*)	2/10, n/30	June 4	June 8
(*b*)	2/10, 1/15, n/30	June 4	June 8
(*c*)	2/10, n/30, ROG	June 4	June 8
(*d*)	2/10, n/30, EOM	June 4	June 8

SOLUTION

(*a*) June 14
(*b*) June 14 (full); June 19 (partial discount)
(*c*) June 18
(*d*) July 10

11.7 Determine the amount to be paid under the following different situations:

	Amount	Date of Purchase	Goods Received	Terms	Date of Payment Made
(a)	$600	Apr. 4	Apr. 11	2/10, n/30	Apr. 10
(b)	$700	May 1	May 14	2/10, n/30, ROG	May 23
(c)	$800	June 6	June 12	2/10, 1/20, n/30	June 25
(d)	$900	July 20	July 24	2/10, n/30, EOM	Aug. 9

SOLUTION

(a) $588
(b) $686 Date of receipt determines discount period.
(c) $792 1 percent discount allowed. Paid after 10 days (2 percent) but before 20 days.
(d) $882 10 days after end of month is allowed for discount taking.

11.8 What amount will be paid to the seller if goods bought on September 6 for $500, terms 2/10, 1/15, n/30, were paid on (a) September 10, (b) September 20, (c) September 30?

SOLUTION

(a) $490 ($500 less 2%); (b) $495 ($500 less 1%); (c) $500 (no discount)

11.9 Lester Washington bought equipment for his plant on October 17 for $3,000, subject to terms 2/10, n/30, EOM. What amount will he pay if his payment is made on (a) October 24, (b) October 31, (c) November 6, (d) November 10?

SOLUTION

(a) $2940 ($3,000 − $60); (b) $2940; (c) $2940; (d) $2940

Mr. Washington has 10 days after the end of the month to take advantage of the discount.

11.10 H. Dryer bought $900 of goods for his company on March 5, subject to a 25 percent trade discount, bearing terms 2/10, 1/20, n/30. If the invoice was paid on March 11, how much was his payment?

SOLUTION

$$
\begin{array}{rl}
\$900 & \text{List price} \\
\underline{25\%} & \text{Trade discount} \\
\$225 & \text{Discount}
\end{array}
$$

$$
\$900 - \$225 =
\begin{array}{rl}
\$675.00 & \\
\underline{13.50} & (\$675 - 2\% \text{ discount}) \\
\$661.50 & \text{Net payment}
\end{array}
$$

11.11 (a) Jankowich Corporation sells its $4 pens for $6. What is their percent markup?
(b) Stationary selling for $10 has a markup of 25 percent. What is the cost?

SOLUTION

(a)

$$\text{Percent} = \frac{(\$6 - \$4)}{6} = \frac{2}{6} = 33\tfrac{1}{3}\%$$

(b)
$$25\% = \frac{x}{10}$$
$$x = 25\% \times \$10$$
$$x = \$2.50 \text{ profit}$$
$$\$10 - \$2.50 = \$7.50 \text{ cost}$$

11.12 Textbooks yield a profit of \$3, which represents 20 percent of the selling price. What is the selling price?

SOLUTION

$$20\% = \frac{\$3}{x}$$
$$20\%x = \$3$$
$$x = \$15$$

11.13 Supplies selling for \$25 per box have a markup on cost (markon) of 25 percent. What is the cost of one box?

SOLUTION

Selling price = cost + profit

25 = 100% + 25%

25 = 125% or (1.25)

$\dfrac{\$25}{1.25}$ = \$20 cost

11.14 A necklace that costs \$24 is marked up 25 percent on cost. What is the selling price?

SOLUTION

Selling price = cost + profit

= \$24 + 25%

= \$24 + \$6

= \$30

11.15 Given the following information, determine the merchandise inventory turnover.

Cost of Goods Sold:		
Merchandise Inventory, Jan. 1	\$22,000	
Purchases (net)	73,000	
Available for Sale	\$95,000	
Merchandise Inventory, Dec. 31	34,000	
Cost of Goods Sold		\$61,000

SOLUTION

The formula is:

$$\text{Inventory turnover} = \frac{\text{cost of goods sold}}{\text{average inventory}^*}$$

$$\text{Turnover} = \frac{61,000}{28,000^*} = 2.2$$

---

*$22,000 + $34,000 ÷ 2.

11.16 The Walzck Company has a division that sells three unrelated products. Determine from the information below the turnover for each product. If one product had to be dropped, which would it be? Why?

Product	Sales in Units	Inventory (Beginning)	Inventory (End)
A	700	50	150
B	800	180	140
C	800	500	550

SOLUTION

$$\text{Product A} \quad \frac{700}{100^*} = 7$$

$$\text{Product B} \quad \frac{800}{160^*} = 5$$

$$\text{Product C} \quad \frac{800}{525^*} = 1.5$$

Product C should be eliminated because it has a very low turnover rate.

---

*Average of beginning and ending inventory.

11.17 From the selected information below, determine:

(a) Turnover of inventory

(b) Average daily cost of goods sold

(c) Number of days' sales in inventory

Cost of Goods Sold	$800,000
Inventory (Beginning)	104,000
Inventory (Ending)	96,000

SOLUTION

(a) $\dfrac{800,000 \text{ (cost of goods sold)}}{100,000 \text{ (average inventory)}} = 8$

(b) $\dfrac{\$800,000}{365 \text{ days}} = \$2,192$

(c) $\dfrac{\$96,000}{\$2,192} = 43.8$ days' sales in inventory

Examination III

1. For each individual situation below, determine the missing figures.

	Beginning Inventory	Purchases During Period	Return Purchases	Ending Inventory	Cost of Goods Sold
(a)	$22,000	$16,000	$1,000	$ 7,000	?
(b)	41,000	23,000	3,000	?	$37,000
(c)	?	22,000	1,000	26,000	40,000

2. (a) Construct the cost of goods sold section of the income statement based on the following information: Sales Income, $84,000; Inventory (Beginning), $28,000; Inventory (Ending), $22,000; Purchases, $51,000; Purchases Returns, $2,000.

   (b) What is the gross profit of the firm?

3. Journalize the following adjusting data as of December 31:

   (a) Merchandise inventory, January 1, $46,000; December 31, $48,000.

   (b) Office supplies physically counted on December 31 were $1,250. The original balance of supplies on hand was $2,100.

   (c) Prepaid insurance before adjustment, $3,850. It was found that $2,700 had expired during the year.

   (d) Salaries for a 5-day week ending on Friday were $3,500. The last payday was on the previous Friday, December 28.

4. Based on the following worksheet's income statement columns, prepare an income statement.

Expense and Income Summary	26,400	28,200
Sales		62,500
Purchases	31,400	
Rent Expense	6,000	
Salaries Expense	18,300	
Depreciation Expense	500	
	82,600	90,700

5. From the trial balance of the J. C. Company on the following page, complete the eight-column worksheet. Use the following data for adjustments: (a) Merchandise Inventory, June 30, 19X5, $1,900; (b) Supplies on Hand, $150; (c) Expired Insurance, $200.

J.C. Company
Trial Balance
June 30, 19X5

	Debit	Credit
Cash	$12,300	
Accounts Receivable	16,000	
Merchandise Inventory	2,700	
Supplies	450	
Prepaid Insurance	500	
Accounts Payable		$ 3,200
Notes Payable		7,100
J.C., Capital		14,750
Sales		39,800
Purchases	17,200	
Salaries Expense	11,400	
Advertising Expense	2,300	
General Expense	2,000	
	$64,850	$64,850

J.C. Company
Worksheet
Year Ended June 30, 19X5

Account Title	Trial Balance		Adjustments		Income Statement		Balance Sheet	
	Dr.	Cr.	Dr.	Cr.	Dr.	Cr.	Dr.	Cr.
Cash	12,300							
Accounts Receivable	16,000							
Merchandise Inventory	2,700							
Supplies	450							
Prepaid Insurance	500							
Accounts Payable		3,200						
Notes Payable		7,100						
J.C., Capital		14,750						
Sales		39,800						
Purchases	17,200							
Salaries Expense	11,400							
Advertising Expense	2,300							
General Expense	2,000							
	64,850	64,850						
Expense and Income Summary								
Supplies Expense								
Insurance Expense								
Net Income								

6. The beginning inventory and various purchases of product B were as follows:

Jan. 1	Balance	8 units @ $10.00
Mar. 5	Purchase	12 units @ 11.00
June 9	Purchase	16 units @ 12.00
Aug. 20	Purchase	15 units @ 13.00
Nov. 1	Purchase	18 units @ 14.00

An inventory count under the periodic system disclosed that 30 units of product B were on hand. Determine the ending inventory cost by (*a*) first-in, first out; (*b*) last-in, first-out; (*c*) weighted average.

7. Estimate the cost of inventory of May 31 by the retail method.

	Cost	Retail
May 1, merchandise	$18,000	$24,000
May purchases	34,000	41,000
Sales for May		37,000

8. Determine the amount to be paid in each transaction below.

	Amount	Invoice Date	Receipt of Goods	Terms	Date of Payment
(*a*)	$600	June 16	June 19	2/10, n/30, ROG	June 27
(*b*)	$700	Aug. 15	Aug. 15	2/10, n/30, EOM	Sept. 10
(*c*)	$800	Aug. 19	Aug. 21	2/10, n/30, EOM	Sept. 12

9. (*a*) Ink selling for $10 a case cost $8. What is the percent markup based on (1) selling price and (2) cost?

   (*b*) If an item has a 30 percent markup on cost and sells for $260, what is the cost?

10. A partial income statement is reproduced below. Determine:

   (*a*) Turnover rate
   (*b*) Average daily cost of goods sold
   (*c*) Number of days' sales in inventory

Cost of Goods Sold:		
Inventory (Jan.)	$ 80,000	
Net Purchases	160,000	
Available for Sale	$240,000	
Inventory (Dec.)	40,000	
Cost of Goods Sold		$200,000

Answers to Examination III

1. (a) $30,000

   (b) $24,000

   (c) $45,000

2. (a)

Cost of Goods Sold:		
Inventory (Beginning)		$28,000
Purchases	$51,000	
Purchase Returns	2,000	49,000
Goods Available for Sale		$77,000
Inventory (Ending)		22,000
Cost of Goods Sold		$55,000

   (b)

Sales	$84,000
Cost of Goods Sold	− 55,000
Gross Profit	$29,000

3. (a)

Expense and Income Summary	46,000	
Merchandise Inventory		46,000
Merchandise Inventory	48,000	
Expense and Income Summary		48,000

   (b)

Office Supplies Expense	850	
Office Supplies		850

   (c)

Insurance Expense	2,700	
Prepaid Insurance		2,700

   (d)

Salaries Expense	700	
Salaries Payable		700

(Monday, December 31, $3,500 ÷ 5)

4.

Sales		$62,500
Cost of Goods Sold		
Merchandise Inventory (Beginning)	$26,400	
Purchases	31,400	
Goods Available for Sale	$57,800	
Merchandise Inventory (Ending)	28,200	
Cost of Goods Sold		29,600
Gross Profit		$32,900
Operating Expenses		
Salaries Expense	$18,300	
Rent Expense	6,000	
Depreciation Expense	500	
Total Expenses		24,800
Net Income		$ 8,100

5.

J.C. Company
Worksheet
Year Ended June 30, 19X5

Account Title	Trial Balance Dr.	Cr.	Adjustments Dr.	Cr.	Income Statement Dr.	Cr.	Balance Sheet Dr.	Cr.
Cash	12,300						12,300	
Accounts Receivable	16,000						16,000	
Merchandise Inventory	2,700		(a) 1,900	(a) 2,700			1,900	
Supplies	450			(b) 300			150	
Prepaid Insurance	500			(c) 200			300	
Accounts Payable		3,200						3,200
Notes Payable		7,100						7,100
J.C., Capital		14,750						14,750
Sales		39,800				39,800		
Purchases	17,200				17,200			
Salaries Expense	11,400				11,400			
Advertising Expense	2,300				2,300			
General Expense	2,000				2,000			
	64,850	64,850						
Expense and Income Summary			(a) 2,700	(a) 1,900	2,700	1,900		
Supplies Expense			(b) 300		300			
Insurance Expense			(c) 200		200			
			5,100	5,100	36,100	41,700	30,650	25,050
Net Income					5,600			5,600
					41,700	41,700	30,650	30,650

6. (a)

Most recent purchase (Nov. 1)	18 units @ $14 =	$252
Next most recent (Aug. 20)	12 units @ 13 =	156
Total units	30 Total cost	$408

(b)

Earliest cost (Jan. 1)	8 units @ $10 =	$ 80
Next earliest (Mar. 5)	12 units @ 11 =	132
Next earliest (June 9)	10 units @ 12 =	120
Total units	30 Total cost	$332

(c)

	8 units @ $10 =	$ 80
	12 units @ 11 =	132
	16 units @ 12 =	192
	15 units @ 13 =	195
	18 units @ 14 =	252
Total units	69 Total cost	$851
Total units	30 Total cost	$370*

The weighted average cost per unit is $851 ÷ 69 = $12.33. The cost of 30 units on hand is calculated as $12.33 × 30 = $370.*

---

*Rounded to the nearest dollar.

7.

	Cost	Retail
May 1, Merchandise	$18,000	$24,000
May Purchases	34,000	41,000
Goods available for sale	$52,000	$65,000
($52,000 ÷ $65,000 = 80% ratio)		
Sales for May		37,000
May 31, inventory at retail		$28,000
May 31, inventory at estimated cost	$22,400*	

———————————

*($28,000 × 80%).

8. (a) $588; (b) $686; (c) $800—no discount allowed

9. (a) (1) $\frac{2}{10} = 20\%$

  (2) $\frac{2}{8} = 25\%$

  (b) $260 = cost + 30%

  $260 = 130%

  $200 = cost

10. (a) 200,000 ÷ 60,000 = 3.3

  (b) $200,000 ÷ 365 = $548 average daily cost of goods sold

  (c) $40,000 ÷ 548 = 73 days' sales in inventory

PART IV: Specific Bookkeeping and Accounting Topics

Chapter 12

Negotiable Instruments

12.1 INTRODUCTION

A large proportion of all business transactions are credit transactions. One way of extending credit is by the acceptance of a promissory note, a contract in which one person (the maker) promises to pay another person (the payee) a specific sum of money at a specific time, with or without interest. A promissory note is used for the following reasons:

1. The holder of a note can usually obtain money by taking the note to the bank and selling it (discounting the note).

2. The note is a written acknowledgment of a debt and is better evidence than an open account. It takes precedence over accounts in the event that the debtor becomes bankrupt.

3. The note facilitates the sale of merchandise on long-term or installment plans.

For a note to be negotiable, it must meet the requirements of the Uniform Negotiable Instrument Law. This legislation states that the instrument:

1. Must be in writing and signed by the maker

2. Must contain an order to pay a definite sum of money

3. Must be payable to order on demand or at a fixed future time

EXAMPLE 1

The promissory note below contains the following information:

(1) Face or principal—the amount of the note

(2) Date of the note—date note was written

(3) Term period—time allowed for payment

(4) Payee—individual to whom payment must be made

(5) Face or principal—[see (1)]

(6) Interest—percentage of annual interest

(7) Maturity date—date the note is to be paid

(8) Maker—person liable for payment of the note

$2,000 (1)   New York, NY   April 4, (2)   19 X5

90 days (3)   after date 1 promise to pay to

the order of Barbara Ledina (4)

Two thousand and 00/100 (5)   Dollars

at 14 percent per annum at Second National Bank (6)

Value received
          Due July 3, 19X5 (7)   J. Lerner (8)

255

12.2 METHODS OF COMPUTING INTEREST

For the sake of simplicity, interest is commonly computed on the basis of a 360-day year divided into 12 months of 30 days each. Two widely used methods are (1) the cancellation method and (2) the 6 percent, 60-days method.

The Cancellation Method

The basic formula is

$$\text{Interest} = \text{principal} \times \text{rate} \times \text{time}$$

EXAMPLE 2

Consider a note for $400 at 6 percent for 90 days. The principal is the face amount of the note ($400). The rate of interest is written as a fraction: 6%/100% = 6/100. The time, if less than a year, is expressed as a fraction by dividing the number of days the note runs by the number of days in a year: 90/360. Thus,

$$\text{Interest} = \$400 \times \frac{6}{100} \times \frac{90}{360} = \$6$$

The 6 Percent, 60-Days Method

The 6 percent, 60-days Method is a variation of the cancellation method, based on the fact that 60 days, or $\frac{1}{6}$ year, at 6 percent is equivalent to 1 percent, so that the interest is obtained simply by shifting the decimal point of the principal two places to the left.

EXAMPLE 3

The method also applies to other time periods or other interest rates. For instance:

$400 Note	30 Days		6%
(a) Determine the interest for 60 days.			$4.00
(b) Divide the result by 2 (30 days is one-half of 60 days)		*Ans.*	$2.00

$400 Note	45 Days		6%
(a) Determine the interest for 30 days.			$2.00
(b) Determine the interest for 15 days.			$1.00
(c) Add the interest for 30 days and 15 days.		*Ans.*	$3.00

$400 Note	60 Days		5%
(a) Determine the interest at 6 percent.			$4.00
(b) Determine the interest at 1 percent by taking one-sixth of the above amount.			$0.67
(c) Multiply the interest at 1 percent by the rate desired, 0.67 × 5.		*Ans.*	$3.35

Determining Maturity Date

The maturity days are the number of days after the note has been issued and may be determined by:

1. Subtracting the date of the note from the number of days in the month in which it was written.

2. Adding the succeeding full months (in terms of days), stopping with the last full month before the number of days in the note are exceeded.

3. Subtracting the total days of the result of steps 1 and 2 above from the time of the note. The resulting number is the due date in the upcoming month.

EXAMPLE 4

The maturity date of a 90-day note dated April 4 would be computed as follows:

Time of note:		90
April	30	
Date of note:	4	26
May		31
June		30
Total:		87
Maturity date:	July	3

If the due date of a note is expressed in months, the maturity date can be determined by counting that number of expressed months from the date of writing:

EXAMPLE 5

A 5-month note dated March 17 would be due for payment on August 17. A 1-month note dated March 31 would mature on April 30.

12.3 ACCOUNTING FOR NOTES PAYABLE AND NOTES RECEIVABLE

A promissory note is a note payable from the standpoint of the maker; it is a note receivable from the standpoint of the payee.

Notes Payable

A note payable is a written promise to pay a creditor an amount of money in the future. Notes are used by a business to (1) purchase items, (2) settle an open account, or (3) borrow money from a bank.

1. *Purchase items*

EXAMPLE 6

Office Equipment costing $2,000 was purchased by giving a note.

Office Equipment	2,000	
Notes Payable		2,000

2. *Settle an open account*

EXAMPLE 7

There are times when a corporation must issue a note payable for settlement of an account payable. Assume that the Harmin Agency bought merchandise from Laska Corporation for $500, terms 2/10, n/30. The entry would be recorded in the purchases journal and would appear in the general ledger as:

Purchases		Accounts Payable	
500			500

However, 30 days later, the agency is unable to pay and gives to the Laska Company a 12 percent, 60-day note for $500 to replace its open account. When the Harmin Agency issues the note payable, an entry is made in the general journal that will decrease the accounts payable and increase the notes payable.

	Accounts Payable	500	
	Notes Payable		500

Accounts Payable		Notes Payable	
500	500		500

Note that the Harmin Agency still owes the debt to the Laska Company. However, it now becomes a different form of an obligation, as it is a written, signed promise in the form of a note payable.

When the maker pays the note in 60 days at 12 percent, the amount of his payment will be the total of the principal and interest will be recorded in the cash disbursements journal.

3. *Borrow money from a bank.*   On occasions, businesses find that it may be necessary to borrow money by giving a note payable to the bank. Frequently, banks require the interest that will be owed to them to be paid in advance. This is accomplished by deducting the amount of the interest from the principal immediately when the loan is made and is known as *discounting a note payable.* The proceeds will be that amount of money that the maker of the note receives after the discount has been taken from the principal.

EXAMPLE 8

Assume that the Rhulen Agency seeks to borrow $3,000 for 60 days at 14 percent from the Commercial National Bank. The bank will deduct the interest ($70.00) from the $3,000 principal and will give the difference of $2,930 (proceeds) to the Rhulen Agency.

The entry recorded in the cash receipts journal of the Rhulen Agency would be

Cash	2,930	
Interest Expense	70	
Notes Payable		3,000

Sixty days after the issuance of the instrument, the note becomes due, and the Rhulen Agency sends a check for the face of the note ($3,000). Because the interest was deducted immediately when the loan was made, no further interest will be paid at that time. The entry to record the payment of the note will be made in the cash payments journal:

Notes Payable	3,000	
Cash		3,000

Note: When a business issues many notes payable, a special subsidiary book, known as the notes payable register, may be used. This register will give the complete data for all notes issued and paid by the business. It must be noted, however, that this is merely a source of information and not a journal, as no postings are made from it to the ledger.

Notes Receivable

A note received from a customer is an asset because it becomes a claim against the buyer for the amount due.

EXAMPLE 9

Assume that Ira Sochet owes S. Wyde $400 and gives him a 15 percent, 90-day note in settlement. On Mr. Wyde's books, the entry is

Notes Receivable	400	
Accounts Receivable		400

Only the principal ($400) is recorded when the note is received, since it represents the amount of the unpaid account. The interest is not due until the date of collection, 90 days later. At that time, the interest earned (income) will be part of the entry recognizing the receipt of the proceeds from the note:

Cash	415	
Notes Receivable		400
Interest Income		15

12.4 DISCOUNTING

The negotiability of a notes receivable based upon its maturity value, enables the holder to receive cash from the bank before the due date. This is known as *discounting*.

Once the interest to be paid has been determined, the procedure for discounting a note is quite simple. We define the maturity value of a note by

1.   Maturity value = face of note + interest income

where the face is the principal and the interest income is computed as in Section 12.2. The holder of a note may discount it at the bank prior to its due date. He or she will receive the maturity value, less the discount, or interest charge imposed by the bank for holding the note for the unexpired portion of its term. In other words,

2.   Discount = maturity value × discount rate × unexpired time

and

3.   Net proceeds = maturity value − discount

EXAMPLE 10

Mr. Wyde holds a $400, ninety-day, 15 percent note written on April 10. (See Example 9.) As the holder of the note, he decides to discount it on May 10. The bank's rate of discount will be assumed to be 15 percent. The interest on the note, as found in Example 9, amounts to $15. Hence,

1.   Maturity value = $400 + $15 = $415

Since, at the time of discounting, Mr. Wyde has held the note for only 30 days, the bank will have to wait 90 − 30 = 60 days until it can receive the maturity value. The discount charge is then

2. $$\text{Discount} = \$415 \times \frac{15}{100} \times \frac{60}{360} = \$10.38$$

and Mr. Wyde receives

3.   Net proceeds = $415 − $10.38 = $404.62

In this example, the bank's discount rate happened to be equal to the interest rate of the note; this need not always be the case.

12.5 DISHONORED NOTES RECEIVABLE

If the issuer of a note does not make payment on the due date, the note is said to be dishonored. It is no longer negotiable, and the amount is charged back to Accounts Receivable. The reasons for transferring the dishonored notes receivable to the Accounts Receivable account are: (1) the Notes Receivable account is then limited to current notes that have not yet matured; and (2) the Accounts Receivable account will then show the dishonoring of the note, giving a better picture of the transaction.

EXAMPLE 11

A $600, sixty-day, 14 percent note written by C. Babcock was dishonored on the date of maturity. The entry is:

Accounts Receivable, C. Babcock	614	
Notes Receivable		600
Interest Income		14

Observe that the interest income is recorded and is charged to the customer's account.

When a payee discounts a note receivable, he or she creates a contingent (potential) liability. This occurs because there is a possibility that the maker may dishonor the note. Bear in mind that the payee has already received payment from the bank in advance of the maturity date. The payee is, therefore, contingently liable to the bank to make good on the amount (maturity value) in the event of default by the maker. Any protest fee arising from the default of the note is charged to the maker of the note and is added to the amount to be charged against his or her account.

EXAMPLE 12

An $800, ninety-day, 14 percent note, dated May 1, is discounted on May 31 at 14 percent. Upon presentation on the due date, the note is dishonored. The entry will be:

Accounts Receivable	828*	
Cash		828

*$800   (face)
 28   (interest)
$828   (maturity value)

Had the bank issued a protest fee of $20, the amount charged to the customer would be $848.

12.6   RECORDING UNCOLLECTIBLE ACCOUNTS

Businesses must expect to sustain some losses from uncollectible accounts and should therefore show on the balance sheet the *net amount of accounts receivable,* the amount expected to be collected, rather than the gross amount. The difference between the gross and net amounts represents the estimated *uncollectible accounts,* or bad debts. These expenses are attributed to the year in which the sale is made, though they may be realized at a later date.

There are two methods of recording uncollectible accounts, the direct write-off method and the allowance method.

Direct Write-Off Method

In small businesses, losses that arise from uncollectible accounts are recognized in the accounts *in the period in which they become uncollectible.* Under this method, when an account is deemed uncollectible, it is written off the books by a debit to the expense account. Uncollectible Accounts Expense, and a credit to the individual customer's account and to the controlling account.

EXAMPLE 13

If William Anderson's $300 account receivable, dated May 15, 19X4, was deemed uncollectible in January 19X5, the entry in 19X5 would be:

Uncollectible Accounts Expense	300	
Accounts Receivable, William Anderson		300

Allowance Method

As has been stated before, one of the fundamentals of accounting is that revenue be matched with expenses in the same year. Under the direct write-off method, in Example 13, the loss was not recorded until a year after the revenue had been recognized. The allowance method does not permit this. The income statement for each period must include all losses and expenses related to the income earned *in that period*. Therefore, losses from uncollectible accounts should be deducted in the year the sale was made. Since it is impossible to predict which particular accounts will not be collected, an adjusting entry is made, usually at the end of the year.

EXAMPLE 14

Assume that in the first year of operation a firm has estimated that $2,000 of accounts receivable will be uncollectible. The adjusting entry would be:

Uncollectible Accounts Expense	2,000	
Allowance for Uncollectible Accounts		2,000

The credit balance of Allowance for Uncollectible Accounts (contra asset) appears on the balance sheet as a deduction from the total amount of Accounts Receivable:

Accounts Receivable	$29,920	
Less: Allowance for Uncollectible		
Accounts	2,000	$27,920

The $27,920 will become the estimated realizable value of the accounts receivable at that date. The uncollectible accounts expense will appear as an operating expense in the income statement.

12.7 COMPUTING UNCOLLECTIBLE ACCOUNTS

There are two generally accepted methods of calculating the amount of uncollectible accounts. One method is to use a flat percentage of the net sales for the year. The other method takes into consideration the ages of the individual accounts at the end of the fiscal year.

Percentage of Sales Method

Under the percentage of sales method, a fixed percentage of the total sales on account is taken. For example, if charge sales were $200,000 and experience has shown that approximately 1 percent of such sales will become uncollectible at a future date, the adjusting entry for the uncollectible accounts would be:

Uncollectible Accounts Expense	2,000	
Allowance for Uncollectible Accounts		2,000

The same amount is used whether or not there is a balance in Allowance for Uncollectible Accounts. However, if any substantial balance should accumulate in the allowance account, a change in the percentage figure would become appropriate.

Balance Sheet Method

Under the balance sheet method, every account is "aged"; that is, each item in its balance is related to the sale date. The further past due the account, the more probable it is that the customer is unwilling or unable to pay. A typical analysis is shown in Example 15.

EXAMPLE 15

Age of Account	Accounts Receivable Balance	Estimated Percent Uncollectible	Amount
1–30 days	$ 8,000	1%	$ 80
31–60 days	12,000	3%	360
61–90 days	6,000	5%	300
91–180 days	3,000	20%	600
Over 180 days	920	50%	460
	$29,920		$1,800

The calculated allowance for uncollectible accounts ($1,800 in Example 15) is reconciled at the end of the year with the actual balance in the allowance account, and an adjusting entry is made. The amount of the adjusting entry must take into consideration the balance of the Allowance for Uncollectible Accounts. The percentage of sales method does not follow this procedure.

EXAMPLE 16

The analysis showed that $1,800 would be required in the Allowance for Uncollectible Accounts at the end of the period. The Allowance for Uncollectible Accounts has a credit balance of $200. The adjusting entry at the end of the year would be:

Uncollectible Accounts Expense	1,600*	
Allowance for Uncollectible Accounts		1,600

*($1,800 − $200)

If, however, there had been a debit balance of $200, a credit to Allowance for Uncollectible Accounts of $2,000 would be necessary to bring the closing balance to $1,800.

When it becomes evident that a customer's account is uncollectible, it is written off the books. This is done by crediting Accounts Receivable (and the individual customer's account in the subsidiary ledger for the amount deemed uncollectible) and by debiting Allowance for Uncollectible Accounts. Note that there is no expense at this time, as it had already been estimated as a loss in the previous year.

EXAMPLE 17

John Andrew's account (a) was deemed uncollectible.

Allowance for Uncollectible Accounts	600	
Accounts Receivable, John Andrew		600

General Ledger   **Accounts Receivable Ledger**

Allowance for Uncollectible Accounts   John Andrew

(a)	600	Bal.	1,800

Bal.	600	(a)	600

Accounts Receivable

Bal.	29,920	(a)	600

12.8   RECOVERY OF UNCOLLECTIBLE ACCOUNTS

If a written-off account is later collected in full or in part (a *recovery of bad debts*), the write-off will be reversed for the amount received.

EXAMPLE 18

At a later date, Mr. Andrew (see Example 17) pays his account in full. The reversing entry (b) to restore his account will be:

Accounts Receivable, John Andrew	600	
Allowance for Uncollectible Accounts		600

A separate entry, (c), will then be made in the cash receipts journal to record the collection, debiting Cash $600 and crediting Accounts Receivable, John Andrew. If a partial collection was made, the reversing entry should be made for the amount recovered.

General Ledger   **Accounts Receivable Ledger**

Cash   John Andrew

(c)	600	

Bal.	600	(a)	600
(b)	600	(c)	600

Accounts Receivable

	29,200	(a)	600
(b)	600	(c)	600

Allowance for Uncollectible Accounts

(a)	600	Bal.	1,800
		(b)	600

Summary

1. If Robert Glatt issues an $800 note to Richard Tobey, Glatt is called the _____ and Tobey the _____ .

2. What effect does the acceptance of a note receivable, in settlement of an account, have on the total assets of a firm?

3. The holder of a note can usually obtain money by taking it to a bank and _____ it.

4. A note is written evidence of a _____.

5. When a payee discounts a note receivable, he or she creates a _____ liability.

6. The face of a note plus the interest due is known as _____.

7. Banks will normally take their discount on the _____ of the note.

8. A written promise to pay a creditor an amount of money in the future is known as a _____.

9. The _____ will be that amount of money that the maker of the note receives after the discount has been taken from the principal.

10. If many notes are issued by a firm, a _____ may be needed.

11. The two methods of recording uncollectible accounts are the _____ method and the _____ method.

12. There are two methods of calculating the amount of uncollectible accounts. They are the _____ method and the _____ method.

Answers: 1. maker, payee; 2. no effect—both are current assets; 3. discounting; 4. debit (obligation); 5. contingent; 6. maturity value; 7. maturity value; 8. note payable; 9. proceeds; 10. notes payable register; 11. direct write-off, allowance; 12. percentage of sales, balance sheet

Solved Problems

12.1 Below is an example of a note receivable.

> July 1, 19X5
>
> I, Ruth Brent, promise to pay Concord, Inc., $900, 90 days from date, at 14 percent interest.
>
> Ruth Brent

(*a*) Who is the maker of the note? (*b*) Who is the payee of the note? (*c*) What is the maturity date of the note? (*d*) What is the maturity value of the note?

SOLUTION

(*a*) Ruth Brent; (*b*) Concord, Inc.; (*c*) September 29; (*d*) $931.50

12.2 A note written on August 1 and due on November 15 was discounted on October 15. (*a*) How many days was the note written for? (*b*) How many days did the bank charge for in discounting the note?

SOLUTION

(*a*)	Aug. 2–31	30 days		(*b*)	Oct. 16–31	16 days
	Sept. 1–30	30 days			Nov. 1–15	15 days
	Oct. 1–31	31 days				31 days *Ans.*
	Nov. 1–15	15 days				
		106 days *Ans.*				

12.3 Determine the interest on the following notes: (*a*) $750 principal, 14 percent interest, 96 days; (*b*) $800 principal, 12 percent interest, 90 days.

SOLUTION

(*a*)	$750	14%	60 days	$17.50		(*b*)	$800	12%	60 days	$16
		14%	30 days	8.75				12%	30 days	8
		14%	6 days	1.75					90 days	$24 *Ans.*
			96 days	$28.00 *Ans.*						

12.4 A $4,000, ninety-day, 14 percent note receivable in settlement of an account, dated June 1, is discounted at 14 percent on July 1. Compute the proceeds of the note.

SOLUTION

$4,000.00	Principal
140.00	Interest income (90 days, 14%)
$4,140.00	Maturity value
96.60	Discount (60 days, 14% of maturity value)
$4,043.40	Proceeds

12.5 What are the entries needed to record the information in Problem 12.4 (*a*) on June 1? (*b*) on July 1?

(*a*)		
(*b*)		

SOLUTION

(a)	Notes Receivable	4,000.00	
	Accounts Receivable		4,000.00
(b)	Cash	4,043.40	
	Interest Income		43.40
	Notes Receivable		4,000.00

12.6 A $6,000, 120-day, 14 percent note receivable, dated September 1, is discounted at 14 percent on October 1. What is the entry needed on October 1?

SOLUTION

$6,000.00	Principal
280.00	Interest income (120 days at 14%)
$6,280.00	Maturity value
219.80	Discount (90 days, 14% of maturity value)
$6060.20	Proceeds

Cash	6,060.20	
Notes Receivable		6,000.00
Interest Income		60.20

12.7 Based on the information in Problem 12.6, what entry would be needed if the note were discounted immediately?

SOLUTION

$6,000.00	Principal
280.00	Interest income (120 days at 14%)
$6,280.00	Maturity value
293.07	Discount (120 days, 14% of maturity value)
$5,986.93	Proceeds

Cash	5,986.93	
Interest Expense	13.07	
Notes Receivable		6,000.00

Note: The proceeds are less than the principal because the note was discounted immediately at the same rate.

12.8 Record the following transactions in the books of John Agin Company:

    (*a*)   May 1   Received a $6,000, ninety-day, 15 percent note in settlement of the Stolloff account.

    (*b*)   May 31   Discounted the note at 15 percent at the bank.

    (*c*)   July 30   Stolloff paid the note in full.

(*a*)

(*b*)

(*c*)

SOLUTION

(*a*)	Notes Receivable	6,000.00	
	Accounts Receivable, Stolloff Company		6,000.00
(*b*)	Cash	6,069.37*	
	Interest Income		69.37
	Notes Receivable		6,000.00

*$6,000.00	Principal
225.00	Interest income
$6,225.00	Maturity value
155.63	Discount
$6,069.37	Proceeds

    (*c*)   No entry

12.9 If, in Problem 12.8, Stolloff dishonored his obligation on July 30 and a $15 protest fee was imposed by the bank, what entry would be required to record this information?

SOLUTION

Accounts Receivable, Stolloff Company	6,240*	
Cash		6,240

    *6,225 (maturity value) + $15 (protest fee) = $6,240.

12.10 Record the following transactions in the books of Carl Bresky:

    (*a*)   Sept. 5   Received an $8,000, ninety-day, 12 percent note in settlement of the M. Ribble account and immediately discounted it at 12 percent at the bank.

    (*b*)   Dec. 4   M. Ribble dishonored the note, and a protest fee of $20 was imposed.

    (*c*)   Dec. 31   M. Ribble paid her obligation, including the protest fee.

(a)

(b)

(c)

SOLUTION

(a)	Notes Receivable	8,000.00	
	Accounts Receivable—M. Ribble		8,000.00
	Cash	7,992.80*	
	Interest Expense	7.20	
	Notes Receivable		8,000.00

*$8,000.00	Principal
240.00	Interest income
$8,240.00	Maturity value
247.20	Discount
$7,992.80	Proceeds

(b)	Accounts Receivable—M. Ribble	8,260*	
	Cash		8,260
	*(Maturity value + protest fee)		
(c)	Cash	8,260	
	Accounts Receivable—M. Ribble		8,260

12.11 The Erin Corporation borrowed $5,000 for 90 days at 16 percent from the Sullivan National Bank. What entries are needed to (a) record the loan and (b) record the repayment?

(a)

(b)

SOLUTION

(a)	Cash	4,800	
	Interest Expense	200*	
	Notes Payable		5,000

*Interest for 90 days at 16 percent deducted in advance.

(b)	Notes Payable	5,000	
	Cash		5,000

12.12 Based on the information in Problem 12.11, what entry would be necessary if, after 90 days, Erin Corp. was unable to repay the loan and was granted another 90-day renewal?

SOLUTION

Interest Expense	200*	
Cash		200

*Only the interest has to be paid, since the note was renewed.

12.13 Record the following transactions in the books of B. K. Logging:

(a) June 1   Received a $10,000, ninety-day, 14% note in settlement of the McGraw account (dated June 1).
(b) July 1   Discounted the note at 16% at local bank.
(c) Aug. 30   Received notice that McGraw dishonored the note; paid the bank on the note plus $10 protest fee.
(d)   30   Contacted McGraw and received full payment on the same day.

Journal Entries

June 1			
July 1			
Aug. 30			
30			

SOLUTION

Journal Entries

June 1	Notes Receivable	10,000	
	Accounts Receivable		10,000
July 1	Cash	10,074	
	Interest Income		74
	Notes Receivable		10,000

Aug. 30	Accounts Receivable	10,360	
	Cash		10,360
30	Cash	10,360	
	Accounts Receivable		10,360

July 1: $10,000 \times 14\% = \$1,400 \times \dfrac{90 \text{ days}}{360 \text{ days}} = \$350$ interest

$10,000 Principal
     350 Interest
$10,350 Maturity value
     276 Discount
$10,074 Proceeds

August 30: $10,350 + $10 (protest fee)

12.14 Hill Top Diner borrowed $8,000 for 120 days at 15.75 percent from the local bank. The note was dated January 1. Show the entries recording the loan and the payback of the note.

Journal Entries

Jan. 1			
May 1			

SOLUTION

Journal Entries

Jan. 1	Cash	7,580	
	Interest Expense	420	
	Notes Payable		8,000
May 1	Notes Payable	8,000	
	Cash		8,000

12.15 Received a $20,000, ninety-day, 14.50 percent note from Sun Town Company on account (note was dated November 1). Sun Town paid the note on the due date. Show the entries for this transaction.

Journal Entries

Nov. 1			
Jan. 30			

SOLUTION

Journal Entries

Nov. 1	Notes Receivable	20,000	
	Accounts Receivable		20,000
Jan. 30	Cash	20,725	
	Interest Income		725
	Notes Receivable		20,000

12.16 From the preceding problem, what would the adjusting entry be on December 31 if that was the last day of the accounting period?

Journal Entry

Dec. 31			

SOLUTION

Journal Entry

Dec. 31	Interest Receivable	483.33	
	Interest Income		483.33*

*$20,000 \times 14.5\% \times \frac{1}{6}$ (November and December).

12.17 Record the following transactions in the books of Carl Klein:

(a) Sept. 5 Received an $8,000, ninety-day, 6 percent note in settlement of the Jeff Willens account and immediately discounted it at 6 percent at the bank.

(b) Dec. 4 Jeff Willens dishonored the note, and a protest fee of $20 was imposed.

(c) Dec. 31 Jeff Willens paid his obligation, including the protest fee.

(a)			
(b)			
(c)			

SOLUTION

(a)	Notes Receivable	8,000	
	Accounts Receivable, Jeff Willens		8,000

Cash	7,998.20*	
Interest Expense	1.80	
Notes Receivable		8,000

*$8,000.00	Principal
120.00	Interest income
$8,120.00	Maturity value
121.80	Discount
$7,998.20	Proceeds

(b)	Accounts Receivable, Jeff Willens	8,140*	
	Cash		8,140

*(Maturity value + protest fee)

(c)	Cash	8,140	
	Accounts Receivable, Jeff Willens		8,140

12.18 Shown are balances for Prurient Press:

Accounts Receivable	Sales	Allowance for Uncollectible Accounts
120,000	350,000	400

What is the adjusting entry needed to record the provision for uncollectible accounts if the uncollectible expense is estimated (a) as 1 percent of net sales? (b) by aging the accounts receivable, the allowance balance being estimated as $3,600?

(a)			
(b)			

SOLUTION

(a)	Uncollectible Accounts Expense	3,500*	
	Allowance for Uncollectible Accounts		3,500

(b)	Uncollectible Accounts Expense	3,200**	
	Allowance for Uncollectible Accounts		3,200

*1% of $350,000
**$3,600 − $400. The credit balance of $400 in allowance must be taken into consideration.

12.19 Below are some accounts of the Jay Balding Company, as of January 19X5.

General Ledger	Accounts Receivable Ledger
Accounts Receivable	**D. Grego**
210,000	1,400

General Ledger	Accounts Receivable Ledger
Allowance for Uncollectible Accounts	**J. Philips**
2,600	1,200

Prepare entries needed to record the following information:

(a) Mar. 5   D. Grego account was determined to be uncollectible
(b) Apr. 14 Wrote off J. Philips account as uncollectible

(a)

(b)

SOLUTION

(a)	Allowance for Uncollectible Accounts	1,400	
	Accounts Receivable, D. Grego		1,400

(b)	Allowance for Uncollectible Accounts	1,200	
	Accounts Receivable, J. Philips		1,200

12.20 If, in Problem 12.19, J. Philips later paid his account in full, what entries would be necessary?

SOLUTION

Accounts Receivable, J. Philips	1,200	
Allowance for Uncollectible Accounts		1,200
Cash	1,200	
Accounts Receivable, J. Philips		1,200

12.21 Using the aging schedule below, prepare the adjusting entry providing for the uncollectible accounts expense.

Amount	Age	Estimated Percent Uncollectible
$24,000	1–30 days	1%
18,000	31–60 days	3%
10,000	61–180 days	25%
6,000	181 days and over	60%

SOLUTION

Uncollectible Accounts Expense	6,880*	
Allowance for Uncollectible Accounts		6,880

*$ 240   1–30 days ($24,000 × 1%)

$ 540   31–60 days ($18,000 × 3%)

$2,500   61–180 days ($10,000 × 25%)

$3,600   181 days and over ($6,000 × 60%)

$6,880

Chapter 13

Controlling Cash

13.1 INTRODUCTION

In most firms, transactions involving the receipt and disbursement of cash far outnumber any other kinds of transactions. Cash is, moreover, the most liquid asset and most subject to theft and fraud. It is therefore essential to have a system of accounting procedures and records that will maintain adequate control over cash.

Cash is a medium of exchange and includes such items as currency, coin, demand deposits, savings deposits, petty cash funds, bank drafts, cashier's checks, personal checks, and money orders.

13.2 CONTROLLING CASH RECEIPTS

In a very small business, the owner-manager can maintain control through personal contact and supervision. In a larger firm, this kind of direct intervention must be replaced by a system of internal control, exercised through accounting reports and records.

The specific controls applied to cash receipts may be summarized as:

1. All receipts should be banked promptly.
2. Receipts from cash sales should be supported by sales tickets, cash register tapes, and so on.
3. Accountability should be established each time cash is transferred.
4. Persons receiving cash should not make disbursements of cash, record cash transactions, or reconcile bank accounts.

13.3 CONTROLLING CASH DISBURSEMENTS

Payments must be made only by properly authorized persons, equivalent value must be received, and documents must support the payment adequately. Following are specific internal controls relating to cash disbursements:

1. All disbursements, except petty cash payments, should be made by prenumbered check.
2. Vouchers and supporting documents should be submitted for review when checks are signed.
3. Persons who sign checks should not have access to cash receipts, should not have custody of funds or record cash entries, and should not reconcile bank accounts.

13.4 CONTROLLING CASH BALANCES

The basic principle of separation of duties is evident in the specific controls for cash balances:

1. Bank reconciliations should be prepared by persons who do not receive cash or sign checks.
2. Bank statements and paid checks should be received unopened by the person reconciling the account.
3. All cash funds on hand should be closely watched and surprise counts made at intervals.

If the rules of Section 13.2, 13.3, and 13.4 are followed, then it is clear that the monthly bank statement can be made a powerful control over cash balances—hence, the importance of reconciling bank balances.

13.5 BANK STATEMENTS

Checks

A business opens a checking account to gain the privilege of placing its deposits in a safe place and the ability also to write checks. When an account is opened, each person who is authorized to write checks on that account must sign a signature card. The bank keeps the signature card on file and compares it when checks are submitted. The check becomes a written notice by the depositor directing the bank to deduct a specific sum of money from the checking account and to pay that amount to the person or company written on the check. A check involves three parties:

1. Drawer—the firm that writes the check
2. Drawee—the bank on which the check is drawn
3. Payee—the person or company to whom the check is to be paid

Checks offer several advantages. The checkbook stubs provide a record of the cash paid out, while the cancelled checks provide proof that money has been paid to the person legally entitled to it. Also, the use of checks is the most convenient form of paying bills, because checks can be sent safely through the mail. If a check is lost or stolen, the depositors can request the bank not to pay (a stop order).

Endorsements

When a check is given to the bank for deposit, the depositor signs the check on the back to show that he or she accepts responsibility for the amount of that check. The depositor's signature is known as an *endorsement*. This endorsement transfers the ownership of the check and guarantees to the individual that the depositor will guarantee its payment. Different kinds of endorsements serve different needs:

1. ***Blank endorsement.***   A blank endorsement consists only of the name of the endorser. Its disadvantage lies in the fact that a lost or stolen check with a blank endorsement may be cashed by the finder or thief. Therefore, this type of endorsement should not be used unless the depositor is at the bank ready to make a deposit (Fig. 13-1).
2. ***Endorsement in full.***   Endorsement in full states that the check can be cashed or transferred only on the order of the person named in the endorsement (Fig. 13-2).
3. ***Restrictive endorsement.***   A restrictive endorsement limits the receiver of the check as to the use he or she can make of the funds collected. Usually this type of endorsement is done when checks are prepared for deposit (Fig. 13-3).

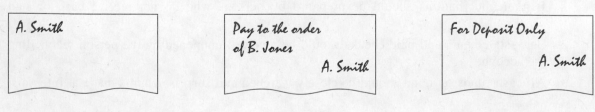

Fig. 13-1   Fig. 13-2   Fig. 13-3

Reconciliation

Banks customarily mail monthly statements to those firms that have checking accounts with them. These statements show the cash balance from the beginning of the month, all the deposits and payments recorded during the month, daily balances, and the ending balance. Cancelled checks, records of deposit, and other documents that support the data shown on the bank statement are forwarded to the depositor along with the statement. Examples of such documents might be a deduction (debit memorandum) for a bank service charge or an addition (credit memorandum) for the proceeds of a note collected by the bank for the depositor.

Usually the balance of the bank statement and the balance of the depositor's account will not agree. To prove the accuracy of both records, the reconciling differences have to be found and any necessary entries made. The reconciling items will fall into two broad groups: (1) those on the depositor's books but not recorded by the bank, and (2) those on the bank statement but not on the depositor's books. The statement used to reconcile this difference is known as the *bank reconciliation statement.*

Items on Books but Not on Bank Statement

Deposits in transit. Deposits in transit comprise cash receipts recorded by the company but too late to be deposited. The total of such deposits is added to the bank balance.

Outstanding checks. Outstanding checks are those issued by the depositor but not yet presented to the bank for payment. The total of these checks is deducted from the bank balance.

Errors. Bookkeeping errors arise in recording amounts of checks—for example, a transposition of figures. The item should be added to the bank balance if it was overstated and deducted if it was understated.

Items on Bank Statement but Not on Books

Service charges. The bank generally deducts amounts for bank services. The exact amount is usually not known by the depositor until the statement is received. The amount should be deducted from the book balance.

NSF (nonsufficient funds) checks. NSF checks have been deposited but cannot be collected because of insufficient funds in the account of the drawer of the check. The bank then issues a debit memorandum charging the depositor's account. The amount should be deducted from the book balance.

Collections. The bank collects notes and other items for a small fee. The bank then adds the proceeds to the account and issues a credit memorandum to the depositor. Often there are unrecorded amounts at the end of the month. The amounts should be added to the book balance.

Bank errors. Bank errors should not be entered on the books. They should be brought to the attention of the bank and corrected by the bank. Journal entries should be made for any adjustments to the book accounts. The statement used in accounting for the differences between the bank balance and the depositor's balance is known as a *bank reconciliation.*

EXAMPLE 1

The following information was available when the L. Etkind Company began to reconcile its bank balance on June 30, 19X5: balance per depositor's books, $1,640; balance per bank statement, $2,420; deposit in transit, $150; checks outstanding—no. 650 for $300 and no. 645 for $240; collection of $400 note plus interest of $8, $408; collection fee for note, $10; bank service charge, $6.

L. Etkind Company
Bank Reconciliation
June 30, 19X5

Balance per bank	$2,420	Balance per books	$1,638
Add: Deposit in transit	150	Add: Proceeds of note ($400 + 8)	408
	$2,570		$2,046
Less:		Less:	
Outstanding checks		Collection fee $10	
No. 650 $300		Service charge 6	
No. 645 240	540		16
Adjusted balance	$2,030	Adjusted balance	$2,030

Only reconciling items in the depositor's section (right side, above) are recorded on the books. The reconciling items in the bank section (left side, above) have already been recorded on the books and merely have not yet reached the bank. They will normally be included in the next bank statement.

To complete the reconcilement, the following two journal entries will be needed:

Entry 1	Cash	408	
	Notes Receivable		400
	Interest Income		8
Entry 2	Service Charge Expense	16	
	Cash		16

13.6 PETTY CASH

To eliminate the necessity of writing checks in very small amounts, it is customary to maintain a petty cash fund from which small disbursements are made. Examples are postage, delivery expense, telegrams, and so on.

Each disbursement from the petty cash fund should be accounted for by a receipt (a bill presented and signed by the payee at the time of payment). If no bill is presented, the one responsible for the fund should prepare a receipt similar to the one illustrated below and have the payee sign it. This is known as a *petty cash voucher*.

The face of the voucher should contain the following data:

(1) Receipt number
(2) Date of disbursement
(3) Name of payee
(4) Amount of the expenditure
(5) Purpose for which the expenditure was made
(6) Account affected by the expenditure
(7) Signature of payee

Petty Cash Voucher

(1) No. _____	(2) Date _____	
(3) Paid to _____	(4) Amount $ _____	
(5) Reason _____		
(6) Account to be charged _____		
(7) Received by _____		

Under the *imprest* system, a fund is established for a fixed petty cash amount, and this fund is periodically reimbursed by a single check for amounts expended. The steps in setting up and maintaining the petty cash fund are as follows:

1. An estimate is made of the total of the small amounts likely to be disbursed over a short period, usually a month. A check is drawn for the estimated total and put into the fund. The only time an entry is made in the petty cash account is to establish the fund initially, unless at some later time it is determined that this fund must be increased or decreased.

EXAMPLE 2   A Petty Cash Fund of $100 Is Established.

$$\text{Petty Cash} \qquad 100$$
$$\qquad \text{Cash} \qquad\qquad 100$$

2. The individual in charge of petty cash usually keeps the money in a locked box along with petty cash vouchers. The petty cash voucher, when signed by the recipient, acts as a receipt and provides information concerning the transaction. As each payment is made, the voucher is entered in the petty cash record under the heading, "Payments."

3. The amount paid is then distributed to the account affected.

4. The columns are totaled in order to determine the amount chargeable to each account.

EXAMPLE 3

Petty Cash Record

Date	Explanation	Voucher	Receipts	Payments	Postage	Del.	Sundry
Jan. 1	Established		$100.00				
2	Postage on sales	1		$ 10.00	$10.00		
4	Telegram	2		6.00	6.00		
8	Taxi fare	3		10.00		$10.00	
10	Coffee for overtime	4		4.00			$ 4.00
15	Stamps	5		18.00	18.00		
26	Cleaning windows	6		12.00			12.00
			$100.00	$ 60.00	$34.00	$10.00	$16.00
	Balance			40.00			
			$100.00	$100.00			
Feb. 1	Balance		$ 40.00				
	Replenished fund		60.00				

5. A check is then drawn in an amount equaling the total amount disbursed.

6. When the check is cashed, the money is replaced in the fund to restore it to the original amount.

7. Each amount listed in the distribution section of the petty cash fund is entered as a debit to the individual expense. The total amount of the check is credited to Cash.

   The petty cash record established in Example 3 would yield the following entry for the first month:

Postage Expense	34	
Delivery Expense	10	
Sundry Expense	16	
Cash		60

8. Proof of petty cash is obtained by counting the currency and adding the amount of all the vouchers in the cash box. The total should agree with the amount in the ledger for the petty cash fund. If it does not, the entry in the cash disbursements journal that records the reimbursement of the petty cash fund will have to include an account known as *Cash Short and Over*. A cash shortage is debited, a cash overage is credited to this account. Cash Short and Over is closed out at the end of the year into the expense and income account and is treated as a general expense (if a debit balance) or miscellaneous income (if a credit balance).

EXAMPLE 4

If, in Example 3, the amount of cash remaining was not $40 but $38, the $2 difference would be the amount considered to be short. The entry would then become:

Postage Expense	34	
Delivery Expense	10	
Sundry Expense	16	
Cash Short and Over	2	
Cash		62

Summary

1. The most liquid asset and also the one most subject to theft and fraud is _____ .

2. All disbursements, except petty cash payments, should be made by _____ .

3. A written notice by a depositor instructing his bank to deduct a specific sum from his account and to pay it to the person assigned is known as a _____ .

4. A check involves three parties: the _____ , who writes the check; the _____ , the bank on which it is drawn; and the _____ , the person to whom it is to be paid.

5. The signature on the back of a check showing that the individual accepts responsibility for that amount is known as an _____ .

6. The _____ endorsement poses the greatest threat in the event of a lost or stolen check.

7. A bank service charge is evidenced by a _____ .

8. A check that has been deposited but cannot be collected because of insufficient funds is labeled _____ and is deducted from the _____ balance.

9. Under the _____ , a fund is established for a fixed petty cash amount that is reimbursed by a single check for amounts expended.

10. If a proof of petty cash is impossible, the account _____ will have to be used.

Answers: 1. cash; 2. prenumbered check; 3. check; 4. drawer, drawee, payee; 5. endorsement; 6. blank; 7. debit memorandum; 8. NSF, book; 9. imprest system; 10. Cash Short and Over

Solved Problems

13.1 Below is an example of a check.

> No. 136
>
> 70-4217 / 711
>
> *January 25,* 19 *X5*
>
> Pay to the Order of *Jason Sloane* _____ $ *75⁰⁰/₁₀₀*
>
> *Seventy-five and* ⁰⁰/₁₀₀ _____ Dollars
>
> WHITESIDE COUNTY BANK
> Rock Falls, Illinois 61071   *B. Smith*
>
> ⑈07⑈⑈⑈42⑈7⑈⑈ 89⑈⑈7602⑈⑈

(a) Who is the drawer?

(b) Who is the drawee?

(c) Who is the payee?

SOLUTION

(a) B. Smith

(b) Whiteside County Bank

(c) Jason Sloane

13.2 (*a*) Assume that J. Lerner, banking at 1st City Bank, wishes a full endorsement for A. Levy. Present below the needed endorsement.

(*b*) A blank endorsement is needed instead.

(*c*) A restrictive endorsement for a deposit is needed instead.

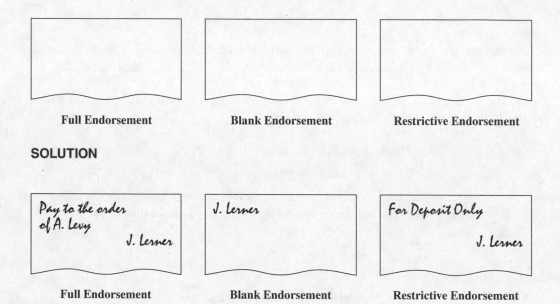

| Full Endorsement | Blank Endorsement | Restrictive Endorsement |

SOLUTION

Pay to the order of A. Levy J. Lerner	J. Lerner	For Deposit Only J. Lerner
Full Endorsement	**Blank Endorsement**	**Restrictive Endorsement**

13.3 In order to produce equal adjusted balances for A & J Company, indicate whether each of items 1–8 below should be:

(*a*) Added to the bank statement balance

(*b*) Deducted from the bank statement balance

(*c*) Added to the depositor's balance

(*d*) Deducted from the depositor's balance

(*e*) Exempted from the bank reconciliation statement

1. Statement includes a credit memorandum, representing the collection of the proceeds of a note left at the bank.

2. A credit memorandum representing the proceeds of a loan made to A & J Company by the bank.

3. Deposits in transit.

4. Seven outstanding checks were not recorded on the statement.

5. A customer's check that A & J Company had deposited was returned with "nonsufficient funds" stamped across the face.

6. The bank erroneously charged someone else's check against A & J's account.

7. A & J Company was credited on the bank statement with the receipt from another depositor.

8. A $96 check was erroneously recorded in A & J's check stubs as $69.

SOLUTION

1. (*c*); 2. (*c*); 3. (*a*); 4. (*b*); 5. (*d*); 6. (*a*); 7. (*b*); 8. (*d*)

13.4 At the close of the day, the total cash sales as determined by the sales registers were $1,580. However, the total cash receipts amounted to only $1,570. The error cannot be located at the present time. What entry should be made to record the cash sales for the day?

SOLUTION

Cash	1,570	
Cash Short and Over	10	
Sales Income		1,580

13.5 Of the following transactions involving the bank reconciliation statement, which ones necessitate an adjusting entry on the depositor's books?

(a) Outstanding checks of $3,000 did not appear on the bank statement.

(b) The last 2 days' deposited receipts, $2,850, did not appear on the bank statement.

(c) The depositor's check for $120 for supplies was written in her records as $210.

(d) Bank service charge, $4.

(e) A note left at the bank for collection, $822, was paid and credited to the depositor's account.

SOLUTION

(c)	Cash	90	
	Supplies		90
(d)	Service Charge Expense	4	
	Cash		4
(e)	Cash	822	
	Notes Receivable		822

13.6 Using the following data, reconcile the bank account of the Kemper Motor Company.

    1. Bank balance, $7,780.

    2. Depositor's balance, $6,500.

    3. Note collected by bank, $1,000, plus interest of $30; a collection charge of $10 was made by the bank.

    4. Outstanding checks, $410.

    5. Deposit in transit, $150.

SOLUTION

Balance per bank statement	$7,780	Balance per Kemper's books		$6,500
Add: Deposit in transit	150	Add: Note collected by bank		
	$7,930	Note	$1,000	
Less:		Interest	30	1,030
				$7,530
Outstanding checks	410	Less: Collection charge		10
Adjusted balance	$7,520	Adjusted balance		$7,520

13.7 Prepare the adjusting entries needed for Problem 13.6.

SOLUTION

Cash	1,030	
Notes Receivable		1,000
Interest Income		30
Service Charge Expense	10	
Cash		10

13.8 Correct the following incorrect bank reconciliation proof.

Kaney Company
Bank Reconciliation
December 31, 19X5

Balance per depositor's books		$7,250
Add:		
Note collected by bank including interest	515	
Deposit in transit	1,200	
Bank error charging Kane's check to Kaney account	860	
Total		$9,825
Deduct:		
Check from customer of J. Brown deposited and		
returned by bank as NSF	$ 150	
Service charge	5	
Check for $250 written in Kaney's ledger for		
supplies and checkbook stubs as $150	100	
Outstanding checks	1,100	1,355
		$8,470
Less: Unexplained difference		1,920
Balance per bank statement		$6,550

SOLUTION

Kaney Company
Bank Reconciliation
December 31, 19X5

Balance per bank statement	$6,550		Balance per depositor's books		$7,250
Add:			Add:		
Deposit in transit	1,200		Note collected by bank		515
Error	860				$7,765
	$8,610		Less:		
			NSF	$150	
Less:			Bank Service Charge	5	
Outstanding checks	1,100		Error	100	255
Adjusted balance	$7,510		Adjusted balance		$7,510

13.9 Prepare the adjusting entries needed for Problem 13.8.

SOLUTION

Cash	515	
Notes Receivable		515
Service Charge Expense	5	
Accounts Receivable—J. Brown	150	
Supplies	100	
Cash		255

13.10 Halls Gift Shop prepares monthly bank reconciliations. From the following data, prepare the July bank reconciliation.

1. Balance per bank statement, $21,700
2. Balance per checkbook, $15,178
3. Note collected by bank, $525 plus $41 interest
4. Outstanding checks:

No. 947	$1,117
No. 953	2,728
No. 957	573
No. 963	1,789
No. 971	770

5. Bank service charge, $19
6. Deposit in transit, $1002

Halls Gift Shop
Bank Reconciliation
July 31, 19X5

Balance per bank statement	
Balance per checkbook	

SOLUTION

Halls Gift Shop
Bank Reconciliation
July 31, 19X5

Balance per bank statement	$21,700
Add: Deposit in transit	1,002
	$22,702
Less: Outstanding checks	6,977
Correct bank balance	$15,725
Balance per checkbook	$15,178
Note plus interest collected by bank	566
	$15,744
Less: Bank service charge	19
Correct book balance	$15,725

13.11 From the following data, prepare a bank reconciliation for the Big Red Company for the month of May:

1. Balance per bank statement, $7,915.

2. Balance per checkbook, $5,140.

3. Deposit in transit, $475.

4. Outstanding checks, $2,170.

5. Note collected by bank, $1,000 plus $110 interest.

6. Bank service charge, $21.

7. A check written in the amount of $98 for supplies was entered in the checkbook as $89.

Big Red Company
Bank Reconciliation
May 31, 19X5

BANK		CHECKBOOK	

SOLUTION

Big Red Company
Bank Reconciliation
May 31, 19X5

BANK		CHECKBOOK		
Balance per bank statement	$7,915	Balance per checkbook		$5,140
Add: Deposit in transit	475	Add: Note and interest		1,110
	8,390			$6,250
Less: Outstanding checks	2,170	Less: Checkbook error	9	
		Bank Service Charge	21	
				30
Correct bank balance	$6,220			$6,220

13.12 Transactions for the Fred Saltzman Co. for the month of January, pertaining to the establishment of a petty cash fund, were as follows:

Jan. 1 Established an imprest petty cash fund of $50.

31 Box contained $6 cash and paid vouchers for transportation, $14; freight, $16; charity, $4; office supplies, $6; miscellaneous expense, $4.

What are the journal entries necessary to record the petty cash information?

SOLUTION

Petty Cash	50	
Cash		50
Transportation Expense	14	
Freight Expense	16	
Charity Expense	4	
Office Supplies Expense	6	
Miscellaneous Expense	4	
Cash		44

13.13 If, in Problem 13.12, the cash on hand was $9, record the January 31 reimbursement.

SOLUTION

Transportation Expense	14	
Freight Expense	16	
Charity Expense	4	
Office Supplies Expense	6	
Miscellaneous Expense	4	
Cash		41
Cash Short and Over		3

13.14 If, in Problem 13.12, the cash on hand was only $2, record the January 31 reimbursement. What will happen to the Cash Short and Over account?

SOLUTION

Transportation Expense	14	
Freight Expense	16	
Charity Expense	4	
Office Supplies Expense	6	
Miscellaneous Expense	4	
Cash Short and Over	4	
Cash		48

Chapter 14

Payroll

14.1 GROSS PAY

The pay rate at which employees are paid is generally arrived at through negotiations between the employer and the employees. The employer, however, must conform with all applicable federal and state laws (minimum wage, and so on). One law requires that workers, excluding salaried workers or workers in industries such as hotels and restaurants, be compensated at one and one-half times their regular pay for hours worked over 40.

Gross pay for wage earners is generally computed by using an individual time card.

Time Card

Name _____		Pay Rate/Hour _____
Week Ended _____		
	Time In	Time Out	Hours
Monday	_____	_____	_____
Tuesday	_____	_____	_____
Wednesday	_____	_____	_____
Thursday	_____	_____	_____
Friday	_____	_____	_____
Approved _____	Total Hours for Week		_____

EXAMPLE 1

The computation of Carol Johnson's gross pay appears below.

Time Card

Name	Carol Johnson	Pay Rate/Hour	$7.50
Week Ended	7/18/X5		
	Time In	Time Out	Hours
Monday	8:00 A.M.	4:00 P.M.	8
Tuesday	8:00 A.M.	6:00 P.M.	10
Wednesday	8:00 A.M.	7:00 P.M.	11
Thursday	8:00 A.M.	4:00 P.M.	8
Friday	8:00 A.M.	5:00 P.M.	9
Approved _____	Total Hours for Week		46

$$\begin{aligned}
\text{Regular pay: } 40 \text{ hours} \times \$7.50 &= \$300.00 \\
\text{Overtime pay: } 6 \text{ hours} \times 1\tfrac{1}{2} \times \$7.50 &= \underline{67.50} \\
\text{Gross pay: } &= \underline{\$367.50}
\end{aligned}$$

14.2 DEDUCTIONS FROM GROSS PAY

Federal Withholding Taxes

Federal income taxes are withheld from gross pay on a pay-as-you-go-system. The amount to withhold from each employee is determined after consideration of the following four factors:

1. The amount of gross pay
2. The taxpayer's filing status (married or single)
3. The number of exemptions claimed by the taxpayer
4. The payroll period

The employee's filing status and number of exemptions claimed is determined by referring to Form W 4, filled out by each employee when he or she began to work (see Fig. 14-1).

Form **W-4** Department of the Treasury Internal Revenue Service	**Employee's Withholding Allowance Certificate** ▶ For Privacy Act and Paperwork Reduction Act Notice, see reverse.	OMB No. 1545-0010 **199–**
1 Type or print your first name and middle initial Last name		2 Your social security number
Home address (number and street or rural route)	3 ☐ Single ☐ Married ☐ Married, but withhold at higher Single rate **Note:** *If married, but legally separated, or spouse is a nonresident alien, check the Single box.*	
City or town, state, and ZIP code	4 If your last name differs from that on your social security card, check here and call 1-800-772-1213 for more information ⋯ ▶ ☐	

5 Total number of allowances you are claiming (from line G above or from the worksheets on page 2 if they apply) . **5**
6 Additional amount, if any, you want withheld from each paycheck . . . . **6** $
7 I claim exemption from withholding and I certify that I meet **ALL** of the following conditions for exemption:
  • Last year I had a right to a refund of **ALL** Federal income tax withheld because I had **NO** tax liability; **AND**
  • This year I expect a refund of **ALL** Federal income tax withheld because I expect to have **NO** tax liability; **AND**
  • This year if my income exceeds $600 and includes nonwage income, another person cannot claim me as a dependent.
  If you meet all of the above conditions, enter "EXEMPT" here . . . . ▶ **7**

Under penalties of perjury, I certify that I am entitled to the number of withholding allowances claimed on this certificate or entitled to claim exempt status.

Employee's signature ▶	Date ▶ , 19	
8 Employer's name and address (Employer: Complete 8 and 10 only if sending to the IRS)	9 Office code (optional)	10 Employer identification number

Fig. 14-1

How many exemptions can an employee claim? An employee is entitled to one personal exemption and one for his or her spouse and each dependent.

EXAMPLE 2

Bill MacDonald's gross pay for the week is $545. He is married and claims four exemptions. The federal tax to be withheld is $35. (Tables may be used for computation of federal income tax withholding. The two tables that follow are used for example only.)

MARRIED Persons—WEEKLY Payroll Period

If the wages are-		And the number of withholding allowances claimed is—										
At least	But less than	0	1	2	3	④	5	6	7	8	9	10
		The amount of income tax to be withheld is—										
400	410	42	35	28	21	14	7	0	0	0	0	0
410	420	44	37	30	23	16	9	2	0	0	0	0
420	430	45	38	31	24	17	10	3	0	0	0	0
430	440	47	40	33	26	19	12	5	0	0	0	0
440	450	48	41	34	27	20	13	6	0	0	0	0
450	460	50	43	36	29	22	15	8	0	0	0	0
460	470	51	44	37	30	23	16	9	2	0	0	0
470	480	53	46	39	32	25	18	11	3	0	0	0
480	490	54	47	40	33	26	19	12	5	0	0	0
490	500	56	49	42	35	28	21	14	6	0	0	0
500	510	57	50	43	36	29	22	15	8	1	0	0
510	520	59	52	45	38	31	24	17	9	2	0	0
520	530	60	53	46	39	32	25	18	11	4	0	0
530	540	62	55	48	41	34	27	20	12	5	0	0
540	550	63	56	49	42	㉟	28	21	14	7	0	0
550	560	65	58	51	44	37	30	23	15	8	1	0

EXAMPLE 3

Barbara Ledina earns $545 for the week. She is single and claims zero exemptions. The amount of the tax to be withheld is $85.

SINGLE Persons—WEEKLY Payroll Period

If the wages are-		And the number of withholding allowances claimed is—										
At least	But less than	⓪	1	2	3	4	5	6	7	8	9	10
		The amount of income tax to be withheld is—										
400	410	53	46	39	32	25	18	11	4	0	0	0
410	420	55	48	41	34	27	19	12	5	0	0	0
420	430	56	49	42	35	28	21	14	7	0	0	0
430	440	58	51	44	37	30	22	15	8	1	0	0
440	450	59	52	45	38	31	24	17	10	3	0	0
450	460	61	54	47	40	33	25	18	11	4	0	0
460	470	63	55	48	41	34	27	20	13	6	0	0
470	480	65	57	50	43	36	28	21	14	7	0	0
480	490	68	58	51	44	37	30	23	16	9	2	0
490	500	71	60	53	46	39	31	24	17	10	3	0
500	510	74	61	54	47	40	33	26	19	12	5	0
510	520	77	63	56	49	42	34	27	20	13	6	0
520	530	79	66	57	50	43	36	29	22	15	8	1
530	540	82	69	59	52	45	37	30	23	16	9	2
540	550	㊴	72	60	53	46	39	32	25	18	11	4

Social Security Taxes (Federal Insurance Contributions Act—FICA)

The FICA tax helps pay for federal programs for old age and disability benefits, Medicare, and insurance benefits to survivors. During the working years of an employee, funds will be set aside from his or her earnings (Social Security taxes). When the employee's earnings cease because of disability, retirement, or death, the funds are made available to his or her dependents or survivors.

Currently (1994), a combined tax rate of 7.65 percent [6.2 percent for old-age, survivors, and disability insurance (OASDI) and 1.45 percent for hospital insurance (Medicare)] is imposed on both employer and employee. The OASDI rate (6.2 percent applies to wages within the OASDI wage base, which is $60,600 for 1994. The Medicare rate (1.45 percent) applies to all wages earned during the year regardless of the amount earned.

EXAMPLE 4

Carol's earnings prior to this week were $50,000. This week her salary was $500. Her FICA deduction is:

$$\$500 \times 0.062\% = \$31.00$$
$$\$500 \times 0.0145\% = \underline{7.25}$$
$$\$38.25$$

If she had earned $60,600 prior to the pay period, her FICA deduction would be:

$$\$100^* \times 0.062\% = \$\ 6.20$$
$$\$500 \times 0.0145\% = \underline{7.25}$$
$$\$\ 13.45$$

---

*Maximum is based on $60,600.

If an individual works for more than one employer during a year, each employer must withhold and pay taxes on the first $60,600. The employee is granted a refund from the government if he or she exceeds the $60,600 Social Security base.

Notice that the withholding of any wages represents, from the employer's viewpoint, a liability, because the employer must pay to the government the amount withheld from the employee.

State and Local Withholding Taxes

Most states and some cities impose a tax on the gross earnings of each residential employee. These taxes are also withheld from the employee's pay and turned over periodically by the employer to the appropriate agency.

Other Deductions

All the deductions discussed so far have been mandatory. Often, through agreement with the employer, amounts will be withheld for retirement plans, union dues, savings bonds, insurance, and other deductions.

EXAMPLE 5

Harold Eccleston earned $575 for the week. Deductions from his pay were: federal withholding, $82.00; total FICA, $43.99; state tax, $23; and union dues, $16. What is his net pay?

$$\text{Net pay} = \$575 - (\$82 + \$43.99 + \$23 + \$16)$$
$$= \$575 - \$164.99$$
$$= \$410.01$$

14.3 THE PAYROLL SYSTEM

The payroll system generally consists of input data (time cards), a payroll register (to compute the payroll each payroll period), individual earnings cards (a separate record for each employee), paychecks, and a system for recording both the payroll and the related employer taxes with appropriate liabilities.

Individual Time Card

Although the overall payroll is recorded in a payroll register, it is also necessary to know both the earnings and the deductions for *each* employee separately. These individual records facilitate the preparation of required governmental reports and assist the employer in maintaining control over payroll expenditures. They also act as convenient references to basic employee information such as earnings to date, exemptions, filing status, and employee classification. Information from the payroll register is posted *immediately* after recording the payroll to the individual earnings cards.

Individual Earnings Card

Name _____	Filing Status _____
Address _____	Exemptions Claimed _____
_____	Position _____
S.S. No. _____	Pay Rate ____ Per _____

First Quarter

| Payroll Period | Gross | | | Deductions | | | | | | Net | |
	Reg.	Ot.	Total	FICA Soc. Sec.	Medicare	Fed. With.	State With.	Oth. Ded.	Total Ded.	Net Pay	Ck. No.
First quarter											

Payroll Register

A payroll register is a specially designed form used at the close of each payroll period (weekly, biweekly, and so on) to summarize and compute the payroll for the period. Although the design of this form may vary slightly depending on desired information and the degree of automation, most contain the same basic information.

Refer to the payroll register (Table 14.1) and note that it is broken into five sections:

(1) Computation of gross earnings (regular, overtime, total).

(2) Taxable earnings (information only), used as a reference to computer FICA tax withheld or paid by the employer and unemployment tax payable by the employer.

(3) Deductions from gross pay—a place is provided for each tax withheld and for miscellaneous deductions (coded).

(4) Net pay. This is the employee's take-home pay. This may be checked by adding the total of deductions to the net pay. The result should be the gross pay.

(5) Gross salaries charged to specific accounts.

EXAMPLE 6

Using the data in Table 14.2, record the payroll as of June 15 for Atlas Company in Table 14.3.

14.4 RECORDING THE PAYROLL

The payroll is generally recorded initially in the general journal. Since the payroll register is the input for the entry, it is generally totaled for the payroll period and proved before any entry is made.

Table 14.1　Payroll Register

Date	Name	(1) Gross Pay			(2) Taxable		(3) Deductions							(4) Net		(5) Distribution	
		Reg.	Ot.	Total	FICA	Unemp.	FICA Social Security	Medicare	Fed. With.	State With.	Code	Oth. Ded.	Total Ded.	Net Pay	Ck. No.	Office Salaries	Factory Salaries

Table 14.2　Payroll Data

Name	(Prior to Payroll) Earnings to Date	Gross Pay			Classification	Fed. With.	FICA		State With.	Other Deductions
		Reg.	Ot.	Total			Social Security	Medicare		
P. Smith	$5,800	$360	$45	$405	Office	$38.00	$25.11	$5.87	$17.00	Union A, $11.00
S. Jones	8,200	320	—	320	Office	45.00	19.84	4.64	15.30	—
R. Campbell	6,900	280	84	364	Factory	31.00	22.57	5.28	13.30	Union A, $9.00

Table 14.3　Payroll Register

Date	Name	Gross Pay			Taxable		Deductions							Net		Distribution	
		Reg.	Ot.	Total	FICA	Unemp.	FICA Social Security	Medicare	Fed. With.	State With.	Code	Oth. Ded.	Total Ded.	Net Pay	Ck. No.	Office Salaries	Factory Salaries
6/15	P. Smith	360	45	405	405	$405*	25.11	5.37	38.00	17.00	A	11.00	96.98	308.02	44	405	
6/15	S. Jones	320	—	320	320	-0-*	19.84	4.64	45.00	15.30		-0-	84.78	235.22	45	320	
6/15	R. Campbell	280	84	364	364	100*	22.57	5.28	31.00	13.30	A	9.00	81.15	282.85	46		364
	Total	960	129	1,089	1,089	$505	67.52	15.79	114.00	45.60		20.00	262.91	826.09		725	364

*Only first $7,000 is subject to unemployment tax.

EXAMPLE 7

From the data summarized in Example 6, record the payroll in general journal form.

General Journal

Date	Description	P.R.	Debit	Credit
June 15	Office Salaries Expense		725.00	
	Factory Salaries Expense	.	364.00	
	FICA—Social Security Payable			67.52
	FICA—Medicare Payable			15.79
	Federal Withholding Tax Payable			114.00
	State Withholding Tax Payable			45.60
	Union Dues Payable			20.00
	Salaries Payable			826.09
	To record the payroll for the week ended June 15			

Payroll Taxes Imposed on the Employer

Social Security (Federal Insurance Contributions Act).   Not only is Social Security (FICA) withheld from the employee's pay, but a matching amount is paid in by the employer and is reported quarterly by the employer on the federal form 941 along with federal withholding tax. This tax payment is made at a member bank of the Federal Reserve.

Unemployment Taxes.   Employers are required to pay unemployment taxes to both the federal and state governments. Under current legislation, the tax is imposed only on the first $7,000 of each employee's earnings. Although the typical state unemployment tax rate is 5.4 percent, rates vary depending on the state, the nature of the business, and the employer's experience with unemployment. For the current year (1994), the official federal unemployment tax rate is 6.2 percent. However, as long as the employer is up to date on the state tax, the employer is allowed an automatic credit of 5.4 percent no matter what rate the employer actually pays. The effective federal unemployment tax rate is therefore 0.8 percent.

Table 14.4   Payroll Taxes

Tax	Paid by		Rate
	Employee	Employer	
FICA—Social Security	Yes	Yes	6.2% on first $60,600 of employee's wages each year*
FICA—Medicare	Yes	Yes	1.45% on all wages earned*
Fed. Income	Yes	No	Varies with exemptions; based on table
Fed. Unemp.	No	Yes	0.8% of first $7,000
State Unemp.	No	Yes	Up to 5.4% of first $7,000

*Subject to statutory change.

Recording the Employer's Taxes

When the payroll entry is recorded, the employer's contribution is also recorded.

EXAMPLE 8

From the data summarized in the payroll register in Table 14.3, record the employer's taxes for the payroll period. (Assume a 5 percent state unemployment tax rate and a 0.8 percent federal rate.)

General Journal

Date	Description	P.R.	Debit	Credit
June 15	Payroll Tax Expense		112.60	
	FICA—Social Security Payable*			67.52
	FICA—Medicare Payable*			15.79
	State Unemployment Insurance Payable†			25.25
	Federal Unemployment Insurance Payable†			4.04
	To record the employers taxes for the week ended June 15			

*Must match employee's contribution.

†Note that by reference to the payroll register (taxable unemployment), only $505.00 is subject to the tax.

Summary

1. Compensation is paid at the rate of time and one-half when an employee works more than _____ hours.

2. The amount of federal income tax withheld from a person is based on the individual's _____ and _____ .

3. Form _____ will yield information pertaining to the number of exemptions an employee is filing.

4. The rate of the total FICA tax is _____ percent.

5. FICA is reported _____ by the employer on Form _____ .

6. The payroll _____ is the input for the payroll entry.

7. Generally, all payroll entries are recorded in the _____ journal.

8. The two types of payroll taxes imposed on the employer are _____ and _____ .

9. The payroll tax expense entry is recorded in the _____ journal.

10. The one tax that is paid by the employee and matched by the employer is _____ .

Answers: 1. 40; 2. filing status, number of exemptions; 3. W-4; 4. 7.65%; 5. quarterly, 941; 6. register; 7. general; 8. FICA, unemployment; 9. general; 10. FICA

Solved Problems

14.1   Below is a time card for Laura Anthony. Complete the hours section of her time card and compute her gross pay.

Time Card

Name	Laura Anthony		Pay Rate/Hour	$8.00
Week Ended	9/20/X5			
	Time In	**Time Out**		**Hours**
Monday	8:00 A.M.	4:00 P.M.		
Tuesday	8:00 A.M.	4:00 P.M.		
Wednesday	8:00 A.M.	6:00 P.M.		
Thursday	8:00 A.M.	7:30 P.M.		
Friday	8:00 A.M.	6:30 P.M.		
Approved		Total Hours for Week		

SOLUTION

Time Card

Name	Laura Anthony		Pay Rate/Hour	$8.00
Week Ended	9/20/X5			
	Time In	**Time Out**		**Hours**
Monday	8:00 A.M.	4:00 P.M.		8
Tuesday	8:00 A.M.	4:00 P.M.		8
Wednesday	8:00 A.M.	6:00 P.M.		10
Thursday	8:00 A.M.	7:30 P.M.		$11\frac{1}{2}$
Friday	8:00 A.M.	6:30 P.M.		$10\frac{1}{2}$
Approved		Total Hours for Week		48

Regular pay: 40 hours × $8.00   = $320.00
Overtime pay: 8 hours × $12.00* =   96.00
Total gross pay   = $416.00

*Time and one-half rate.
8 hours overtime × 1.5 = $12.00 per hour for overtime
$12.00 × 8 hours overtime = $96.00 for overtime

14.2   How many exemptions are permitted to be claimed on Form W-4 in the following cases:
   (*a*) Taxpayer and spouse (nonworking)
   (*b*) Taxpayer, spouse, and two children
   (*c*) Taxpayer, spouse, and mother she fully supported

SOLUTION

(a) 2; (b) 4; (c) 3

14.3 How much FICA tax will be withheld from the following employees?

Employee	Amount Earned Prior to Current Payroll	Amount Earned This Week	Amount Withheld for FICA	
			Soc. Sec.	Medicare
(a) I. Blanton	$26,000	$600	?	?
(b) P. Burday	60,200	700	?	?
(c) M. Fleming	61,000	750	?	?

SOLUTION

	Soc. Sec.	Medicare
(a)	$37.20	$8.70
(b)	$24.80*	$10.15
(c)	$ 0 **	$10.88

*$400 balance subject
**Maximum reached

14.4 Complete the table below based on the employer's payroll obligation. Assume a state rate of 4 percent and a federal rate of 0.8 percent.

Employee	Amount Earned This Week	Accumulated Earnings	Total FICA	Federal Unemployment	State Unemployment
(a) B. Orzech	$550	$5,300	$42.07	?	?
(b) M. Felson	475	6,725	36.34	?	?
(c) H. Hendricks	610	7,900	46.66	?	?

SOLUTION

	Federal Unemployment	State Unemployment
(a)	$4.40	$22.00
(b)	2.20*	11.00†
(c)	None	None

*Federal rate is 0.8 percent on first $7,000; balance subject to tax is $275.00.
†State rate is 4 percent on first $7,000; balance subject to tax is $275.00.

14.5 Judy Bagon worked 44 hours during the first week in February of the current year. The pay rate is $9.00 per hour. Withheld from her wages were FICA; federal income tax $47.00; hospitalization $7.20. Prepare the necessary payroll entry.

SOLUTION

Salaries Expense	414.00*	
FICA—Social Security Payable		25.67
FICA—Medicare Payable		6.00
Federal Income Tax Payable		47.00
Hospitalization Payable		7.20
Salaries Payable		328.13

*40 hours × $9 = $360.00 (regular)
4 hours × $13.50 = 54.00 (overtime)
$414.00

14.6 Based on the information in Problem 14.5, what is the entry to record the employer's payroll tax if it is assumed the state tax rate is 4 percent and the federal unemployment rate is 0.8 percent? (Prior to payroll) earnings to date = $5,100.00.

SOLUTION

Payroll Tax Expense	51.54	
FICA—Social Security Payable		25.67
FICA—Medicare Payable		6.00
Federal Unemployment Insurance Payable		3.31
State Unemployment Insurance Payable		16.56

14.7 The total payroll for the Berchid Realty Company for the week ending May 30 was $26,000. Of the total amount, $19,000 was subject to FICA Social Security tax, $3,800 held for federal income tax, $1,500 held for pension saving plan, and the balance paid in cash. Present the journal entry necessary to record the payroll for this week.

Salaries Expense		
FICA—Social Security Payable		
FICA—Medicare Payable		
Federal Income Taxes Payable		
Pension Savings Payable		
Cash		

SOLUTION

Salaries Expense	26,000	
FICA—Social Security Payable		1,178*
FICA—Medicare Payable		377**
Federal Income Taxes Payable		3,800
Pension Savings Payable		1,500
Cash		19,145

*$19,000 × 6.2%
**$26,000 × 1.45%, no limit as to earnings

14.8 Based on Problem 14.7, present the employer's payroll tax entry, assuming a state tax rate of 4 percent and federal unemployment 0.8 percent and that the total payroll, $12,000 was subject to federal and state unemployment insurance.

Payroll Tax Expense		
FICA—Social Security Payable		
FICA—Medicare Payable		
Federal Unemployment Insurance Payable		
State Unemployment Insurance Payable		

SOLUTION

Payroll Tax Expense	2,131	
FICA—Social Security Payable		1,178*
FICA—Medicare Payable		377**
Federal Unemployment Insurance Payable		96
State Unemployment Insurance Payable		480

*Matched.

14.9 For the week ending June 30, the Benezran Company had a total gross payroll of $54,000. Of that amount, earnings subject to FICA Social Security tax were $41,500, and the amount subject to unemployment compensation tax was $11,200. Present the journal entry to record the employer's payroll tax for the week, assuming the following rates: state unemployment, 4 percent; federal unemployment, 0.8 percent.

SOLUTION

Payroll Tax Expense	3,893.60	
FICA—Social Security Payable		2,573.00
FICA—Medicare Payable		783.00
State Unemployment Insurance Payable		448.00
Federal Unemployment Insurance Payable		89.60

14.10 Below is the payroll data for three of the employees of the S. Board Company:

Employee	Amount Earned to Date	Gross Pay for Week
L. Benjamin	$7,400	$500.00
R. Hochian	6,800	400.00
C. Murphy	5,400	300.00

The company is located in a state that imposes an unemployment insurance tax of 3 percent on the first $7,000. Federal unemployment tax is 0.8 percent. Present the entry necessary to record the employer's payroll tax expense.

SOLUTION

	FICA Social Security	Medicare	State	Federal
Benjamin	$ 31.00	$ 7.25	None	None
Hochian	24.80	5.80	$ 6.00 (200 × 3%)	$1.60 (200 × 0.8%)
Murphy	18.60	4.35	9.00 (300 × 3%)	2.40 (300 × 0.8%)
	$74.40	$17.40	$15.00	$4.00

Payroll Tax Expense	110.80	
FICA—Social Security Payable		74.40
FICA—Medicare Payable		17.40
State Unemployment Insurance Payable		15.00
Federal Unemployment Insurance Payable		4.00

14.11 Based on the information below, complete the March 28 payroll register for the J. Rakosi Medical Center.

Name	Earnings to Date	Gross Pay Reg.	Ot.	Total	Federal Withholding	Other Deductions
J. Erin	$7,400	$280	$63	$343	$35	Union, $12
M. Ribble	6,900	400	75	475	77	Union, $10
W. Mondstein	7,100	380	—	380	42	—
M. Yamura	3,700	410	—	410	44	—

Payroll Register

Date	Name	Gross Pay Reg.	Ot.	Total	Taxable FICA	Unemp.	Deductions FICA Social Security	Medicare	Fed. With.	Oth. Ded.	Net Net Pay

SOLUTION

Payroll Register

Date	Name	Gross Pay			Taxable		Deductions				Net
		Reg.	Ot.	Total	FICA	Unemp.	FICA		Fed. With.	Oth. Ded.	Net Pay
							Social Security	Medicare			
3/28	J. Erin	280	63	343	343	—	21.27	4.97	35.00	U-12.00	269.76
	M. Ribble	400	75	475	475	100	29.45	6.89	77.00	U-10.00	351.66
	W. Mondstein	380	—.	380	380	—	23.56	5.51	42.00	—	308.93
	M. Yamura	410	—	410	410	410	25.42	5.95	44.00	—	334.63
	Totals	1,470	138	1,608	1,608	510	99.70	23.32	198.00	22.00	1,264.98

14.12 Based on the information in Problem 14.11, present the payroll journal entry needed.

SOLUTION

Salaries Expense	1,608.00	
FICA—Social Security Payable		99.70
FICA—Medicare Payable		23.32
Federal Income Taxes Payable		198.00
Union Dues Payable		22.00
Salaries Payable		1,264.98

14.13 Based on the information presented in the payroll register of Problem 14.11, present the necessary payroll tax expense entry for the employer. Assume a state tax rate of 5 percent and a federal rate of 0.8 percent.

SOLUTION

Payroll Tax Expense	152.60	
FICA—Social Security Payable		99.70
FICA—Medicare Payable		23.32
Federal Unemployment Insurance Payable		4.08*
State Unemployment Insurance Payable		25.50*

*The total amount of the payroll subject to the $7,000 maximum earned limitation for unemployment insurance is $510 (M. Ribble, $100.00; M. Yamura, $410.00).

14.14 Below is the payroll information for the Link Company for the week ending June 9, 19X5. Office salaries were $68,400, of which $54,200 was subject to FICA Social Security tax, $6,740 was withheld for federal withholding tax, and $2,960 was withheld for state taxes. Prepare the necessary journal entry.

SOLUTION

Office Salaries Expense	68,400.00	
FICA—Social Security Payable		3360.40
FICA—Medicare Payable		991.80
Federal Taxes Payable		6,740.00
State Taxes Payable		2,960.00
Salaries Payable		54,347.80

14.15 From the information in Problem 14.14, what would be the journal entry to record the employer's payroll tax expense for the week if $44,700 was subject to unemployment tax? Use a 3.5% state tax and 0.8% federal rate.

SOLUTION

Payroll Tax Expense	6,274.30	
FICA—Social Security Payable		3360.40
FICA—Medicare Payable		991.80
State Unemployment Taxes Payable		1,564.50
Federal Unemployment Taxes Payable		357.60

*Employer has to match FICA tax.

Chapter 15

Property, Plant, and Equipment: Depreciation

15.1 FIXED ASSETS

Tangible assets that are relatively permanent and are needed for the production or sale of goods or services are termed *property, plant, and equipment,* or *fixed assets.* These assets are not held for sale in the ordinary course of business. The broad group is usually separated into classes according to the physical characteristics of the items (e.g., land, buildings, machinery and equipment, furniture and fixtures).

The cost of property, plant, and equipment includes all expenditures necessary to put the asset into position and ready for use.

EXAMPLE 1

For a lathe purchased by AB Optical Company, the data were: invoice price, $11,000; cash discount, $220; freight-in, $300; trucking, $200; electrical connections and installation, $720. The total cost is $11,000 − $220 + $300 + $200 + $720 = $12,000. Therefore, the entry is

Machinery and Equipment	12,000	
Cash		12,000

15.2 DEPRECIATION AND SCRAP VALUE

Though it may be long, the useful life of a fixed asset is limited. Eventually the asset will lose all productive worth and will possess only salvage value (scrap value). The accrual basis of accounting demands a period-by-period matching of costs against derived revenues. Hence, the cost of a fixed asset (over and above its scrap value) is distributed over its entire estimated lifetime. This spreading of the cost over the periods that receive benefits is known as *depreciation.*

To determine depreciation expense for a fixed asset, we need the following information:

1. *Cost.* The total purchase price of the item, including its initial cost, transportation, sales tax, installation and any other expense to make it ready for use.

2. *Estimated useful life.* The projected life during which the business expects the asset to function. This may be expressed in years, miles, units of production, or other measures appropriate to the particular equipment. For example, a building or store may be depreciated over years, an automobile by mileage, a printing press by the number of units it prints or hours it is used.

3. *Residual value.* Also called scrap or salvage value, residual value is the estimated value of the asset when it is fully depreciated. When subtracted from the cost of the asset, it produces the "depreciable cost." For example, a $14,000 press with a scrap value of $4,000 has a depreciable cost of $10,000 ($14,000 − $4,000). If the business expects the asset to have no value at the end of the depreciation period, the asset's entire cost ($14,000 for the press) should be depreciated.

Depreciation decreases the fixed asset's book value and also decreases capital. Depreciation is considered an operating expense of the business. It may be recorded by an entry at the end of each month or at the end of the year, usually depending on the frequency with which financial statements are prepared. Fixed assets are recorded at cost and remain at that figure as long as they are held. The depreciation taken to date is shown as a credit in the offset account Accumulated Depreciation and is deducted from the asset account on the balance sheet, as shown in Example 2 below.

An *offset* (or *contra*) *account* is an account with a credit balance that is offset against (deducted from) an asset account to produce the correct balance sheet book value. The offset account appears in the general ledger directly after its companion account. Generally, every depreciable asset has its own account and an accumulated depreciation account. To determine the asset's book, or carrying, value, the accumulated depreciation account is subtracted from the asset account.

EXAMPLE 2

Equipment	$10,000	
Less: Accumulated Depreciation	4,000	$6,000

The book value of the equipment has gone from $10,000 to $6,000.

There is one exception to the above considerations: land. This fixed asset is nondepreciable; it is usually carried on the books permanently at cost.

15.3 DEPRECIATION METHODS

The depreciable amount of a fixed asset—that is, cost minus scrap value—may be written off in different ways. For example, the amount may be spread evenly over the years affected, as in the straight-line method. Two accelerated methods, the double-declining-balance method and the sum-of-the-years'-digits method, provide for larger amounts of depreciation in the earlier years. Repairs, on the other hand, are generally lower in the earlier years, so the total cost of depreciation and repairs should be about the same each year. The units-of-production method bases depreciation each period on the amount of output.

Straight Line (SL)

The straight-line method is the simplest and most widely used depreciation method. Under this method, an equal portion of the cost of the asset is allocated to each period of use. The periodic charge is expressed as

$$\frac{\text{Cost} - \text{scrap value}}{\text{Useful life (in years)}} = \text{annual depreciation charge}$$

EXAMPLE 3

Cost of machine, $17,000; scrap value, $2,000; estimated life, 5 years.

$$\frac{\$17,000 - \$2,000}{5} = \$3,000 \text{ per year}$$

The entry to record the depreciation would be:

Depreciation Expense, Machinery	3,000	
Accumulated Depreciation, Machinery		3,000

In order to have sufficient documentation for an asset's depreciation, a schedule should be prepared showing the asset's cost, depreciation expense, accumulated depreciation, and, most important of all, its "book value." *Book value* (or *undepreciated cost*) is the balance of an asset's cost less its accumulated depreciation to date. Based on Example 3, the book value at the end of each year would be:

	Cost		Accumulated Depreciation		Book Value
Year 1	$17,000	−	$ 3,000	=	$14,000
2	$17,000	−	$ 6,000	=	$11,000
3	$17,000	−	$ 9,000	=	$ 8,000
4	$17,000	−	$12,000	=	$ 5,000
5	$17,000	−	$15,000	=	$ 2,000

Book value should not be confused with market value. The book value is the difference between cost and accumulated depreciation. *Market value* is what the asset can actually be sold for on a given date.

As an asset is used, accumulated depreciation increases while book value decreases. The last column shows the asset's book value in any year. In the fifth and final year, 19X7, book value is the same as scrap value. At this point, the asset is said to be fully depreciated.

In the preceding example, we assumed that the machine was purchased at the beginning of the year, permitting depreciation of the asset for the full 12 months. Usually, however, machines are bought during the year. When this happens, the amount of depreciation is recorded not for the entire year, but only for the number of months it is used, to the nearest whole month.

If an asset is held for more than half a month, that month is counted. If it is held for less than 15 days in any month, that month is not counted. An asset bought on or before the 15th of the month is considered to be in use and therefore can be depreciated for the entire month. If it is bought on or after the 16th, it cannot be depreciated for that month. Depreciation will begin the following month.

Units of Production (UOP)

Units-of-production depreciation is based on an asset's usage. This can be expressed in

1. Units produced
2. Hours consumed
3. Mileage driven

This method is used when an asset's usage varies from year to year.

Units produced.   Under the first variation of the UOP method, a fixed amount of depreciation is allocated to each unit of output produced by the machine. The per-unit depreciation expense is multiplied by the number of items produced in each accounting period. This depreciation method accurately reflects the depreciation expense for the asset because it is based on the number of units produced in each period. Depreciation per unit is computed in two steps:

$$\frac{\text{Cost of asset} - \text{scrap value}}{\text{Total estimated units of output}} = \text{depreciation per unit}$$

Units produced $\times$ unit depreciation $=$ annual depreciation expense

EXAMPLE 4

Cost of machine $17,000; scrap value $2,000; total estimated units produced during lifetime 300,000.

First-year production: 25,000 units
Second-year production: 30,000 units

The depreciation expense for the first and second years is calculated as:

$$\frac{\$17,000 - \$2,000}{300,000} = \$0.05 \text{ depreciation per unit}$$

Year 1:   25,000 units $\times$ $0.05 = $1,250

Year 2:   30,000 units $\times$ $0.05 = $1,500

Entry for first year:

Depreciation Expense, Machine	1,250	
Accumulated Depreciation, Machine		1,250

Entry for second year:

Depreciation Expense, Machine	1,500	
Accumulated Depreciation, Machine		1,500

The machine will continue to be depreciated until the 300,000 units have been produced. Since only production (not time) is considered when using this method, it gives a clearer picture of the machine's true cost.

Hours used. In this second variation of UOP, a fixed amount of depreciation is allocated, based on the number of hours a machine is used. (Under straight-line depreciation, the depreciation expense is based on the passage of time, regardless of actual use.)

EXAMPLE 5

Determine the depreciation for the following machines in the first year using straight-line depreciation.

	Machine A	Machine B
Cost	$22,000	$22,000
Scrap value	$ 2,000	$ 2,000
Estimated life	5 years	5 years
	(18,000 hours)	(18,000 hours)

Machine A was in use 3,000 hours in the first year. Machine B was in use 1,000 hours in the first year. To calculate:

$$\frac{\$22,000 - \$2,000}{5 \text{ years}} = \$4,000 \text{ annual depreciation expense}$$

Both machines A and B have the same annual depreciation cost of $4,000, because the straight-line method does not consider hours of use, only the estimated life of the machine.

EXAMPLE 6

Using the information in Example 5, determine the depreciation cost of (*a*) machine A and (*b*) machine B using the units-of-production method based on hours used.

$$\frac{\$22,000 - \$2,000}{18,000 \text{ hours}} = \$1.11 \text{ depreciation rate per hour of operation}$$

(a) Machine A: 3,000 hours $\times$ \$1.11 = \$3,330 first-year depreciation expense

(b) Machine B: 1,000 hours $\times$ \$1.11 = \$1,110 first-year depreciation expense

The difference in first-year depreciation when using the straight-line (Example 5) or units-of-production (Example 6) method is considerable. Under the UOP method, machine B's limited use results in its having one-third the depreciation expense of machine A. Under the straight-line method, both machines carry the same depreciation expense, regardless of use. In this case, UOP is the more logical choice for reporting depreciation, because it more accurately matches depreciation expense against periodic income. Under UOP, both machines will be fully depreciated when they have completed 18,000 hours of use.

Mileage driven.   Under the third variation of UOP depreciation, instead of using time to calculate depreciation, the number of miles driven are the "units." The depreciation expense per mile will remain constant over the life of the truck and will be multiplied by the actual miles the truck is driven in each accounting period.

EXAMPLE 7

A truck costing \$24,000 with a salvage value of \$4,000 has an estimated useful life of 80,000 miles. If, in the first year, it is driven 18,000 miles, what is the entry needed to record depreciation expense?

$$\frac{\$24,000 \text{ (cost)} - \$4,000 \text{ (salvage value)}}{80,000 \text{ total estimated miles}} = \$0.25 \text{ per mile}$$

18,000 (miles driven) $\times$ \$.25 = \$4,500   First-year depreciation expense

Depreciation Expense, Truck	4,500	
Accumulated Depreciation, Truck		4,500

Double Declining Balance (DDB)

The declining-balance method is an accelerated method of depreciation because a greater amount of depreciation expense is taken in the early years of an asset's life and less is taken in later years. This method is preferred for the following reasons:

1. Technology can make an asset obsolete or inadequate before the asset wears out.

2. Most plant assets decline in value more quickly in their early years than in later years.

3. Often, an asset contributes most to a business during its first years of operation.

4. The expenditure for equipment is made at the beginning of the asset's life.

5. It is good accounting practice to charge more depreciation in the early years of an asset's useful life, because in later years repair and maintenance expenses are incurred as the asset gets older.

The double-declining-balance (DDB) method produces the highest amount of depreciation in the earlier years. It does not recognize scrap value. Instead, the book value of the asset remaining at the end of the depreciation period becomes the scrap value. Under this method, the straight-line rate is doubled and applied to the declining book balance each year. Many companies prefer the double-declining-balance method because of the faster write-off in the earlier years, when the asset contributes most to the business and when the expenditure was actually made. The procedure is to apply a fixed rate to the declining book value of the asset each year. As the book value declines, the depreciation becomes smaller.

EXAMPLE 8

A $17,000 asset is to be depreciated over 5 years; the double-declining-balance rate is thus 40 percent per year.

Year	Book Value at Beginning of Year	Rate	Depreciation for Year	Book Value at End of Year
1	$17,000	40%	$6,800	$10,200
2	10,200	40%	4,080	6,120
3	6,120	40%	2,448	3,672
4	3,672	40%	1,469	2,203
5	2,203	40%	881	1,322

The $1,322 book value at the end of the fifth year becomes the scrap value. If, however, a scrap value had been estimated at $2,000, the depreciation for the fifth year would be $203 ($2,203 − $2,000) instead of $881.

The date of purchase should also be considered. Up to this point it has been assumed that the equipment was purchased at the beginning of the year, which is usually not a common occurrence. Therefore a change in the computation for the first, partial year of service is needed.

EXAMPLE 9

If, in Example 8, the equipment had been purchased and placed into use at the end of the ninth month of the fiscal year, the pro-rata portion of the first full year's depreciation would be:

$$\frac{3}{12}(40\% \times 17,000) = \$1,700$$

The method of computation for the remaining years would not be affected. Thus,

$$40\% (\$17,000 - \$1,700) = \$6,120$$

would be the depreciation for the second year, and $9,180 ($17,000 − $7,820) would be its book value.

Sum-of-the-Years'-Digits (SYD)

The fourth method of computing depreciation is sum-of-the-years'-digits. Like DDB, it is an accelerated method that allows more depreciation expense to be recorded in the early years of an asset's life and less in later years. Like DDB, depreciation expense declines over the life of the asset, but unlike DDB, it declines by the same amount each year.

To determine depreciation expense under SYD, the asset's cost (minus scrap value) is multiplied by a fraction. The numerator of the fraction is the years remaining in the asset's life, but in reverse order. It changes each year. The denominator is the sum of all the digits (hence its name) making up the life of the asset. It remains constant. Here is what the fraction looks like:

$$\frac{\text{Numerator (years in reverse)}}{\text{Denominator (life of asset)}}$$

Example 10 shows how to compute depreciation expense with the SYD method using this fraction.

The years of the asset's lifetime are labeled 1, 2, 3, etc., and the depreciation amounts are based on a series of fractions having the sum of the years' digits as the common denominator. The largest digit is used as the numerator for the first year, the next largest digit for the second year, and so forth.

EXAMPLE 10

Cost of machine, $17,000; scrap value, $2,000; estimated life, 5 years.

The depreciable amount is $17,000 − $2,000 = $15,000. To find the fraction of this amount to be written off each year, proceed as follows:

1. Label the years 1, 2, 3, 4, and 5.

2. Calculate the sum of the year's digits: $S = 1 + 2 + 3 + 4 + 5 = 15$.

3. Convert the sum to a series of fractions:

$$\tfrac{1}{15} + \tfrac{2}{15} + \tfrac{3}{15} + \tfrac{4}{15} + \tfrac{5}{15} = 1$$

4. Take the above series of fractions in reverse order as the depreciation rates. Thus:

Year	Fraction	Amount		Depreciation
1	$\tfrac{5}{15}$	× $15,000	=	$ 5,000
2	$\tfrac{4}{15}$	× 15,000	=	4,000
3	$\tfrac{3}{15}$	× 15,000	=	3,000
4	$\tfrac{2}{15}$	× 15,000	=	2,000
5	$\tfrac{1}{15}$	× 15,000	=	1,000
				$15,000

If the life expectancy of a machine were 5 years as stated above, you could follow step 2 by adding $1 + 2 + 3 + 4 + 5 = 15$. However, for a machine that has a long life expectancy, it is simpler to use the formula

$$S = \frac{N(N + 1)}{2}$$

In the above equation,

$$S = \frac{5(5 + 1)}{2} = 15$$

EXAMPLE 11

The life of a piece of equipment is calculated to be 30 years. The sum of the year's digits is:

$$S = \frac{30(30 + 1)}{2} = 465$$

Partial-Year Depreciation

If an asset is purchased during the year rather than at the beginning, each full year's depreciation must be allocated between the two fiscal years affected to assure accurate reporting and accounting.

EXAMPLE 12

If a machine bought on October 2, 19X4, with a 10-year life, costing $30,000, has a scrap value of $2,500, the depreciation for the first two years is determined as follows:

Year 1:

$$19X4: \quad \$27,500 \times \tfrac{10}{55} = \$5,000 \times \tfrac{3*}{12} = \underline{1,250} \text{ depreciation expense}$$

Year 2:

$$19X5: \qquad \$27,500 \times \tfrac{10}{55} = \$5,000 \times \tfrac{9\dagger}{12} = \$3,750 \text{ depreciation expense}$$

$$+$$

$$\$27,500 \times \tfrac{9}{55} = \$4,500 \times \tfrac{3}{12} = \underline{\$1,125} \text{ depreciation expense}$$

$$= \underline{\$4,875} \text{ depreciation expense}$$

---

*Use of the machine for 3 months.
†Balance (12 months − 3 months).

Comparison of Methods

Once you know the four methods of depreciation, the next question is how to select the one that's most appropriate. Under generally accepted accounting principles (GAAP), businesses are encouraged to match the income an asset produces against its expense. This can be accomplished by selecting the correct depreciation method.

The four principal methods of depreciation are compared in Table 15.1. It is assumed that over a 5-year lifetime, the asset was in operation for the following numbers of hours: 1,800, 1,200, 2,000, 1,400, 1,600. Cost of asset, $17,000; scrap value, $2,000.

Table 15.1   Annual Depreciation Charge

Year	Straight Line (SL)	Units of Production (UOP)	Double Declining Balance (DDB)	Sum of the Years' Digits (SYD)
1	$ 3,000	$ 3,375	$ 6,800	$ 5,000
2	3,000	2,250	4,080	4,000
3	3,000	3,750	2,448	3,000
4	3,000	2,625	1,468	2,000
5	3,000	3,000	204	1,000
Total	$15,000	$15,000	$15,000	$15,000

Based on Table 15.1, we can conclude the following:

1. If the asset is expected to generate income evenly over an extended period of time, the *straight-line method* should be used.

2. If the asset will produce a different number of units each year, or if the machine may wear out early, the *units-of-production method* is preferable because it is based on usage rather than time. In other words, the more units are produced in a single year, the higher will be the asset's annual depreciation expense.

3. If the asset is expected to generate high income in its early years, the *double-declining-balance method* is another method of rapid depreciation write-off. Like the sum-of-the-years' digits, this accelerated depreciation process reduces tax liability in the early years and increases available cash to pay for the asset.

4. If the asset is expected to generate high income in its early years, the accelerated method of *sum-of-the-years' digits* should be used, because it will generate greater depreciation expense in its earlier years as it can be matched with the early period's higher revenues, or because it is closer to the date of purchase when the major expenditure was made. This

accelerated depreciation method reduces tax liability in the early years, making more cash available for the asset's purchase.

Summary

1. The main reason for depreciation is _____.

2. Accumulated Depreciation is an example of an _____ account, since the fixed asset remains at cost while the offset builds up.

3. The market value of a fixed asset at the end of its service is known as a _____.

4. The uniform distribution of depreciation over the life of the asset is known as the _____ method.

5. The _____ method is used to write off the asset based on a series of fractions.

6. The method that produces the largest amount of depreciation in the earlier years, then rapidly declines, is known as the _____ method.

7. Under SYD depreciation, (less/more) _____ depreciation expense is recorded in the early years and (less/more) _____ depreciation expense is recorded as the asset gets older.

8. Under SYD, the final year's book value must be the same as its _____ value.

9. When income produced by an asset is the same each year, the recommended method of depreciation is _____.

10. When use rather than time is the key factor, _____ is the preferred method of depreciation.

11. If the largest amount of depreciation is taken in the first year of an asset's operation, then the business is using the _____ method of depreciation.

12. Two accelerated methods of depreciation are _____ and _____.

Answers: 1. aging; 2. contra, offset, or valuation; 3. scrap or salvage; 4. straight-line; 5. sum-of-the-years'-digits; 6. double-declining-balance; 7. more, less; 8. scrap; 9. SL; 10. UOP; 11. DDB; 12. SYD, DDB

Solved Problems

15.1 Hacol Company acquired an asset on January 1, 19X5, at a cost of $38,000, with an estimated useful life of 8 years and a salvage value of $2,000. What is the annual depreciation based on the straight-line method for the first two years?

SOLUTION

Cost	$38,000
Scrap value	2,000
Amount to be depreciated	$36,000

Year 1: $36,000 ÷ 8 years = $4,500 depreciation
Year 2: $36,000 ÷ 8 years = $4,500 depreciation

15.2 For the asset of Problem 15.1, compute the depreciation for the first 2 years by the sum-of-the-years'-digits method.

SOLUTION

$$S = 8\left(\frac{8+1}{2}\right) = 36$$

Year 1: $\frac{8}{36} \times \$36,000 = \$8,000$

Year 2: $\frac{7}{36} \times \$36,000 = \$7,000$

15.3 Repeat Problem 15.2, but using the double-declining-balance method.

SOLUTION

For the depreciation rate we take twice the straight-line rate; that is,

$$2 \times \frac{100\%}{8 \text{ years}} = 25\% \text{ per year}$$

Therefore,

Year 1: $38,000 × 25% = $9,500
Year 2:   ($38,000 − $9,500) × 25% = $7,125

15.4 A truck was purchased on January 1, 19X5, for $8,500, with an estimated scrap value of $500. It will be depreciated for 8 years using the straight-line method. Show how the Truck account and the related Accumulated Depreciation account would appear on the balance sheet on (a) December 31, 19X5; (b) December 31, 19X6.

(a)

(b)

SOLUTION

(a)	Truck	$8,500	
	Less: Accumulated Depreciation	1,000*	$7,500
(b)	Truck	$8,500	
	Less Accumulated Depreciation	2,000†	$6,500

*($8,500 − $500) ÷ 8 years = $1,000 per year.
†$1,000 per year × 2.

15.5 Based on Problem 15.4, what amount will appear in the income statement for Depreciation Expense, Truck, (a) for the year 19X5? (b) for the year 19X6?

SOLUTION

(a) $1,000 (1 year's depreciation)
(b) $1,000 (1 year's depreciation)

15.6 Equipment costing $9,600, with an estimated scrap value of $1,600, was bought on July 1, 19X5. The equipment is to be depreciated by the straight-line method for a period of 10 years. The company's fiscal year is January through December. Show how the equipment account and the related Accumulated Depreciation account would appear in the balance sheet on (a) December 31, 19X5; (b) December 31, 19X6.

(a)			
(b)			

SOLUTION

(a)	Equipment	$9,600	
	Less: Accumulated Depreciation	400*	$9,200

($9,600 − $1,600) ÷ 10 years = $800 depreciation per year; $\frac{1}{2}$ year (July 1 to Dec. 31) × $800 per year = $400.

(b)	Equipment	$9,600	
	Less: Accumulated Depreciation	1,200*	$8,400

*$1\frac{1}{2}$ years × $800 per year = $1,200.

15.7 What amount will appear in the income statement for Depreciation Expense, Equipment (Problem 15.6), (a) for the year 19X5? (b) for the year 19X6?

SOLUTION

(a) $400 ($\frac{1}{2}$ year's depreciation);   (b) $800 (1 year's depreciation)

15.8 A machine was purchased for $28,000 and had an estimated scrap value of $4,000. What would the year-end entry be if the units-of-production method was used, and it had an estimated life of 32,000 hours? In the first year of operation, it was used 7,200 hours.

SOLUTION

Depreciation Expense, Machine	5,400	
Accumulated Depreciation, Machine		5,400

$$\frac{\$28,000 - \$4,000}{32,000 \text{ hours est. life}} = 0.75 \times 7,200 \text{ hours} = \$5,400$$

15.9 See Thru Glass Company purchased a new glass-cutting machine on May 19, 19X5, for $28,000. The machine has an estimated scrap value of $4,000 and will be depreciated by the straight-line method over 5 years. The See Thru Glass Company year ends on December 31, 19X5. What would the entry be on December 31, 19X5?

SOLUTION

Depreciation Expense, Machine	2,800*	
Accumulated Depreciation, Machine		2,800

*$28,000   Cost
−4,000   Scrap value
$24,000

$24,000 ÷ 5 years = $4,800 per year
$4,800 ÷ 12 months = $400 per month
$400 × 7 months = $2,800

Note that the machine was not put into use until after the 15th of the month, so you do not count the month of May.

15.10 Based on the information in Problem 15.9, what would the entry be if the double-declining-balance method was used?

SOLUTION

Depreciation Expense, Machine	6,533.31*	
Accumulated Depreciation, Machine		6,533.31

*$28,000 × 40% = $11,200; $\frac{7}{12}$($11,200) = $6,533.31.

15.11 Based on the information in Problem 15.9, what would the entry be if the sum-of-the-years'-digits method was used?

SOLUTION

Depreciation Expense, Machine	4,666.69*	
Accumulated Depreciation, Machine		4,666.69

*$28,000 cost − $4,000 scrap value = $24,000 × 5/15 = $8,000 per year; $8,000 ÷ 12 months = $666.67 × 7 months = $4,666.69 depreciation expense for the year.

15.12 A fixed asset costing $60,000, with an estimated salvage value of $5,000, has a life expectancy of 10 years. Compare the results of the various depreciation methods by filling in the tables below. Take twice the straight-line rate as the rate for the double-declining-balance method.

Straight-Line Method

Year	Depreciation Expense	Accumulated Depreciation	Book Value at End of Year
1			
2			
3			
4			

Sum-of-the-Years'-Digits Method

Year	Depreciation Expense	Accumulated Depreciation	Book Value at End of Year
1			
2			
3			
4			

Double-Declining-Balance Method

Year	Depreciation Expense	Accumulated Depreciation	Book Value at End of Year
1			
2			
3			
4			

SOLUTION

Straight-Line Method

Year	Depreciation Expense	Accumulated Depreciation	Book Value at End of Year
1	$5,500*	$ 5,500	$54,500†
2	5,500	11,000	49,000
3	5,500	16,500	43,500
4	5,500	22,000	38,000

*($60,000 − $5,000) ÷ 10 = $5,500.
†$60,000 − $5,500 = $54,500.

Sum-of-the-Years'-Digits Method

Year	Depreciation Expense	Accumulated Depreciation	Book Value at End of Year
1	$10,000*	$10,000	$50,000
2	9,000	19,000	41,000
3	8,000	27,000	33,000
4	7,000	34,000	26,000

$*S = 10(10 + 1)/2 = 55; \frac{10}{55} \times \$55,000 = \$10,000.$

Double-Declining-Balance Method

Year	Depreciation Expense	Accumulated Depreciation	Book Value at End of Year
1	$12,000*	$12,000	$48,000
2	9,600†	21,600	38,400
3	7,680	29,280	30,720
4	6,144	35,424	24,576

*(2 × 10%) × $60,000 = $12,000.
†20% × ($60,000 − $12,000) = $9,600.

Examination IV

1. Sandra Sarazzin worked 49 hours during the second week in March of the current year. Her pay rate is $6.40 per hour. Withheld from her wages were FICA Social Security 6.2% and FICA Medicare .0145%; federal income tax, $51; hospitalization, $8; union dues, $6. Determine the necessary payroll entry.

2. The total payroll for the Randolf Company for the week ending April 30 was $17,000. The amount was subject to FICA tax; $2,800 was held for federal income tax; $900 was withheld for hospitalization; and the balance was paid in cash.

   (a) Present the journal entry necessary to record the payroll for this week.

   (b) Present the employer's payroll tax entry, assuming a state unemployment of 4 percent, a federal rate of 0.8 percent, and that the total payroll, $5,000, was subject to federal and state unemployment tax.

3. Journalize the following separate entries:

   (a) W. Schoop discounted his own $4,000 note from City Bank for 120 days at 12 percent.

   (b) W. Schoop discounted at 12 percent E. Orlian's $3,000, ninety-day, 12 percent note immediately upon receipt.

4. Apr. 5   A. Offengender bought $2,100 worth of goods from T. Vadka Company on account.

   May 1   Vadka received a ninety-day, 12 percent note in settlement of A. Offengender's account.

       31   Vadka discounted the note at 12 percent.

   July 30   The bank informed Vadka that the discounted note has been dishonored and will charge Vadka the maturity value plus a protest fee of $5.00.

   Aug. 1   Received the full amount owed from Offengender.

   Prepare all necessary entries on the books of Vadka to reflect the above transactions.

5. Prepare a bank reconciliation statement based on the following information:

   (a) Bank balance, $3,400.

   (b) Checkbook balance, $3,120.

   (c) Outstanding checks, $1,140.

   (d) Deposits in transit, $1,800.

   (e) A $1,000 note was collected by the bank; interest added to it was $15. Bank service charge for collection, $5.

   (f) A $16 check we had deposited was returned for nonsufficient funds.

   (g) Check 12 for $82 was inadvertently recorded in our check stubs as $28.

6. Klein's Logging Company purchased a new truck for $80,000 on January 1, 19X5. The estimated life is 5 years, with an estimated scrap value of $5,000. From this information, prepare three depreciation schedules, using (a) the straight-line method, (b) the double-declining-balance method, (c) the sum-of-the-years'-digits method.

Answers to Examination IV

1.

Salaries Expense	342.40*	
FICA—Social Security Payable		21.23
FICA—Medicare Payable		4.96
Federal Income Tax Payable		51.00
Hospitalization Payable		8.00
Union Dues Payable		6.00
Salaries Payable		251.21

*40 hours × $6.40 = $256.00 (regular)
  9 hours × $9.60 =   86.40 (overtime)
                $342.40 total compensation

2. (*a*)

Salaries Expense	17,000	
FICA—Social Security Payable		1,054
FICA—Medicare Payable		246.50
Federal Income Taxes Payable		2,800
Hospitalization Payable		900
Cash		11,999.50

(*b*)

Payroll Tax Expense	1,540.50	
FICA—Social Security Payable		1,054
FICA—Medicare Payable		246.50
Federal Unemployment Insurance Payable		40
State Unemployment Insurance Payable		200

3. (*a*)

Cash	3,840	
Interest Expense	160	
Notes Payable		4,000

(*b*)

Cash	2,997.30*	
Interest Expense	2.70	
Notes Receivable		3,000.00

*$3,000.00 Principal
    90.00 Interest income
$3,090.00 Maturity value
    92.70 Discount
$2,997.30 Proceeds

4.

Apr. 5	Accounts Receivable	2,100.00	
	Sales Income		2,100.00
May 1	Notes Receivable	2,100.00	
	Accounts Receivable		2,100.00
31	Cash	2,119.74*	
	Notes Receivable		2,100.00
	Interest Income		19.74
July 30	Accounts Receivable	2,168.00[†]	
	Cash		2,168.00

Aug.   1   Cash   2,168.00

               Accounts Receivable   2,168.00

*$2,100.00	Principal
63.00	Interest income (90 days, 12%)
$2,163.00	Maturity value
43.26	Discount (60 days balance, 12%)
$2,119.74	Proceeds

†Maturity value	$2,163.00
Protest fee	5.00
	$2,168.00

5.

Bank Reconciliation Statement

Bank Balance	$3,400	Check balance		$3,120
Add: Deposit in transit	1,800	Add:		
	$5,200	Notes receivable	$1,000	
		Interest income	15	1,015
				$4,135
Less: Outstanding checks	1,140	Less:		
		Service charge	$ 5	
		NSF	16	
		Error	54	75
Bank balance corrected	$4,060	Checkbook balance corrected		$4,060

6. (a) Straight-line method:

Year	Depreciation Expense	Accumulated Depreciation at End of Year	Book Value at End of Year
1	$15,000	$15,000	$65,000
2	15,000	30,000	50,000
3	15,000	45,000	35,000
4	15,000	60,000	20,000
5	15,000	75,000	5,000*

*Note that at the end of 5 full years, you end up with the estimated scrap value.

(b) Double-declining-balance method:

Year	Depreciation Expense	Accumulated Depreciation at End of Year	Book Value at End of Year
1	$32,000	$32,000	$48,000
2	19,200	51,200	28,800
3	11,520	62,720	17,280
4	6,912	69,632	10,368
5	5,368*	75,000	5,000

*Note that at the end of 5 full years, you would have a scrap value of $5,000 because the scrap value had been estimated ($10,368 − $5,000).

(c) Sum-of-the-years'-digits method:

$$S = \frac{5(5 + 1)}{2} = 15$$

Year	Depreciation Expense	Accumulated Depreciation at End of Year	Book Value at End of Year
1	$25,000	$25,000	$55,000
2	20,000	45,000	35,000
3	15,000	60,000	20,000
4	10,000	70,000	10,000
5	5,000	75,000	5,000

Chapter 16

The Partnership

16.1 CHARACTERISTICS OF THE PARTNERSHIP

According to the Uniform Partnership Act, a partnership is "an association of two or more persons to carry on as co-owners of a business for profit." Generally speaking, partnership accounting is like that for the sole proprietorship, except with regard to owners' equity. The partnership uses a capital account and a drawing account for each partner.

The partnership has the following characteristics:

Articles of copartnership. Good business practice calls for a written agreement among the partners that contains provisions on the formation of the partnership, capital contributions of each partner, profit and loss distribution, admission and withdrawal of partners, withdrawal of funds, and dissolution of the business.

Unlimited liability. All partners have unlimited liability and are individually responsible to creditors for debts incurred by the partnership. The debts of the business can be satisfied not only by the assets of the partnership but also by the personal assets of the partners.

Co-ownership of property. All property invested in the business by the partners, as well as that purchased with the partnership's funds, becomes the property of all partners jointly. Therefore, each partner has an interest in the partnership in proportion to his or her capital balance, rather than a claim against specific assets.

Participation in profits and losses. Profits and losses are distributed among the partners according to the partnership agreement. If no agreement exists, profit and losses must be shared equally.

Limited life. A partnership may be dissolved by bankruptcy, death of a partner, mutual agreement, or court order.

16.2 FORMATION OF THE PARTNERSHIP

When a partnership is formed, each partner's capital account is credited for his or her initial investment, and the appropriate asset account is debited. If noncash assets are invested, these should be recorded at an agreed amount.

If liabilities are to be assumed by the partnership, they are credited to the respective liability accounts.

EXAMPLE 1

Walter Gurney has agreed to go into partnership with Ted Drew.

Drew's Accounts	Drew's Ledger Balances	Agreed Valuation
Cash	$18,000	$18,000
Supplies	3,000	2,000
Accounts Receivable	6,000	6,000
Equipment	18,000 ⎫	
Accumulated Depreciation—Equipment	4,000 ⎭	12,000
Notes Payable	8,000	8,000

The entry to record the initial investment of Drew in the firm of Drew and Gurney is:

Cash	18,000	
Supplies	2,000	
Accounts Receivable	6,000	
Equipment	12,000	
Notes Payable		8,000
Drew, Capital		30,000

16.3 DIVISION OF NET INCOME AND LOSS

Partnership profits and losses may be divided in any manner the partners may agree upon. In general, a partner may be expected to share in proportion to the amount of capital and/or services he or she contributes. In the absence of a clear agreement, the law provides that all partners share equally, regardless of the differences in time devoted or capital contributed.

Below are outlined the principal methods for profit and loss distribution. For simplicity, the examples are limited to two partners.

Fixed or Capital Basis

Profits and losses are generally divided equally, in a fixed ratio, or in a ratio based on the amounts of capital contributed by the partners.

EXAMPLE 2

Drew and Gurney have capital balances of $30,000 and $20,000, respectively. The net income for the first year of operations was $15,000. If the partners have decided to share on an equal basis, the journal entry for the allocation of the net income will be:

Expense and Income Summary	15,000	
Drew, Capital		7,500
Gurney, Capital		7,500

If, however, capital investment is to be the determining factor, the entry will run as follows:

Expense and Income Summary	15,000	
Drew, Capital		9,000*
Gurney, Capital		6,000†

$$* \frac{30,000}{30,000 + 20,000}(15,000)$$

$$† \frac{20,000}{30,000 + 20,000}(15,000)$$

Interest Basis

Under this method, each partner is paid interest on his or her capital investment, and the remaining net income is divided in a fixed ratio or on some other basis. Thus, a partner's share depends partially on his or her capital investment.

EXAMPLE 3

Instead of the equal split in Example 2, each partner is to receive 6 percent interest on his or her capital balance, the remaining net income to be shared equally. The entry is

Expense and Income Summary	15,000	
Drew, Capital		7,800
Gurney, Capital		7,200

which is computed as follows:

	Drew	Gurney	Total
Interest on investment	$1,800*	$1,200**	$ 3,000
Balance	6,000	6,000	12,000
Totals	$7,800	$7,200	$15,000

*$30,000 × .06
**$20,000 × .06

Salary Basis

The partners may agree to give recognition to contributions in the form of services, while the remaining net income may be divided equally or in a fixed ratio.

EXAMPLE 4

Assume that the partnership of Drew and Gurney (Example 2) agree that a yearly salary allowance of $4,000 be given to Drew and $3,000 to Gurney, the balance to be divided equally. The entry is

Expense and Income Summary	15,000	
Drew, Capital		8,000
Gurney, Capital		7,000

which is computed as follows:

	Drew	Gurney	Total
Salaries	$4,000	$3,000	$ 7,000
Balance	4,000	4,000	8,000
Totals	$8,000	$7,000	$15,000

Salary-Plus-Interest Basis

Here, services rendered to the business and capital contribution jointly determine the income division. Each partner gets a salary, and, at the same time, interest on capital. If any balance remains, it is divided in an agreed ratio.

EXAMPLE 5

Drew and Gurney (Example 2) decide to allow a credit of 6 percent interest on capital balances, respective salaries of $4,000 and $3,000, and equal division of any remainder. The entry is

Expense and Income Summary	15,000	
Drew, Capital		8,300
Gurney, Capital		6,700

which is computed as follows:

	Drew	Gurney	Total
Interest	$1,800	$1,200	$ 3,000
Salaries	4,000	3,000	7,000
	$5,800	$4,200	$10,000
Balance	2,500	2,500	5,000
Totals	$8,300	$6,700	$15,000

In Example 5, as well as in Examples 3 and 4, the income of the business exceeded the total of the allowances to the partners. However, this may not always be the case. If the net income is less than the total of the allowances, the balance remaining is negative and is divided among the partners as though it were a loss.

EXAMPLE 6

Drew and Gurney (Example 2) decide to allow a credit of 6 percent interest on capital balances, respective salaries of $8,000 and $6,000, and equal division of the remainder. The entry is

Expense and Income Summary	15,000	
Drew, Capital		8,800
Gurney, Capital		6,200

which is computed as follows:

	Drew	Gurney	Total
Interest	$1,800	$1,200	$ 3,000
Salaries	8,000	6,000	14,000
	$9,800	$7,200	$17,000
Balance	− 1,000	− 1,000	− 2,000
Totals	$8,800	$6,200	$15,000

16.4   ADMISSION OF A NEW PARTNER

The Uniform Partnership Act states that a partner may dispose of part or all of his or her interest in the firm without the consent of the remaining partners.

The individual who purchases the interest receives the selling partner's rights to share in income and expense. However, this purchaser is not a full partner, since he or she will have no vote or right to participate in partnership activities unless he or she is admitted to the firm.

Admission by Purchase of Interest

When the incoming partner purchases an interest from another partner, he or she pays the purchase price directly to the old partner. The only change required in the partnership's books is an entry transferring capital from the old partner's account to the account established for the new partner. Assets and liabilities of the business are not affected.

EXAMPLE 7

Drew and Gurney have capital balances of $30,000 and $20,000, respectively. T. Lambert is admitted to the partnership by purchasing half of Drew's interest for $18,000. The only entry required is the changing of the capital balances of the affected partners.

Drew, Capital		Gurney, Capital		Lambert, Capital	
15,000	30,000 Bal.		20,000 Bal.		15,000

Lambert's admission results in the transfer of half of Drew's capital to Lambert, regardless of the amount paid by Lambert for his share of the partnership.

Admission by Contribution of Assets

The new partner may contribute assets to the partnership, thus increasing both the assets and the capital of the firm.

EXAMPLE 8

Assume that Lambert is to be admitted to the partnership of Drew and Gurney, whose total capital is $50,000 ($30,000 and $20,000, respectively) Lambert is to contribute $25,000 for a one-third interest in the new partnership. The entry to record his admission is:

Cash	25,000	
Lambert, Capital		25,000

In Examples 7 and 8 it was assumed that the assets of Drew and Gurney were stated in terms of the current market prices when Lambert was admitted. Because of this, no adjustments were necessary in any of the assets prior to his admission. In some cases, when a new partner is admitted, assets may first have to be revalued or goodwill recognized in order to bring the capital accounts into line with current values.

1. *Revaluation of assets.* The book values of certain assets of the partnership must be adjusted before they agree with current prices. The net amount of the revaluation is then transferred to the capital accounts of the old partners according to their income division agreement. If it appears that a number of assets need revaluation, whether to higher or lower figures, the adjustments may be made in a temporary account, *Asset Revaluation,* which will subsequently be closed to the partners' capital accounts.

EXAMPLE 9

Drew and Gurney share profits and losses equally. It was discovered that the supplies account is understated: The supplies carried on the books at $6,000 have a current replacement cost of $10,000. The following entry would be recorded prior to the admission of Lambert into the partnership:

Supplies	4,000	
Drew, Capital		2,000
Gurney, Capital		2,000

EXAMPLE 10

Before admitting Lambert to partnership, Drew and Gurney decide that: (*a*) $600 is to be written off the Accounts Receivable balance; (*b*) supplies carried at $6,000 are to be revalued at $8,000.

The entry to record the above revaluation is:

Supplies	2,000	
Accounts Receivable		600
Asset Revaluation		1,400

After all adjustments have been made, Asset Revaluation is closed as follows:

Asset Revaluation	1,400	
Drew, Capital		700
Gurney, Capital		700

2. *Recognition of goodwill.* If a firm has the ability to earn more than the normal rate on its investment (because of a favorable location, established reputation, management skills, or better products or services), goodwill may be indicated, and an incoming partner may be charged for it. If so, the goodwill account is debited, while the old partners' accounts are credited in the ratios set up by the articles of partnership. On the other hand, if goodwill is created by the incoming partner, the goodwill account is debited, and the new partner's capital account credited.

EXAMPLE 11   Goodwill to the Old Partners

The capital balances of Drew and Gurney are $30,000 and 20,000, respectively. The partnership agrees to admit Lambert to their firm, who is to contribute cash of $20,000 and is to receive a one-fourth interest in the firm.

Though the total capital of the firm before the admission is $50,000, the parties agree that the firm is worth $60,000. This excess of $10,000 indicates the existence of goodwill; it will be allocated to the old partners in their profit-and-loss ratio, which is 1:1 in this case. The entries to record goodwill and the admission of the new partner are:

Goodwill	10,000	
Drew, Capital		5,000
Gurney, Capital		5,000
Cash	20,000	
Lambert, Capital		20,000*

$*\frac{1}{4}$($30,000 + $20,000 + $20,000 + $10,000)

      Drew   Gurney   Lambert   goodwill

EXAMPLE 12   Goodwill to the New Partner

Drew and Gurney, with capital balances of $30,000 and $20,000, respectively, agree to admit Lambert into the firm for a $15,000 investment, giving him a one-third share in profits and losses and granting him goodwill recognition of $10,000. The entry to record the above information is:

Cash	15,000	
Goodwill	10,000	
Lambert, Capital		25,000*

$*\frac{1}{3}$($30,000 + $20,000 + $25,000)

      Drew   Gurney   Lambert

16.5　LIQUIDATION OF A PARTNERSHIP

If the partners of a firm decide to discontinue the operation of the business, several accounting steps are necessary:

1. The accounts are adjusted and closed.

2. All assets are converted to cash.

3. All creditors are paid in full.

4. Any remaining cash is distributed among the partners according to the balances in their capital accounts (and not according to their profit-and-loss ratios).

EXAMPLE 13　Liquidation at a Gain

After Drew, Gurney, and Lambert have ceased business operations and adjusted and closed the accounts, the general ledger has the following post-closing trial balance:

Cash	$20,000	
Noncash Assets	65,000	
Liabilities		$10,000
Drew, Capital		15,000
Gurney, Capital		25,000
Lambert, Capital		35,000
	$85,000	$85,000

Assume for simplicity that all liabilities are paid at one time and that the noncash assets are sold in one transaction. Then, if the sale price is $80,000 and the partners share equally in profits and losses, we have the following liquidation schedule:

	Assets	=	Liabilities	+	Capital	
	Cash + Other		Accounts Pay.		Drew + Gurney +	Lambert
Balances of capital accounts	$ 20,000　$65,000		$10,000		$15,000　$25,000	$35,000
Sale of assets	+ 80,000　− 65,000				+ 5,000　+ 5,000	+ 5,000
Balance after sale	$100,000		$10,000		$20,000　$30,000	$40,000
Payment of liabilities	− 10,000		10,000			
Balance after payment	$ 90,000				$20,000　$30,000	$40,000
Distribution to partners	− 90,000				− 20,000　− 30,000	− 40,000

The entries to record the liquidation are then:

Sale of Assets

Cash	80,000	
Other Assets		65,000
Gain on Liquidation		15,000
Gain on Liquidation	15,000	
Drew, Capital		5,000
Gurney, Capital		5,000
Lambert, Capital		5,000

Payment of Liabilities

Liabilities	10,000	
Cash		10,000

Final Distribution to Partners

Drew, Capital	20,000
Gurney, Capital	30,000
Lambert, Capital	40,000
Cash	90,000

EXAMPLE 14 Liquidation at a Loss

The data are as in Example 13, except that the noncash assets are now sold for $5,000.

	Assets =		Liabilities	+	Capital		
	Cash +	Other	Accounts Pay.		Drew +	Gurney +	Lambert
Balances of capital accounts	$20,000	$65,000	$10,000		$15,000	$25,000	$35,000
Sale of assets	+ 5,000	− 65,000			− 20,000	− 20,000	− 20,000
Balance after sale	$25,000		$10,000		$(5,000)	$ 5,000	$15,000
Payment of liabilities	− 10,000		−10,000				
Balance after payment	$15,000				$(5,000)	$ 5,000	$15,000
Distribution to partners	− 15,000					− 2,500	− 12,500
					$(5,000)	$2,500	$ 2,500

Notice that in the foregoing liquidation schedule the $60,000 loss on sale of the noncash assets was divided equally among the three partners. However, Drew's capital balance was not sufficient to absorb his share of the loss. This resulted in a debit balance ($5,000) in his capital account and becomes a claim of the partnership against him for that amount. The $5,000 deficit must be borne by the two remaining partners, and thus, in the distribution to partners, Gurney and Lambert each take an additional loss of $2,500.

The entries to record the liquidation are as follows:

Sale of Assets

Cash	5,000	
Loss on Realization	60,000	
Other Assets		65,000
Drew, Capital	20,000	
Gurney, Capital	20,000	
Lambert, Capital	20,000	
Loss on Realization		60,000

Payment of Liabilities

Liabilities	10,000	
Cash		10,000

Distribution to Partners

Gurney, Capital	2,500	
Lambert, Capital	12,500	
Cash		15,000

Since there is a capital deficiency outstanding, one of three different possibilities will arise in the future: (1) Drew pays the deficiency in full; (2) Drew makes a partial payment; (3) Drew makes no payment. The entries corresponding to these possibilities are:

(1) Payment in Full

Cash	5,000	
Drew, Capital		5,000

Gurney, Capital	2,500	
Lambert, Capital	2,500	
Cash		5,000

(2) Partial Payment of $4,000

Cash	4,000	
Drew, Capital		4,000

Settlement of Drew's deficiency

Gurney, Capital	500	
Lambert, Capital	500	
Drew, Capital		1,000

To close out the balance of Drew's account

Gurney, Capital	2,000	
Lambert, Capital	2,000	
Cash		4,000

To distribute cash according to capital balances

(3) No Payment

Gurney, Capital	2,500	
Lambert, Capital	2,500	
Drew, Capital		5,000

Summary

1. Partnership and sole proprietorship accounting are alike except in _____.

2. Noncash assets are recorded at _____ amounts when the partnership is formed.

3. If profits and losses are not to be shared equally, the basis of distribution must be stated in the _____.

4. Salaries and the interest on partners' capital balances are not included on the income statement but are shown on the _____.

5. The book value of the partnership of Acme and Beam is $60,000, with each partner's account showing $30,000. If Caldwell were to purchase Beam's interest for $40,000, the amount credited to Caldwell's equity account would be _____.

6. In order to reflect higher current prices, certain assets of the partnership will be debited, with the corresponding credit to _____ .

7. A firm's superior earning power is recognized as _____ .

8. When a partnership decides to go out of business, the process of selling the assets, paying the creditors, and distributing the remaining cash to the partners is known as _____ .

9. The final distribution of cash to the partners is based on their _____ .

Answers:　1. owners' equity; 2. agreed; 3. partnership agreement; 4. capital statement; 5. $30,000; 6. Asset Revaluation; 7. goodwill; 8. liquidation; 9. capital balances

Solved Problems

16.1　Henderson and Erin have decided to form a partnership. Henderson invests the following assets at their agreed valuations, and he also transfers his liabilities to the new firm.

Henderson's Accounts	Henderson's Ledger Balances	Agreed Valuations
Cash	$17,500	$17,500
Accounts Receivable	7,200	7,000
Merchandise Inventory	12,200	10,000
Equipment	6,000	4,200
Accumulated Depreciation	1,000	
Accounts Payable	3,500	3,500
Notes Payable	3,600	3,600

Erin agrees to invest $26,000 in cash. Record (*a*) Henderson's investment; (*b*) Erin's investment.

(*a*)

(*b*)

SOLUTION

(a)	Cash	17,500	
	Accounts Receivable	7,000	
	Merchandise Inventory	10,000	
	Equipment	4,200	
	Accounts Payable		3,500
	Notes Payable		3,600
	Henderson, Capital		31,600
(b)	Cash	26,000	
	Erin, Capital		26,000

16.2 Adams, Bentley, and Carson have capital balances of $30,000, $25,000, and $20,000, respectively. Adams devotes three-fourths time; Bentley, half time; and Carson, one-fourth time. Determine their participation in net income of $37,500 if income is divided (a) in the ratio of capital investments; (b) in the ratio of time worked.

(a)	Adams	
	Bentley	
	Carson	
	Net Income	$37,500
(b)	Adams	
	Bentley	
	Carson	
	Net Income	$37,500

SOLUTION

(a) Total capital is $75,000. Hence:

Adams	($30,000/$75,000) × $37,500 =	$15,000
Bentley	($25,000/$75,000) × $37,500 =	12,500
Carson	($20,000/$75,000) × $37,500 =	10,000
Net income		$37,500

(b) The ratio is 3:2:1. Hence:

Adams	$\frac{3}{6}$ × $37,500 =	$18,750
Bentley	$\frac{2}{6}$ × $37,500 =	12,500
Carson	$\frac{1}{6}$ × $37,500 =	6,250
Net income		$37,500

16.3 The capital accounts of W. Dunn and S. Evans have balances of $35,000 and $25,000, respectively. The articles of copartnership refer to the distribution of net income as follows:

1. Dunn and Evans are to receive salaries of $9,000 and $6,000, respectively.
2. Each is to receive 6 percent on his capital account.
3. The balance is to be divided equally.

If net income for the firm is $32,000, (a) determine the division of net income and (b) present the entry to close the expense and income summary account.

(a)

	Dunn	Evans	Total
Salaries			
Interest			
Balance			
Share of net income			

(b)

SOLUTION

(a)

	Dunn	Evans	Total
Salaries	$ 9,000	$ 6,000	$15,000
Interest	2,100	1,500	3,600
	$11,100	$ 7,500	$18,600
Balance	6,700	6,700	13,400
Share of net income	$17,800	$14,200	$32,000

(b)

Expense and Income Summary	32,000	
Dunn, Capital		17,800
Evans, Capital		14,200

16.4 Redo Problem 16.3 for a net income of $12,000.

(a)

	Dunn	Evans	Total
Salaries			
Interest			
Balance			
Share of net income			

(b)

SOLUTION

(a)

	Dunn	Evans	Total
Salaries	$ 9,000	$6,000	$15,000
Interest	2,100	1,500	3,600
	$11,100	$7,500	$18,600
Balance	− 3,300	− 3,300	− 6,600
Share of net income	$ 7,800	$4,200	$12,000

(b)

Expense and Income Summary	12,000	
Dunn, Capital		7,800
Evans, Capital		4,200

16.5 The abbreviated income statement of James and Kelly for December 31, 19X5, appears below:

Sales (net)	$240,000
Less: Cost of Goods Sold	105,000
Gross Profit	$135,000
Less: Expenses	65,000
Net Income	$ 70,000

The profit and loss agreement specifies that:

1. Interest of 5 percent is to be allowed on capital balances (James, $25,000; Kelly, $15,000).

2. Salary allowances to James and Kelly are to be $6,000 and $4,000, respectively.

3. A bonus is to be given to James equal to 20 percent of net income without regard to interest or salary.

4. Remaining profits and losses are to be divided in the ratio of capital balances.

(a) Present the distribution of net income.

(b) Present the journal entry required to close the books.

(a)

	James	Kelly	Total
Interest			
Salary			
Bonus			
Balance			
Net income			

(b)

SOLUTION

(a)

	James	Kelly	Total
Interest	$ 1,250	$ 750	$ 2,000
Salary	6,000	4,000	10,000
Bonus	14,000		14,000
	$21,250	$ 4,750	$26,000
Balance	27,500*	16,500*	44,000
Net income	$48,750	$21,250	$70,000

$*$25,000 James $\frac{25}{40} \times \$44,000 = \$27,500$
 15,000 Kelly $\frac{15}{40} \times \$44,000 = \$16,500$
$40,000 Total

(b)

Expense and Income Summary	70,000	
James, Capital		48,750
Kelly, Capital		21,250

16.6 Kupo, Lesser, and Morton, with capital balances of $20,000, $30,000, and $25,000, respectively, split their profits and losses based on their capital balances. If the net profit for the year was $150,000, determine the distribution to each partner.

Kupo	
Lesser	
Morton	
Total cash	$150,000

SOLUTION

Kupo	$ 40,000	$(\frac{20}{75} \times \$150,000)$
Lesser	60,000	$(\frac{30}{75} \times \$150,000)$
Morton	50,000	$(\frac{25}{75} \times \$150,000)$
Total cash	$150,000	

16.7 The capital accounts in the partnership of Frank Buck and John Doe are $57,500 and $87,500, respectively. The partnership agreement calls for a 15 percent interest on their capital accounts and the remaining sum to be shared equally. Net income for the year was $30,000. Show the division of the net income in good report form.

	Buck	Doe	Combined
Interest on capital balance			
Buck			
Doe			
Subtotal			
Balance			
Totals			

SOLUTION

	Buck	Doe	Combined
Interest on capital balance			
Buck, $57,000 × 15%	$ 8,625		$ 8,625
Doe, $87,500 × 15%		$13,125	13,125
Subtotal			$21,750
Balance ($30,000 − $21,750) divided equally	4,125	4,125	8,250
Totals	$12,750	$17,250	$30,000

16.8 From the information in Problem 16.7, show the journal entry to close the Income Summary account.

	Dr.	Cr.

SOLUTION

	Dr.	Cr.
Expense and Income Summary	30,000	
Buck, Capital		12,750
Doe, Capital		17,250

16.9 If Frank Buck and John Doe had the same partnership agreement and capital balances as above but incurred a net loss of $2,000, show the distribution in good report form.

	Buck	Doe	Combined
Buck			
Doe			
Subtotal			
Deficiency			
Totals			

SOLUTION

	Buck	Doe	Combined
Buck	$ 8,625		$ 8,625
Doe		$13,125	13,125
Subtotal			$21,750
Deficiency ($2,000 + 21,750) divided equally	(11,875)	(11,875)	23,750
Totals	($3,250)	$1,250	($2,000)

16.10 From the information above, show the journal entry to close the Income Summary account.

	Dr.	Cr.

SOLUTION

	Dr.	Cr.
Buck, Capital	3,250	
Expense & Income Summary		2,000
Doe, Capital		1,250

16.11 The partnership of Klein, Cross, and Budd had net income of $60,000 for the current year. The partnership agreement called for interest of 10 percent on average capital accounts, salaries of $5,000, $5,000, and $10,000, respectively, and the remaining sum divided in a 2:2:1 ratio. Average capital accounts were as follows:

Klein, Capital, $20,000

Cross, Capital, $20,000

Budd, Capital, $10,000

Show the division of the net income in good report form.

	Klein	**Cross**	**Budd**	**Combined**
Subtotal				
Salaries				
2:2:1 ratio balance				
Totals				

SOLUTION

	Klein	**Cross**	**Budd**	**Combined**
Klein ($20,000 × 10%)	$ 2,000			$ 2,000
Cross ($20,000 × 10%)		$ 2,000		2,000
Budd ($10,000 × 10%)			$ 1,000	1,000
Subtotal				5,000
Salaries	5,000	5,000	10,000	20,000
	$ 7,000	$ 7,000	$11,000	$25,000
2:2:1 ratio balance	14,000	14,000	7,000	35,000
Totals	$21,000	$21,000	$18,000	$60,000

16.12 From the above information, show the journal entry to close the Expense and Income Summary account.

	Dr.	Cr.

SOLUTION

	Dr.	Cr.
Expense and Income Summary	60,000	
Klein, Capital		21,000
Cross, Capital		21,000
Budd, Capital		18,000

16.13 From the preceding problem, if there was a net income of $20,000 and the agreement was the same that income and losses were shared in a ratio of 2:2:1, show the division of the net income in good report form.

	Klein	Cross	Budd	Combined
Klein				
Cross				
Budd				
Subtotal				
Salaries				
Deficiency ratio 2:2:1				

SOLUTION

	Klein	Cross	Budd	Combined
Klein ($20,000 × 10%)	$ 2,000			$ 2,000
Cross ($20,000 × 10%)		$ 2,000		2,000
Budd ($10,000 × 10%)			$ 1,000	1,000
Subtotal				$ 5,000
Salaries	5,000	5,000	10,000	20,000
	$ 7,000	$ 7,000	$11,000	$25,000
Deficiency ratio 2:2:1	(2,000)	(2,000)	(1,000)	(5,000)
	$ 5,000	$ 5,000	$10,000	$20,000

16.14 Show the closing entry from the above information.

	Dr.	Cr.

SOLUTION

	Dr.	Cr.
Expense and Income Summary	20,000	
Klein, Capital		5,000
Cross, Capital		5,000
Budd, Capital		10,000

16.15 The capital accounts of J. Phillips and J. Willens have balances of $25,000 each. E. Kurlander joins the partnership. What entry is necessary (a) if Kurlander purchases half of Phillip's investment for $15,000? (b) if Kurlander invests $15,000 in the firm?

(a)

(b)

SOLUTION

		Dr.	Cr.
(a)	J. Phillips, Capital	12,500	
	E. Kurlander, Capital		12,500
(b)	Cash	15,000	
	E. Kurlander, Capital		15,000

16.16 The financial position of the partnership of Eccleston and Kapela, who share income in the ratio 3:2, is shown below:

Eccleston-Kapela Company
Balance Sheet
April 30, 19X5

ASSETS		LIABILITIES AND CAPITAL	
Current Assets	$ 65,000	Liabilities	$ 50,000
Equipment (net)	125,000	Eccleston, Capital	85,000
		Kapela, Capital	55,000
Total Assets	$190,000	Total Liabilities and Capital	$190,000

Both partners agree to admit a new partner, Graves, into the firm. Prepare the necessary entries corresponding to each of the following options:

(a) Graves purchases half of Kapela's interest for $30,000.

(b) Graves invests $70,000 in the partnership and receives a one-third interest in capital and income.

(c) The original partners feel that goodwill should be recorded at $20,000. Graves' investment is to gain her a one-third interest in capital and income.

(a)

(b)

(c)

SOLUTION

(a) Kapela, Capital	27,500	
Graves, Capital		27,500
(b) Cash	70,000	
Graves, Capital		70,000
(c) Goodwill	20,000	
Eccleston, Capital		12,000
Kapela, Capital		8,000
Cash	80,000	
Graves, Capital		80,000*

*Eccleston and Kapela = $160,000; Capital = $\frac{2}{3}$; Graves must put in $\frac{1}{3}$ or $80,000.

16.17 Before admitting Goldsmith to the partnership, Klapper and Babcock, who share profits and losses equally, decide that (a) Merchandise Inventory, recorded at $26,000, is to be revalued at $29,000; (b) $500 of Accounts Receivable is to be written off. Present journal entries to record the revaluations.

(a)

(b)

SOLUTION

(a)	Merchandise Inventory	3,000	
	Accounts Receivable		500
	Asset Revaluation		2,500
(b)	Asset Revaluation	2,500	
	Klapper, Capital		1,250
	Babcock, Capital		1,250

16.18 After the assets of the partnership have been adjusted to reflect current prices, the capital balances of B. Trane and J. Hochian are each $25,000. However, both partners agree that the partnership is worth $60,000. They decide to admit R. Berechad as an equal partner into their firm for a $30,000 investment. (*a*) Record the recognition of goodwill. (*b*) Record Berechad's investment. (*c*) What is the total capital of the firm?

(a)

(b)

(c)

SOLUTION

(a)	Goodwill	10,000	
	B. Trane, Capital		5,000
	J. Hochian, Capital		5,000
(b)	Cash	30,000	
	R. Berechad, Capital		30,000

(c)	B. Trane, Capital	$30,000
	J. Hochian, Capital	30,000
	R. Berechad, Capital	30,000
	Total Capital	$90,000

16.19 If, in Problem 16.18, R. Berechad invested $20,000 for an equal share of equity, what would the entry be to record her admittance into the firm?

SOLUTION

Cash	20,000	
Goodwill	10,000	.
R. Berechad, Capital		30,000

Since the total capital prior to Berechad's admittance was $60,000, an equal share would require an investment of $30,000, as in Problem 16.18. Therefore, the owners must have agreed to recognize the new partner's ability and awarded her capital credit (goodwill) of $30,000 − $20,000 = $10,000.

16.20 The following T accounts show the balances of the partnership of Bigelow and Holand as of June 30, 19X5, prior to dissolution:

Cash		Merchandise Inventory	
35,000		12,600	

Equipment		Accumulated Depreciation	
15,000			12,000

Prepaid Insurance		Account Payable	
1,400			16,000

Bigelow, Capital		Holand, Capital	
	18,000		18,000

The partners share profits and losses equally. The terminating transactions are:

(a) Sold the merchandise for its market value, $16,500
(b) Realized $1,100 from the surrender of the insurance policies
(c) Sold the equipment for $2,000
(d) Distributed the gain to the partners' capital accounts
(e) Paid all liabilities
(f) Distributed the remaining cash

Present journal entries to record the above information.

(a)

(b)

(c)			
(d)			
(e)			
(f)			

SOLUTION

(a)	Cash	16,500	
	Merchandise Inventory		12,600
	Loss or Gain on Realization*		3,900
(b)	Cash	1,100	
	Loss or Gain on Realization	300	
	Prepaid Insurance		1,400
(c)	Cash	2,000	
	Accumulated Depreciation	12,000	
	Loss or Gain on Realization	1,000	
	Equipment		15,000
(d)	Loss or Gain on Realization	2,600	
	Bigelow, Capital		1,300
	Holand, Capital		1,300
(e)	Accounts Payable	16,000	
	Cash		16,000
(f)	Bigelow, Capital	19,300	
	Holand, Capital	19,300	
	Cash		38,600

*Used to show the difference between value and sale.

Summary of Transactions

Transaction	Cash	Other Assets	Liabilities	Bigelow, Capital	Holand, Capital
Balance	$35,000	$17,000	$16,000	$18,000	$18,000
(a)–(d)	+ 19,600	− 17,000		+ 1,300	+ 1,300
	$54,600		$16,000	$19,300	$19,300
(e)	− 16,000		− 16,000		
(f)	$38,600			$19,300	$19,300
	− 38,600			− 19,300	− 19,300

16.21 Sochet, Carlin, and Stadler, who divide profits and losses equally, have the following ledger balances as of December 31:

Cash	$36,000	Sochet, Capital	$15,000
Other Assets	18,000	Carlin, Capital	10,000
Liabilities	16,000	Stadler, Capital	13,000

The partners decide to liquidate and sell their noncash assets at a loss of $6,000. After meeting their obligations, they divide the remaining cash. Present all necessary entries.

(a) **Loss on realization:**

(b) **Division of loss:**

(c) **Payment of liabilities:**

(d) **Division of remaining cash:**

SOLUTION

(a)	**Loss on realization:**		
	Cash	12,000	
	Loss on Realization	6,000	
	Other Assets		18,000
(b)	**Division of loss:**		
	Sochet, Capital	2,000	
	Carlin, Capital	2,000	
	Stadler, Capital	2,000	
	Loss on Realization		6,000
(c)	**Payment of liabilities:**		
	Liabilities	16,000	
	Cash		16,000
(d)	**Division of remaining cash:**		
	Sochet, Capital	13,000	
	Carlin, Capital	8,000	
	Stadler, Capital	11,000	
	Cash		32,000

Summary of Transactions

Transaction	Cash	Other Assets	Liabilities	Sochet, Capital	Carlin, Capital	Stadler, Capital
Balance	$36,000	$18,000	$16,000	$15,000	$10,000	$13,000
(a), (b)	+ 12,000	− 18,000		− 2,000	− 2,000	− 2,000
	$48,000		$16,000	$13,000	$ 8,000	$11,000
(c)	− 16,000		− 16,000			
	$32,000			$13,000	$ 8,000	$11,000
(d)	− 32,000			− 13,000	− 8,000	− 11,000

16.22 Shambley, Sudol, and Harmin, who share income and losses in the ratio 2:1:1, decide to liquidate their business on April 30. As of that date their post-closing trial balance reads:

Cash	$ 38,000	
Other Assets:	82,000	
Liabilities		$ 48,000
Shambley, Capital		30,000
Sudol, Capital		22,000
Harmin, Capital		20,000
	$120,000	$120,000

Present the entries to record the following liquidating transactions:

(a) Sold the noncash assets for $12,000

(b) Distributed the loss to the partners

(c) Paid the liabilities

(d) Allocated the available cash to the partners

(e) The partner with the debit balance pays the amount he owes

(f) Any additional money is distributed

(a)			
(b)			
(c)			
(d)			
(e)			
(f)			

SOLUTION

(a)	Cash	12,000	
	Loss on Realization	70,000	
	Other Assets		82,000
(b)	Shambley, Capital	35,000	
	Sudol, Capital	17,500	
	Harmin, Capital	17,500	
	Loss on Realization		70,000
(c)	Liabilities	48,000	
	Cash		48,000
(d)	Sudol, Capital	2,000	
	Cash		2,000

(e)	Shambley, Capital	5,000	
	Cash		5,000
(f)	Cash	5,000	
	Sudol, Capital		2,500
	Harmin, Capital		2,500

Summary of Transactions

Transaction	Cash	Other Assets	Liabilities	Shambley, Capital	Sudol, Capital	Harmin, Capital
Balance	$38,000	$82,000	$48,000	$30,000	$22,000	$20,000
(a), (b)	+ 12,000	− 82,000		− 35,000	− 17,500	− 17,500
	$50,000		$48,000	$(5,000)	$ 4,500	$ 2,500
(c)	− 48,000		− 48,000			
	$ 2,000			$(5,000)	$ 4,500	$ 2,500
(d)	− 2,000				− 2,000	
				$(5,000)	$ 2,500	$ 2,500
(e)	+ 5,000			+ 5,000		
	$ 5,000				$ 2,500	$ 2,500
(f)	− 5,000				− 2,500	− 2,500

16.23 The trial balance of Blake and Carson, who share profits and losses equally, is as follows:

Cash	$ 40,000	
Other Assets:	60,000	
Accounts Payable		$ 30,000
Blake, Capital		45,000
Carson, Capital		25,000
	$100,000	$100,000

Both partners had decided to admit Davidoff into the partnership, as the business had grown steadily. Prior to Davidoff's admittance, the partners had agreed to record goodwill of $20,000. After this adjustment had been made, Davidoff invested sufficient cash so that he would have a one-third interest in the firm. However, the partners could not work together, and they decided to liquidate. The business, exclusive of the cash balance but including their liabilities, was sold for $32,000. Assuming that, at the time of the sale, the balances of the accounts were as they appear above, prepare journal entries to record (a) the recognition of goodwill, (b) the acceptance of Davidoff into the partnership, (c) the sale of the business, (d) the distribution of the loss on realization, (e) the final division of cash.

(a)			

(b)

(c)

(d)

(e)

SOLUTION

(a)	Goodwill	20,000	
	Blake, Capital		10,000
	Carson, Capital		10,000
(b)	Cash	45,000	
	Davidoff, Capital		45,000*
	*To produce three equal parts, Davidoff must invest one-half of the existing capital ($70,000 + $20,000 goodwill).		
(c)	Cash	32,000	
	Accounts Payable	30,000	
	Loss on Realization	18,000	
	Other Assets		60,000
	Goodwill		20,000
(d)	Blake, Capital	6,000	
	Carson, Capital	6,000	
	Davidoff, Capital	6,000	
	Loss on Realization		18,000
(e)	Blake, Capital	49,000	
	Carson, Capital	29,000	
	Davidoff, Capital	39,000	
	Cash		117,000

Summary of Transactions

Transaction	Cash	Other Assets	Goodwill	Accounts Payable	Blake, Capital	Carson, Capital	Davidoff, Capital
Balance	$ 40,000	$60,000		$30,000	$45,000	$25,000	
(a)			$20,000		+ 10,000	+ 10,000	
	$ 40,000	$60,000	$20,000	$30,000	$55,000	$35,000	
(b)	+ 45,000						$45,000
	$ 85,000	$60,000	$20,000	$30,000	$55,000	$35,000	$45,000
(c), (d)	+ 32,000	− 60,000	− 20,000	− 30,000	− 6,000	− 6,000	− 6,000
	$117,000				$49,000	$29,000	$39,000
(e)	117,000				− 49,000	− 29,000	− 39,000

Chapter 17

The Corporation

17.1 CHARACTERISTICS OF THE CORPORATION

In essence, the corporation is an artificial being, created by law and having a continuous existence regardless of its changing membership. The members are the stockholders; they own the corporation but are distinct from it. As a separate legal entity, the corporation has all the rights and responsibilities of a person, such as entering into contracts, suing and being sued in its own name, and buying, selling, or owning property.

17.2 CORPORATE TERMINOLOGY

The *stockholders*, as owners of the business, have the right (1) to vote (one vote for every share of stock held), (2) to share in profits, (3) to transfer ownership, (4) to share in the distribution of assets in case of liquidation.

The *board of directors* is elected by the stockholders within the framework of the articles of incorporation. The board's duties include the appointing of corporate officers, determining company policies, and the distribution of profits.

A *share of stock* represents a unit of the stockholders' interest in the business. The par value of a share is an arbitrary amount established in the corporation's charter and printed on the face of each stock certificate. It bears no relation to the *market value*, that is, the current purchase or selling price. There are several categories of stock shares:

Authorized shares are shares of stock that a corporation is permitted to issue (sell) under its articles of incorporation.

Unissued shares are authorized shares that have not yet been offered for sale.

Subscribed shares are shares that a buyer has contracted to purchase at a specific price on a certain date. The shares will not be issued until full payment has been received.

Treasury stock represents shares that have been issued and later reacquired by the corporation.

Outstanding stock represents shares authorized, issued, and in the hands of stockholders. (Treasury stock is not outstanding, as it belongs to the corporation and not to the stockholders.)

17.3 ADVANTAGES OF THE CORPORATE FORM

The corporate form of business in the United States, when compared to the sole proprietorship or partnership, has several important advantages:

1. *Limited liability of stockholders.* Each stockholder is accountable only for the amount he or she invests in the corporation. If the company should fail, the creditors cannot ordinarily look beyond the assets of the corporation for settlement of their claims.

2. *Ready transfer of ownership.* Ownership of a corporation is evidenced by stock certificates; this permits stockholders to buy or sell their interests in a corporation without interfering with the management of the business. Through the medium of organized exchanges, millions of shares of stock change hands each day.

3. **Continued existence.** The death or incapacity of a partner may dissolve a partnership, but the corporation's existence is independent of the stockholders.

4. **Legal entity.** The corporation can sue and be sued, make contracts, buy and sell in its own name. This is in contrast to the sole proprietorship, which must, by law, use individual names in all legal matters.

5. **Ease of raising capital.** Advantages 1 and 2 on the preceeding page make the corporation an attractive investment for stockholders. Compare this to the partnership, where capital raising is restricted by the number of partners, the amounts of their individual assets, and the prospect of unlimited liability.

17.4 DISADVANTAGES OF THE CORPORATE FORM

Although the corporate form of business has the advantages listed above, it also has some disadvantages, such as the following:

1. **Taxation.** The corporation must pay federal income taxes in the same manner as an individual, and this results in double taxation of corporate income. Double taxation develops first from the taxing of the net profits and second from that portion of the profits distributed to the stockholders as individual income.

2. **Cost of organization.** The corporation must secure state approval and legal assistance in forming this type of ownership. Requirements vary from state to state, but all states require (a) a minimum number of stockholders, (b) a minimum amount of capital, and (c) a payment of incorporation fees and taxes. The legal fees involved may run to thousands of dollars in large firms and must be added to the costs of state fees and taxes.

3. **Legal restrictions.** The charter of the corporation of a state is the basis of the corporation's transactions and permits it to engage in only those activities that are stated or implied in the document. If the corporation wishes to operate in another state, it must either incorporate in that state also or pay a tax to the state. It is, therefore, apparent that the corporation is the most restricted form of business ownership.

17.5 EQUITY ACCOUNTING FOR THE CORPORATION

Accounting for the corporation is distinguished from accounting for the sole proprietorship or the partnership by the treatment of owners' (stockholders') equity, which, in the corporation, is separated into paid-in capital and retained earnings. The reason for this separation is that most states prohibit corporations from paying dividends from other than retained earnings. Paid-in capital is further divided, and so we have three major capital accounts:

Capital Stock. This account shows the par value of the stock issued by the corporation.

Additional Paid-in Capital. Amounts paid in beyond the par value of stock.

Retained Earnings. The accumulated earnings arising from profitable operation of the business.

EXAMPLE 1 Operation at a Profit

Assume that on January 1, two separate businesses are formed, a sole proprietorship operated by Ira Sochet and a corporation having four stockholders. Assume further that the single owner invested $20,000, while the four stockholders each bought 500 shares of common stock at $10 per share. The entries to record the investments are as follows:

	Sole Proprietorship			*Corporation*	
Cash	20,000		Cash	20,000	
Ira Sochet, Capital		20,000	Common Stock		20,000

After a year's operations, the net income of each enterprise was $5,000. In the sole proprietorship, the Expense and Income Summary balance is transferred to the capital account; in the corporation, the balance is transferred to Retained Earnings. Thus:

	Sole Proprietorship			*Corporation*	
Expense and			Expense and		
Income Summary	5,000		Income Summary	5,000	
Ira Sochet, Capital		5,000	Retained Earnings		5,000

The balance sheets of the two firms are identical except for the owners' equity sections, which appear as follows:

	Sole Proprietorship			*Corporation*	
Ira Sochet, Capital, January 1	$20,000		Common Stock, $10 par (2,000 shares authorized and issued)		$20,000
Add: Net Income	5,000		Retained Earnings		5,000
Ira Sochet, Capital, December 31	$25,000		Stockholders' Equity		$25,000

EXAMPLE 2 Operation at a Loss

During the second year of operations, both firms in Example 1 lost $7,000, an amount that exceeds the first year's profits. Observe the difference in the two balance sheets:

	Sole Proprietorship			*Corporation*	
Ira Sochet, Capital, January 1	$25,000		Common Stock, $10 par (2,000 shares authorized and issued)		$20,000
Deduct: Net Loss	(7,000)		Deduct: Deficit		(2,000)*
Ira Sochet, Capital, December 31	$18,000		Stockholders' Equity		$18,000

Retained Earnings	
7,000	5,000

The $7,000 was treated as a net loss in the sole proprietorship; in the corporation, it was reduced by the net profit from the first year and titled "Deficit."

17.6 COMMON STOCK

If a corporation issues only one class of stock, it is known as *common stock,* with all shares having the same rights. The ownership of a share of common stock carries with it the right to:

1. Vote in the election of directors and in the making of certain important corporate decisions
2. Participate in the corporation's profits
3. Purchase a proportionate part of future stock issues
4. Share in assets upon liquidation

17.7 PREFERRED STOCK

In order to appeal to a broader market, the corporation may also issue *preferred stock*. This class of stock does not ordinarily carry voting rights (although such rights are sometimes conferred by a special provision in the charter); however, as its name implies, this stock does take preference over common stock in several respects.

Prior claim against earnings.   The board of directors has the power to declare and distribute dividends to the stockholders. In such distributions, the claims of preferred stock are honored before those of common stock. However, the amount of dividends paid to preferred stock is usually placed on the amount paid to common stock. From an accounting viewpoint, the priority in receiving dividends constitutes the most important benefit of preferred stock.

EXAMPLE 3

Eppy Corporation has outstanding 1,000 shares of preferred stock with a preference of a $5 dividend (5 percent of $100 par value) and 3,000 shares of common stock. Net income was $20,000 and $40,000 for the first 2 years of operations. The board of directors has authorized the distribution of all profits.

	Year 1	Year 2
Net Profit	$20,000	$40,000
Dividends on Preferred		
(1,000 shares, $5 per share)	5,000	5,000
Balance to Common	$15,000	$35,000
Number of Common Shares	÷3,000	÷3,000
Common Stock Dividend per Share	$5.00	$11.67

Prior claim to assets.   If, upon liquidation of a corporation, the assets that remain after payment of all creditors are not sufficient to return the full amount of the capital contribution of preferred and common stockholders, payment must first be made to preferred stockholders. Any balance would then go to common stockholders.

Preferred stock may also carry the following options:

Call privilege.   The issuing company will have the right to redeem (all) the stock at a later date for a predetermined price. This call price would be in excess of the original issue price, such as 105 percent of par value.

Conversion privilege.   The stockholders, at their option, may convert preferred stock into common stock. This might be done if the corporation's common stock should become more desirable than the preferred stock because of large earnings (see Example 3).

17.8 ISSUE OF STOCK

Issue at Par

When a corporation is organized, the charter will state how many shares of common and preferred stock are authorized. Often more stock is authorized than is intended to be sold immediately. This will enable the corporation to expand in the future without applying to the state for permission to issue more shares. When stock is sold for cash and issued immediately, the entry to record the security has the usual form: Cash is debited, and the particular security is credited.

EXAMPLE 4

Carey Corporation, organized on January 1 with an authorization of 10,000 shares of common stock ($40 par), issues 8,000 shares at par for cash. The entry to record the stockholders' investment and the receipt of cash is:

Cash	320,000	
Common Stock		320,000

If, in addition, Carey Corporation issues 1,000 shares of preferred 5 percent stock ($100 par) at par, the combined entry would be:

Cash	420,000	
Preferred Stock		100,000
Common Stock		320,000

A corporation may accept property other than cash in exchange for stock. If this occurs, the assets should be recorded at fair market value, usually as determined by the board of directors of the company.

EXAMPLE 5

In exchange for 1,000 shares of $100-par common stock, Walker Corporation receives, at fair market value, machinery worth $50,000, and land and buildings worth $30,000 and $20,000, respectively. The transaction is recorded as:

Machinery	50,000	
Land	30,000	
Buildings	20,000	
Common Stock		100,000

Issue at a Premium or a Discount

The market price of stock is influenced by many factors, such as:

1. Potential earning power
2. General business conditions and other prospects
3. Financial condition and earnings record
4. Dividend record

Stock will be sold at a price above par if investors are willing to pay the excess, or premium. The premium is not profit to the corporation but rather part of the investment of the stockholders.

EXAMPLE 6

Carey Corporation issues 8,000 shares of its authorized 10,000 shares of common stock ($40 par) for $45 a share. The entry to record the transaction is:

Cash	360,000	
Common Stock		320,000
Premium on Common Stock		40,000

If the purchaser will not pay par value, the corporation may issue the stock at a price below par. The difference between par value and the lower price is called the *discount*.

EXAMPLE 7

Carey Corporation issues 1,000 shares of 5 percent preferred stock ($100 par) at 98.

Cash	98,000	
Discount on Preferred Stock	2,000	
Preferred Stock		100,000

EXAMPLE 8

Based on Examples 6 and 7, the stockholders' equity section of the balance sheet of Carey Corporation is as follows:

Paid-in Capital		
Preferred Stock, 5%, $100 par		
(1,000 shares authorized and		
issued)	$100,000	
Less: Discount on Preferred Stock	2,000	$ 98,000
Common Stock, $40 par		
(10,000 shares authorized,		
8,000 shares issued)	$320,000	
Premium on Common Stock	40,000	360,000
Total Paid-in Capital		$458,000
Retained Earnings		22,000*
Stockholders' Equity		$480,000

*Assumed.

17.9 BOOK VALUE

The book value per share of stock is obtained by dividing the stockholders' equity amount by the number of shares outstanding. It thus represents the amount that would be distributed to each share of stock if the corporation were to be dissolved.

Individual book values for common and preferred stock are defined by separating the stockholders' equity amount into two parts and dividing each part by the corresponding number of shares. All premiums and discounts, as well as retained earnings or deficits, go to common stock only.

EXAMPLE 9

Suppose that the balance sheet reads:

Common Stock, $40 par	
(10,000 shares authorized,	
8,000 shares issued)	$320,000
Retained Earnings	22,000
Stockholders' Equity	$342,000

Then we would have

$$\text{Book value} = \frac{\$342,000}{8,000 \text{ shares}} = \$42.75 \text{ per share}$$

EXAMPLE 10

For the data in Example 8, the allocation of the total equity between preferred and common stock would be

Total equity	$480,000
Allocation to preferred stock	100,000
Balance to common stock	$380,000

and the book values would be

$$\text{Book value of preferred} = \frac{\$100,000}{1,000 \text{ shares}} = \$100 \text{ per share}$$

$$\text{Book value of common} = \frac{\$380,000}{8,000 \text{ shares}} = \$47.50 \text{ per share}$$

17.10   EARNINGS PER SHARE

To find earnings per share (EPS), take the net profit after taxes, less any preferred dividends. This will equal the earnings available for common stockholders. Divide by the number of shares of common stock outstanding to arrive at EPS:

$$\text{Earnings Per Share} = \frac{\text{earnings available for common stockholders}}{\text{number of shares of common stock outstanding}}$$

EXAMPLE 11

ABC Corporation, with 200,000 shares of common stock outstanding, had net income after taxes of $500,000. They declared and paid $100,000 of preferred stock dividends. What is the EPS?

$$\frac{\$400,000}{200,000} = \$2.00 \text{ EPS}$$

This figure is the dollar amount earned on behalf of each common stock shareholder. Note that this does not mean the stockholders will receive this amount in the form of a dividend: The corporation is not required to pay a dividend to common stockholders.

17.11   BOND CHARACTERISTICS

A corporation may obtain funds by selling stock or by borrowing through long-term obligations. An issue of bonds is a form of long-term debt in which the corporation agrees to pay interest periodically and to repay the principal at a stated future date.

Bond denominations are commonly multiples of $1,000. A bond issue normally has a term of 10 or 20 years, although some issues may have longer lives. The date at which a bond is to be repaid is known as the *maturity date*. In an issue of serial bonds, the maturity dates are spread in a series over the term of the issue. This relieves the corporation from the impact of total payment at one date.

17.12 FUNDING BY STOCK VERSUS FUNDING BY BONDS

The major differences between stocks and bonds may be summarized as follows:

	Stocks	Bonds
Representation	Ownership in the corporation	A debt of the corporation
Inducement to Holders	Dividends	Interest
Accounting Treatment	Dividends are a distribution of profits Stocks are equity	Interest is an expense Bonds are a long-term liability
Repayment	By selling in the market at any time	On a predetermined date

These differences give rise to alternative methods of financing, as in Examples 12 and 13 below.

EXAMPLE 12

The board of directors of a new company has decided that $1,000,000 is needed to begin operations. The controller presents three different methods of financing:

	Method 1 (Common Stock)	Method 2 (Preferred and Common Stock)	Method 3 (Bonds, Preferred and Common Stock)
Bonds, 5%	—	—	$ 500,000
Preferred stock, 6%	—	$ 500,000	250,000
Common stock, $100 par	$1,000,000	500,000	250,000
Total	$1,000,000	$1,000,000	$1,000,000

Subsequent profits before interest on bonds and before taxes are estimated at $300,000; taxes are estimated at 40 percent.

	Method 1	Method 2	Method 3
Profit	$300,000	$300,000	$300,000
Less: Interest on bonds	—	—	25,000
Net income before taxes	$300,000	$300,000	$275,000
Less: Income taxes	120,000	120,000	110,000
Net Income	$180,000	$180,000	$165,000
Less: Dividends on preferred stock	—	30,000	15,000
Common stock balance	$180,000	$150,000	$150,000
Number of common shares	÷10,000*	÷5,000†	÷2,500‡
Earnings per common share	$18	$30	$60

---

*$1,000,000 ÷ $100.
†$500,000 ÷ $100.
‡$250,000 ÷ $100.

For the common stockholders, Method 3 (called debt and equity financing) is clearly the best. It gives greater earnings because (1) bond interest is deducted for income tax purposes; (2) bonds are marketed at an interest rate that is lower than the dividend rate on preferred stock.

EXAMPLE 13

As the amount of profit becomes smaller, Method 1 of Example 12 becomes the best financing method. Assume that the same three methods of funding are under consideration for an anticipated net income of $60,000 before interest and taxes.

	Method 1	Method 2	Method 3
Profit	$60,000	$60,000	$60,000
Less: Interest on bonds	—	—	25,000
Net income before taxes	$60,000	$60,000	$35,000
Less: Income taxes	24,000	24,000	14,000
Net Income	$36,000	$36,000	$21,000
Less: Dividends on preferred stock	—	30,000	15,000
Common stock balance	$36,000	$ 6,000	$ 6,000
Number of shares	÷10,000	÷5,000	: 2,500
Earnings per share	$3.60	$1.20	$2.40

Summary

1. The rights to vote and to share in the profits of the company rest with the _____.

2. The greatest disadvantage of the corporate form of business is the _____ on income.

3. The value established for stock is called _____.

4. Shares of stock that a corporation is allowed to sell are called _____.

5. The profit and loss of the corporation is recorded in the _____ account.

6. If a corporation issues only one class of stock, this stock is known as _____.

7. To achieve a broader market and a more attractive issue price, preferred stock may _____ _____ in profits beyond the specified rate.

8. The amount paid in excess of par by a purchaser of newly issued stock is called a _____ _____, whereas the amount paid below par is known as a _____.

Answers: 1. stockholders; 2. tax; 3. par value; 4. authorized shares; 5. Retained Earnings; 6. common stock; 7. participate; 8. premium, discount

Solved Problems

17.1 Two separate business organizations, a partnership and a corporation, were formed on January 1, 19X5.

1. The initial investments of the partners, Blue and Gray, were $25,000 and $20,000, respectively.

2. The Green Corporation have five stockholders, each owning 90 shares of $100-par common.

At the end of the calendar year, the net income of each company was $15,000. (*a*) For each organization, show the proper entry to close the expense and income account. (*b*) Prepare a capital statement for the partnership and a stockholders' equity statement for the corporation, as of December 31, 19X5.

(*a*) **Partnership entry:**

Corporation entry:

(*b*)

Partnership Capital Statement

Stockholders' Equity Statement

SOLUTION

(*a*) **Partnership entry:**

Expense and Income Summary	15,000	
Blue, Capital		7,500*
Gray, Capital		7,500*

*Profits and losses are to be divided equally if no other distribution is specified.

Corporation entry:		
Expense and Income Summary	15,000	
Retained Earnings		15,000

(b)

Partnership Capital Statement

	Blue	Gray	Total
Capital, January 1, 19X5	$25,000	$20,000	$45,000
Add: Net Income	7,500	7,500	15,000
Capital, December 31, 19X5	$32,500	$27,500	$60,000

Stockholders' Equity Statement

Common Stock, $100 par	
(450 shares authorized and issued)	$45,000
Retained Earnings	15,000
Stockholders' Equity	$60,000

17.2 Redo Problem 17.1 assuming that each business suffers a loss of $18,000 in the second year of operations.

(a) **Partnership entry:**

Corporation entry:

(b)   *Partnership Capital Statement*

Stockholders' Equity Statement

SOLUTION

(a) **Partnership entry:**

Blue, Capital	9,000	
Gray, Capital	9,000	
Expense and Income Summary		18,000

Corporation entry:

Retained Earnings	18,000	
Expense and Income Summary		18,000

(b)

Partnership Capital Statement

	Blue	Gray	Total
Capital, January 1, 19X5	$32,500	$27,500	$60,000
Less: Net Loss	9,000	9,000	18,000
Capital, December 31, 19X5	$23,500	$18,500	$42,000

Stockholders' Equity Statement

Common Stock, $100 par	
(450 shares authorized and issued)	$45,000
Less: Deficit*	(3,000)
Stockholders' Equity	$42,000
*Retained Earnings (Dec. 31, 19X5)	$15,000
Less: Net Loss (Dec. 31, 19X5)	18,000
Deficit	($3,000)

17.3 The board of directors' policy is to distribute all profits earned in a year to preferred and common stockholders. During the first 3 years of operations, the corporation earned $68,000, $180,000, and $320,000, respectively. There are outstanding 10,000 shares of 6 percent, $100-par preferred stock and 40,000 shares of common stock. Determine the amount per share applicable to common stock for each of the 3 years.

	Year 1	Year 2	Year 3

SOLUTION

	Year 1	Year 2	Year 3
Net profit (after taxes)	$68,000	$180,000	$320,000
Dividend on preferred stock	60,000	60,000	60,000
Balance to common stock	$ 8,000	$120,000	$260,000
Common dividend per share	$0.20	$3.00	$6.50

17.4 On January 1, the Green Corporation issued for cash 5,000 shares of its authorized 10,000 shares of $10-par common stock. Three months later it was decided to issue another 5,000 shares of common stock at par and also 1,000 shares of 5 percent, $100-par preferred stock. What entries are required to record the January and April transactions?

Jan. 1			
Apr. 1			

SOLUTION

Jan. 1	Cash	50,000	
	Common Stock		50,000
Apr. 1	Cash	150,000	
	Common Stock		50,000
	Preferred Stock		100,000

17.5 In Problem 17.4, present the stockholders' equity section: (*a*) as of January 31; (*b*) as of April 30.

(*a*)

(*b*)

SOLUTION

(*a*) Paid-in Capital:

Common Stock, $10 par		
(10,000 shares authorized, 5,000 shares issued)	$50,000	
Stockholders' Equity		$50,000

(*b*) Paid-in Capital:

Preferred Stock, 5%, $100 par		
(1,000 shares authorized and issued)	$100,000	
Common Stock, $10 par		
(10,000 shares authorized and issued)	100,000	
Stockholders' Equity		$200,000

17.6 Rund Corporation issues 2,000 shares of 6 percent, $50-par preferred stock at $48 and 5,000 shares of $25-par common stock at $30. (*a*) Present the entry needed to record the above information. (*b*) Present the stockholders' equity section.

(*a*)

(*b*)

SOLUTION

(*a*)	Cash	246,000	
	Discount on Preferred Stock	4,000	
	Preferred Stock		100,000
	Common Stock		125,000
	Premium on Common Stock		25,000

(*b*)	Paid-in Capital:		
	Preferred Stock, 6%, $50 par	$100,000	
	Less: Discount on Preferred Stock	4,000	$ 96,000
	Common Stock, $25 par	$125,000	
	Add: Premium on Common Stock	25,000	150,000
	Stockholders' Equity		$246,000

17.7 Boaches, Inc., receives in exchange for 3,000 shares of $100-par preferred stock and 2,000 shares of $50-par common stock the following fixed assets:

	Cost	Fair Market Value
Building	$200,000	$125,000
Land	100,000	80,000
Machinery	150,000	150,000
Equipment	60,000	45,000

Provide the entry to record the above information.

SOLUTION

Building	125,000	
Land	80,000	
Machinery	150,000	
Equipment	45,000	
Preferred Stock		300,000
Common Stock		100,000

17.8 The Tobak Corporation agrees to issue 10,000 shares of common stock in exchange for equipment valued at $250,000. Present the required journal entry if par value of the common stock is (a) $25, (b) $20, (c) $30.

(a)

(b)

(c)

SOLUTION

(a)	Equipment	250,000	
	Common Stock		250,000
(b)	Equipment	250,000	
	Common Stock		200,000
	Premium on Common Stock		50,000
(c)	Equipment	250,000	
	Discount on Common Stock	50,000	
	Common Stock		300,000

17.9 On January 1, P. Henry, Inc., was organized with an authorization of 5,000 shares of preferred 6 percent stock, $100 par, and 10,000 shares of $25-par common stock.

(a) Record the following transactions:

    Jan. 10   Sold half of the common stock at $28 for cash.

           15   Issued 2,000 shares of preferred and 1,000 shares of common at par in exchange for land and building with fair market values of $140,000 and $85,000, respectively.

    Mar. 6   Sold the balance of the preferred stock for cash at $105.

(b) Present the stockholders' equity section of the balance sheet as of March 6.

(*a*)

Jan. 10				
15				
Mar. 6				

(*b*)

SOLUTION

(*a*)	Jan. 10	Cash		140,000	
		Common Stock			125,000
		Premium on Common Stock			15,000
	15	Land		140,000	
		Building		85,000	
		Preferred Stock			200,000
		Common Stock			25,000
	Mar. 6	Cash		315,000	
		Preferred Stock			300,000
		Premium on Preferred Stock			15,000

(*b*)	Paid-in Capital:		
	Preferred Stock, 6%, $100 par		
	(5,000 shares authorized and issued)	$500,000	
	Add: Premium on Preferred Stock	15,000	$515,000
	Common Stock, $25 par		
	(10,000 shares authorized, 6,000 shares issued)	$150,000	
	Add: Premium on Common Stock	15,000	$165,000
	Total Paid-in Capital		$680,000

17.10 Corporations A and B each have 10,000 shares of common stock outstanding. Assuming that the two stocks have the same book value, complete the following table:

	Corporation A	Corporation B
Assets	$350,000	?
Liabilities	100,000	$ 70,000
Common Stock	200,000	175,000
Retained Earnings	?	?

SOLUTION

	Corporation A	Corporation B
Assets	$350,000	$320,000‡
Liabilities	100,000	70,000
Common Stock	200,000	175,000
Retained Earnings	50,000*	75,000†

---

*Assets   = Liabilities + Stockholders' Equity
 $350,000 = $100,000 +   ($200,000 + ?)

†Because the book values of the common stock in both corporations are identical, Corporation B must have the same total for stockholders' equity: $250,000 ($175,000 + $75,000).

‡Assets = Liabilities + Stockholders' Equity
   ?   = $70,000   + $250,000

17.11 The XYZ Corporation had income before taxes of $700,000 (use a 40 percent tax rate) and paid $140,000 to the preferred stockholders. What are the earnings per share for XYZ common stockholders with 70,000 shares of common stock outstanding?

_____
_____
_____
_____

SOLUTION

Earnings before taxes	$700,000
40% tax rate	× 40%
Taxes	$280,000

Income	$700,000
Taxes	− 280,000
	$420,000
Less preferred dividends	140,000
Earnings available to	
common stockholders	$280,000

$$\frac{\$280,000}{70,000} = \$4 \text{ per share}$$

17.12 The corporation's equity accounts appear below:

Preferred Stock, 5%, $100 par	
(5,000 shares authorized, 3,000 shares issued)	$300,000
Discount on Preferred Stock	30,000
Common Stock, $50 par	
(10,000 shares authorized, 4,000 shares issued)	200,000
Premium on Common Stock	10,000
Retained Earnings (credit balance)	35,000

In order to secure additional funds, the board of directors approved the following proposals:

1. To borrow $100,000, with an 8 percent mortgage
2. To sell the remaining common stock at par
3. To issue the balance of the preferred stock in exchange for equipment value at $185,000

Prepare (*a*) journal entries for the transactions, (*b*) the stockholders' equity section.

(*a*) 1.

    2.

    3.

(*b*)

SOLUTION

(*a*)	1.	Cash	100,000	
		Mortgage Payable		100,000
	2.	Cash	300,000	
		Common Stock		300,000
	3.	Equipment	185,000	
		Discount on Preferred Stock	15,000	
		Preferred Stock		200,000

(b) Paid-in Capital:

Preferred Stock, 5%, $100 par (5,000 shares authorized and issued)	$500,000	
Less: Discount on Preferred Stock	45,000	$ 455,000
Common Stock, $50 par (10,000 shares authorized and issued)	$500,000	
Add: Premium on Common Stock	10,000	510,000
Total Paid-in Capital		$ 965,000
Retained Earnings		35,000
Total Stockholders' Equity		$1,000,000

17.13 Determine the equity per share of preferred and of common stock, if the balance sheet shows:

(a)	Preferred Stock, $100 par	$200,000
	Common Stock, $25 par	100,000
	Premium on Common Stock	10,000
	Retained Earnings	40,000
(b)	Preferred Stock, $100 par	$200,000
	Premium on Preferred Stock	10,000
	Common Stock, $25 par	100,000
	Retained Earnings (deficit)	(40,000)

(a)

Preferred Stock	Common Stock

(b)

Preferred Stock	Common Stock

SOLUTION

(a)

Preferred Stock		Common Stock	
$200,000	To preferred stock	$100,000	Common stock
		10,000	Premium
$100.00	Per share	40,000	Retained earnings
		$150,000	To common stock
		$37.50*	Per share

*$150,000 ÷ 4,000 shares. The number of shares outstanding is determined by dividing the value of the stock, $100,000, by its par value, $25.

(b)

Preferred Stock		Common Stock	
$200,000	To preferred stock	$100,000	Common stock
		10,000*	Premium
$100.00	Per share	(40,000)	Deficit
		$ 70,000	To common stock
		$ 17.50	Per share

*The premium on preferred stock is allocated to common stock when computing equity per share.

17.14 Three companies have the following structures:

	G Company	H Company	I Company
Bonds Payable, 5%	$1,000,000	$ 600,000	—
Preferred Stock, 6%, $100 par	—	600,000	$1,000,000
Common Stock, $100 par	1,000,000	800,000	1,000,000
Total	$2,000,000	$2,000,000	$2,000,000

Assuming a tax rate of 40 percent of income, determine the earnings per share of common stock if the net income of each company before bond interest and taxes was (a) $140,000; (b) $500,000.

(a)

	G Company	H Company	I Company

(b)

	G Company	H Company	I Company

SOLUTION

(a)

	G Company	H Company	I Company
Income	$140,000	$140,000	$140,000
Less: Bond interest	50,000	30,000	—
Income before taxes	$ 90,000	$110,000	$140,000
Less: Tax (40%)	36,000	44,000	56,000
Net income	$ 54,000	$ 66,000	$ 84,000
Less: Preferred dividend	—	36,000	60,000.
To common stock	$ 54,000	$ 30,000	$ 24,000
Number of common shares	÷10,000	÷8,000	÷ 10,000
Earnings per share	$ 5.40	$ 3.75	$ 2.40

(b)

	G Company	H Company	I Company
Income	$500,000	$500,000	$500,000
Less: Bond interest	50,000	30,000	—
Income before taxes	$450,000	$470,000	$500,000
Less: Tax (40%)	180,000	188,000	200,000
Net income	$270,000	$282,000	$300,000
Less: Preferred dividend	—	36,000	60,000
To common stock	$270,000	$246,000	$240,000
Number of common shares	÷10,000	÷8,000	÷10,000
Earnings per share	$27.00	$30.75	$24.00

17.15 F. Saltzman Industries has 12,000 shares of common stock outstanding. The board decides to expand existing facilities at a projected cost of $3,000,000. Method 1: issue of $3,000,000 in common stock, $50 par. Method 2: issue of $1,500,000 in preferred stock, 6 percent, $100 par, and $1,500,000 in common stock, $50 par. Method 3: issue of $1,500,000 in 6 percent bonds, $750,000 in preferred stock, 6 percent, $100 par, and $750,000 in common stock, $50 par. Assuming that the net income before bond interest and taxes (40 percent) will be increased to $300,000, find the earnings per share of common stock under each method.

	Method 1	Method 2	Method 3

SOLUTION

	Method 1	Method 2	Method 3
Income	$300,000	$300,000	$300,000
Less: Bond interest	—	—	90,000
Income before taxes	$300,000	$300,000	$210,000
Less: Taxes	120,000	120,000	84,000
Net income	$180,000	$180,000	$126,000
Less: Preferred dividend	—	90,000	45,000
To common stock	$180,000	$ 90,000	$ 81,000
Number of common shares	÷72,000	÷42,000	÷27,000
Earnings per share	$2.50	$2.14	$3.00

17.16 Rework Problem 17.15 for an expected income of $180,000.

	Method 1	Method 2	Method 3

SOLUTION

	Method 1	Method 2	Method 3
Income	$180,000	$180,000	$180,000
Less: Bond interest	—	—	90,000
Income before taxes	$180,000	$180,000	$ 90,000
Less: Taxes	72,000	72,000	36,000
Net income	$108,000	$108,000	$ 54,000
Less: Preferred dividend	—	90,000	45,000
To common stock	$108,000	$ 18,000	$ 9,000
Number of common shares	÷72,000	÷42,000	÷27,000
Earnings per share	$1.50	$0.43	$0.33

Examination V

1. Berg and Kotin have decided to form a partnership. Berg invests the following assets at their original evaluations, and also transfers his liabilities to the new partnership.

Berg's Accounts	Berg's Ledger Balances	Agreed Valuations
Cash	$17,200	$17,200
Accounts Receivable	3,700	3,500
Allowance for Doubtful Accounts	500	400
Merchandise Inventory	11,400	9,300
Equipment	14,600	10,000
Accumulated Depreciation	2,000	
Accounts Payable	4,500	4,500
Notes Payable	2,100	2,100
Mortgages Payable	10,000	10,000

Kotin agrees to invest $42,000 in cash. Record (a) Berg's investment and (b) Kotin's investment into the new partnership.

2. Baggetta and Cohen have capital accounts of $20,000 and $40,000, respectively. The partners divide net income in the following manner:

   (1) Salaries of $10,000 to Baggetta and $12,000 to Cohen.
   (2) Each partner receives 5% on his capital investment.
   (3) The balance is divided in the ratio of 1:2.

   Determine the division of net income if net income is (a) $34,000; (b) $22,000.

3. The accounts of Sully and Todd had the following balances when they decided to discontinue operations:

Accounts Payable	$ 6,700	Lara Todd, Capital	$15,000
Accumulated Depreciation, Equip.	6,150	Merchandise Inventory	19,000
Cash	16,000	Notes Payable	1,500
Equipment	8,800	Supplies	550
Frank Sully, Capital	15,000		

The partners share profits and losses equally. Present the entries to record the following transactions:

(a) Received $400 upon sale of supplies
(b) Disposed of the merchandise inventory, receiving $22,000
(c) Sold the equipment for $3,000
(d) Distributed the loss or gain to the partners
(e) Paid all liabilities
(f) Distributed the remaining cash

373

4. On January 1, B. Clinton, Inc., was organized with an authorization of 5,000 shares of preferred 6% stock, $100 par, and 10,000 shares of $25-par common stock.

(*a*) Record the following transactions:

Jan. 10   Sold half of the common stock at $29 for cash.

Jan. 15   Issued 2,000 shares of preferred and 1,000 shares of common at par in exchange for land and building with fair market values of $140,000 and $85,000, respectively.

Mar. 6   Sold the balance of the preferred stock for cash at $105.

(*b*) Present the stockholders' equity section of the balance sheet as of March 6.

5. Below are data from two different corporations, labeled (*a*) through (*d*). Determine for each corporation the equity per share of preferred and common stock.

(*a*)	Preferred stock, 6%, $100 par	$400,000
	Premium on preferred stock	40,000
	Common stock, $25 par	250,000
	Discount on common stock	20,000
	Retained earnings	100,000
(*b*)	Preferred stock, 6%, $100 par	$500,000
	Common stock, $25 par	100,000
	Premium on common stock	10,000
	Retained earnings	40,000

The corporation is being dissolved and preferred stock is entitled to receive $110 upon liquidation.

6. Shapot Industries has 12,000 shares of common stock outstanding. The board decides to expand existing facilities at a projected cost of $3,000,000. *Method I:* Issue of $3,000,000 in common stock, $50 par. *Method II:* Issue of $1,500,000 in preferred stock, 6 percent, $100 par, and $1,500,000 in common stock, $50 par. *Method III:* Issue of $1,500,000 in 6 percent bonds, $750,000 in preferred stock, 6 percent, $100 par, and $750,000 in common stock, $50 par. Assuming that the net income before bond interest and taxes (50 percent) will be increased to $300,000, find the earnings per share of common stock under each method.

Answers to Examination V

1. (*a*)

Cash	17,200	
Accounts Receivable	3,500	
Merchandise Inventory	9,300	
Equipment	10,000	
Allowance for Doubtful Accounts		400
Accounts Payable		4,500
Notes Payable		2,100
Mortgage Payable		10,000
Berg, Capital		23,000

(*b*)

Cash	42,000	
Kotin, Capital		42,000

2. (*a*)

	Baggetta	Cohen	Total
Salary	$10,000	$12,000	$22,000
Interest	1,000	2,000	3,000
	$11,000	$14,000	$25,000
Balance	3,000	6,000	9,000
Total Share	$14,000	$20,000	$34,000

(*b*)

	Baggetta	Cohen	Total
Salary	$10,000	$12,000	$22,000
Interest	1,000	2,000	3,000
	$11,000	$14,000	$25,000
Balance	− 1,000	− 2,000	− 3,000
Total Share	$10,000	$12,000	$22,000

3. (*a*)

Cash	400	
Loss or Gain on Realization	150	
Supplies		550

(*b*)

Cash	22,000	
Merchandise Inventory		19,000
Loss or Gain on Realization		3,000

(*c*)

Cash	3,000	
Accumulated Depreciation	6,150	
Equipment		8,800
Loss or Gain on Realization		350

(d)	Loss or Gain on Realization	3,200	
	Sully, Capital		1,600
	Todd, Capital		1,600
(e)	Accounts Payable	6,700	
	Notes Payable	1,500	
	Cash		8,200
(f)	Sully, Capital	16,600	
	Todd, Capital	16,600	
	Cash		33,200

Summary of Transactions

Transaction	Cash	Other Assets	Liabilities	Sully, Capital	Todd, Capital
Balance	$16,000	$22,200	$8,200	$15,000	$15,000
(a)–(d)	+25,400	−22,200		+ 1,600	+ 1,600
	$41,400		$8,200	$16,600	$16,600
(e)	− 8,200		−8,200		
	$33,200			$16,600	$16,600
(f)	−33,200			−16,600	−16,600

4. (a)	Jan. 10 Cash	145,000	
	Common Stock		125,000
	Premium on Common Stock		20,000
	Jan. 15 Land	140,000	
	Building	85,000	
	Preferred Stock		200,000
	Common Stock		25,000
	Mar. 6 Cash	315,000	
	Preferred Stock		300,000
	Premium on Preferred Stock		15,000

(b)	Paid-in Capital		
	Preferred Stock, 6%, $100 par		
	(5,000 shares authorized and issued)	$500,000	
	Add: Premium on Preferred Stock	15,000	$515,000
	Common Stock, $25 par		
	(10,000 shares authorized,		
	6,000 shares issued)	$150,000	
	Add: Premium on Common Stock	20,000	170,000
	Total Paid-in Capital		$685,000

5. (*a*)

	Preferred Stock			Common Stock
$400,000	To preferred stock		250,000	Common stock
$100	Per share		40,000	Premium on preferred stock
			(20,000)	Discount on common stock
			100,000	Retained earnings
			$370,000	To common stock
			$37	Per share

(*b*)

	Preferred Stock			Common Stock
$550,000	To preferred stock		$100,000	Common stock
$110	Per share		10,000	Premium
			40,000	Retained earnings
			(50,000)	Preferred liquidation excess
			$100,000	To common stock
			$25	Per share

6.

	Method I	Method II	Method III
Income	$300,000	$300,000	$300,000
Less: Bond Interest	—	—	90,000
Income before Taxes	$300,000	$300,000	$210,000
Less: Taxes (50%)	150,000	150,000	105,000
Net Income	$150,000	$150,000	$105,000
Less: Preferred Dividend	—	90,000	45,000
To Common Stock	$150,000	$ 60,000	$ 60,000
Number of Common Shares	÷72,000	÷42,000	÷27,000
Earnings per Share	$2.08	$1.43	$2.22

Appendix

Mathematics

A.1 OPERATIONS WITH DECIMALS

Addition of Decimals

To add decimals, arrange the numbers to be added in a column with all decimal places underneath one another. This helps to avoid the chance of error when adding tenths, hundredths, and so on. To simplify the process, zeros may be added to the *right* of the decimal place without changing the numbers.

EXAMPLE 1

Three plant machine parts weigh 1.26, 0.00145, and 4.3452 pounds, respectively; their combined weight is:

$$
\begin{array}{r}
1.26000* \\
0.00145 \\
\underline{4.34520*} \\
\underline{5.60665}
\end{array}
$$

---

*Zeros added to simplify the process.

Subtraction of Decimals

To subtract decimals, arrange the two numbers to be subtracted in a column with the higher number on top. Zeros should be added to the number with fewer decimal places to simplify the solution.

EXAMPLE 2

Product A has a shipping weight of 2.49 pounds, while product B weighs 1.234 pounds. What is the difference in weight?

$$
\begin{array}{r}
2.490 \\
-1.234 \\
\underline{1.256}
\end{array}
$$

Multiplication of Decimals

Multiplication of decimals follows the same process used for multiplication of whole numbers with the exception that in the final answer (product), the number of decimal places is equal to the total number of decimal places in the original numbers.

EXAMPLE 3

At $4.50 per ounce, what will 1.235 ounces cost?

$$1.235 \longleftarrow 3 \text{ decimal places}$$
$$\times \$ \quad 4.5 \longleftarrow 1 \text{ decimal places}$$
$$\underline{}$$
$$6175$$
$$\underline{4940}$$
$$\underline{\underline{\$5.5575}} \longleftarrow 4 \text{ decimal places}$$

Division of Decimals

Division of decimals follows the same process as division of whole numbers. The decimal point in the divisor must first be eliminated, however, by moving the decimal point in both the divisor and the dividend to the right by the same number of places. Zeros are added to the dividend if needed. For the final answer, the decimal point is placed directly above the item it has been moved to in the dividend.

EXAMPLE 4

The cost of producing 3.22 pounds of Product A is $7.1162. What does one pound cost?

$$\text{Divide:} \quad 3.22\overline{)7.1162} \quad \$2.21$$

$$\underline{644}$$
$$676$$
$$\underline{644}$$
$$322$$
$$\underline{322}$$

A.2 PERCENTAGES

Percent really means "per hundred." A percentage is simply a manner of expressing the relationship between one number or amount and another in terms of hundredths. It is a convenient, widely used, acceptable method of referring to an amount in terms of another known amount. In order to work mathematically with percentages, you must first translate the percent into a decimal or a fraction.

EXAMPLE 5

To convert a percent to a decimal, simply move the decimal place in the percent two places to the left:

$$1\% = 0.01 \qquad 60\% = 0.60$$

EXAMPLE 6

To convert a percent to a fraction, place 100 under the number:

$$1\% = \frac{1}{100} \qquad 60\% = \frac{60}{100}$$

EXAMPLE 7

To convert a fraction or decimal to a percent, the easiest method is to convert the number first to a decimal and then move the decimal point two places to the right.

$$\text{For fractions:} \qquad \frac{1}{100} = 0.01 = 1\%$$

$$\frac{60}{100} = 0.60 = 60\%$$

$$\text{For decimals:} \qquad 0.01 = 1\%$$

$$0.60 = 60\%$$

The relationship in percent (*rate*) of one number or amount to another may be computed by dividing the *percentage* (the amount whose relationship to a second number you want to find) by the *base* (the number you are comparing to). The formula is expressed mathematically as

$$\text{Percent (rate)} = \frac{\text{percentage}}{\text{base}}$$

EXAMPLE 8

What percent of 80 is 20?

$$\text{Percent (rate)} = \frac{20 \text{ (percentage)}}{80 \text{ (base)}} = \frac{1}{4} = 0.25 = 25\%$$

EXAMPLE 9

If the cost of an item is $75 and the selling price is $100, what percent of the selling price is the cost?

$$\text{Percent (rate)} = \frac{\$75 \text{ (percentage)}}{\$100 \text{ (base)}} = 75\%$$

EXAMPLE 10

Income statement analysis. Determine the percent of each of the amounts listed in the income statement below to net sales:

LAT Company
Income Statement
For Year Ended December 31, 19X5

Net Sales		$10,000
Cost of Sales		4,000
Gross Profit		$ 6,000
Operating Expenses:		
Selling Expenses	$2,000	
General Expenses	1,000	
Total Operating Expenses		3,000
Net Income		$ 3,000

$$\text{Cost of Sales:} \qquad \frac{4,000 \text{ (percentage)}}{10,000 \text{ (base)}} \qquad \text{Cost of Sales} = 0.40 \text{ or } 40\%$$

$$\text{Gross Profit:} \qquad \frac{6,000 \text{ (percentage)}}{10,000 \text{ (base)}} \qquad \text{Gross Profit} = 0.60 \text{ or } 60\%$$

$$\text{Selling Expenses:} \qquad \frac{2,000 \text{ (percentage)}}{10,000 \text{ (base)}} \qquad \text{Selling Expense} = 0.20 \text{ or } 20\%$$

General Expenses: $\dfrac{1,000 \text{ (percentage)}}{10,000 \text{ (base)}}$ General Expense = 0.10 or 10%

Total Operating Expenses: Sell. Exp. + Gen. Exp. or 20% + 10% = 30%

Net Income: $\dfrac{3,000 \text{ (percentage)}}{10,000 \text{ (base)}}$ Net Income = 0.30 or 30%

This would be presented as follows:

LAT Co.
Income Statement
For Year Ended, December 31, 19X5

Net Sales	$10,000		100%
Cost of Sales	4,000		40%
Gross Profit		$6,000	60%
Operating Expenses:			
Selling Expenses	$ 2,000	20%	
General Expenses	1,000	10%	
Total Operating Expenses		3,000	30%
Net Income		$3,000	30%

A.3 STATISTICAL METHODS

The accountant uses information, both internal and external, as a basis from which to make decisions regarding the direction and control of the various activities of the firm. It is important that the financial manager be familiar with certain arithmetic tools that may be used to organize and summarize this data into meaningful forms once it has been accumulated.

Ratios

One of the ways in which numbers can be compared is by expressing the relationship of one number to another (or others). This is known as a *ratio*.

When two numbers are to be compared, the ratio may be found by placing one number (first term) over the other number (second term) and reducing the resulting fraction to lowest terms.

EXAMPLE 11

If there are 80 male employees and 60 female employees in a plant, what is the ratio of male to female?

$$\frac{80}{60} = \frac{4}{3} \quad \text{or} \quad 4:3$$

An alternative way of expressing this relationship is simply to divide the first term by the second term. The answer will therefore always be $x:1$.

EXAMPLE 12

The total assets of Agin Company are $80,000 and their liabilities are $50,000. What is the ratio of assets to liabilities?

$$\frac{\$80,000}{50,000} = \frac{8}{5} = 1.6:1$$

Ratios are often a common means of analyzing relationships, particularly on accounting statements. One of the most common is known as the *current ratio* and represents the ratio of current assets to current liabilities. This is a measure of business liquidity, because it tells how many times over the company could pay its current debts. Another common application of ratios is the ratio of owners' equity to long-term debt. These and other ratios are convenient signposts from which the directions a business is going can be determined.

EXAMPLE 13

Company A has current assets of $50,000 and current liabilities of $20,000. Their current ratio is computed as:

$$\frac{50,000}{20,000} = 2.5:1$$

This shows that the firm has $2.50 of current assets for every $1.00 it owes in current liabilities.

EXAMPLE 14

The total stockholders' equity is $64,000, while the company's liabilities are $135,000. What is the ratio of stockholders' equity to liabilities?

$$\frac{64,000}{135,000} = 0.47:1$$

Averages

A means of presenting large quantities of numbers in summary form is accomplished by the use of an average. Three measures of averages are discussed below.

1. **Mean.** The mean is the most popular and is computed for a particular list of figures by adding the figures and dividing by the number of figures in the list. The equation used to compute the mean is

$$M = \frac{S}{N}$$

   where M = mean
   S = sum of the figures in the list
   N = number of figures in the list

EXAMPLE 15

A group of employees earn the following weekly salaries:

Salary	Number of Employees	Total Amount Earned
$ 90	2	$ 180
100	1	100
110	2	220
120	4	480
130	2	260
140	1	140
150	1	150
	13	$1,530

The mean salary is computed as follows:

$$M = \frac{S}{N} = \frac{\$1,530}{13} = \$118 \qquad \text{(rounded off)}$$

2. **Median.** The median is the number that divides a group in half. In order to calculate the median, it is first necessary to list the figures in ascending or descending order. When there is an odd number of figures, the number that separates the list into two equal groups, so that the number of figures in one group is equal to the number of figures in the other group, must be located. When there is an even number of figures, the number that is midway between the middle two items is located. The formula used in the computation of the median is

$$M = \frac{N + 1}{2}$$

where M = median
N = number of figures in the list

EXAMPLE 16

From Example 15, the median salary is computed as:

$$M = \frac{N + 1}{2} = \frac{13 + 1}{2} = 7 \quad \text{or} \quad \$120$$

because $120 is the seventh salary in the list of salaries, taking into account the number of employees who make each salary.

3. **Mode.** The mode is the number that occurs most frequently in a series of figures.

EXAMPLE 17

In Example 15, the mode salary is $120, because it is the salary that occurs most frequently.

Index Numbers

The index number is used to compare business activities during one time period with similar activities during another time period. If the time period considered is a full year, a value of 100 percent is assigned to the base-year value of the item. Every subsequent year's value for that same item is expressed as a percentage of that base-year value.

EXAMPLE 18

Assume that the cost of food in 1985 (base year) had a value of 100, and 10 years later the value had increased to 142.6. This indicates that the value of the food increased 42.6 percent over that period of time.

EXAMPLE 19

Assume that you wish to construct an index for the number of accounting books sold in a given year. You select 1985 as the base period. In that year, the number of books sold was 6,000,000. Ten years later (in 1995), the sales were 9,000,000. Expressed as a percentage, the index number for 1995 would be 150.0. This figure is derived by dividing the increase in sales by the base period, multiplying by 100 to get the percent, and adding the percent to 100 [that is, (3,000,000/6,000,000) × 100 + 100 = 150].

Summary

1. To help avoid the chance of error while adding decimals, arrange the numbers to be added with all decimal places _____ one another.

2. The relationship between one number and another in terms of hundredths is called a _____ _____ .

3. The relationship of one number to another is known as a _____ .

4. A means of presenting large quantities of numbers in summary form is by the use of an _____ .

5. The most popular form of average is the _____ .

6. The _____ is the number that divides a group in half.

7. In the formula $M = \dfrac{N + 1}{2}$, the letter N is _____ .

8. The _____ is the number that occurs most frequently in a series of figures.

9. The method of comparing business activities during one time period with similar activities during another time period is accomplished by the use of _____ .

10. In computing index numbers, a value of 100 percent is assigned to the _____ year.

Answers: 1. underneath; 2. percent; 3. ratio; 4. average; 5. mean; 6. median; 7. the number of figures in the list; 8. mode; 9. index numbers; 10. base.

Solved Problems

A.1   Add the following decimals:

$$11.24 + 6.535 + 9.4372 + 21.6$$

SOLUTION

$$
\begin{array}{r}
11.2400 \\
6.5350 \\
9.4372 \\
21.6000 \\
\hline
48.8122 \\
\hline
\end{array}
$$

Note: Adding zeros to the right of the decimal does not change the number.

A.2 The cost of three different fuels are (a) $1.41, (b) $1.4129, (c) $1.4253. What would the total be if all three were bought together?

SOLUTION

$$\begin{array}{r} \$1.4100 \\ 1.4129 \\ \underline{1.4253} \\ \$4.2482 = \$4.25 \end{array}$$

A.3 The shipping department has two packages weighing 5.4 pounds and 3.891 pounds, respectively. What is their difference in weight?

SOLUTION

$$\begin{array}{r} 5.400 \\ \underline{-3.891} \\ 1.509 \text{ pounds} \end{array}$$

A.4 A company purchased 400 gallons of fuel at 0.4165 cent per gallon. How much did the fuel cost?

SOLUTION

$$\begin{array}{r} 0.4165 \\ \underline{\times\quad 400} \\ 166.6000 = \$166.60 \end{array}$$

A.5 If the total cost of making 150.5 kilograms of chemicals is $72, what is the cost of 1 kilogram?

SOLUTION

$$0.478 = 48\cancel{c} \text{ per kilogram}$$
$$150.5\overline{)72.0000}$$

$$\begin{array}{r} 6020 \\ \underline{11800} \\ 10535 \\ \hline 12650 \end{array}$$

A.6 Convert the following percentages to decimals: (a) 4%; (b) 14%; (c) 15.5%; (d) 126%.

SOLUTION

(a) 0.04; (b) 0.14; (c) 0.155; (d) 1.26

A.7 Convert the following percentages to fractions: (a) 4%; (b) 14%; (c) 15.5%; (d) 126%.

SOLUTION

(a) 4/100; (b) 14/100; (c) 155/1000; (d) 126/100

A.8 (a) If the cost of an item is $82 and the selling price is $100, what percent of the selling price is the cost? (b) What is the profit on sales in terms of a percent?

SOLUTION

(a) $\dfrac{82 \text{ (percentage)}}{100 \text{ (base)}} = 82\%$ (b) $\begin{array}{r} \$100 \text{ Selling price} \\ -82 \text{ Cost} \\ \hline \$\ 18 \text{ Profit} \end{array}$ $\dfrac{18 \text{ (profit)}}{100 \text{ (sales)}} = 18\% \text{ profit}$

A.9 Determine, based on the information below:

(a) Percent of cost to sales.

(b) Percent of gross profit to sales.

(c) Percent of net profit to sales.

Income Statement

Sales Income	$25,000
Cost of Goods Sold	14,000
Gross Profit	$11,000
Operating Expenses	5,000
Net Profit	$ 6,000

SOLUTION

(a) $\dfrac{14,000}{25,000} = 56\%$ (b) $\dfrac{11,000}{25,000} = 44\%$ (c) $\dfrac{6,000}{25,000} = 24\%$

A.10 (a) The Silvergold Printing Company prints 200 sheets of hot type for every 40 sheets of cold type. What is the ratio of hot type to cold type?

(b) The total assets of G. Miller Co. is $60,000, and their liabilities total $26,000. What is the ratio of assets to liabilities?

SOLUTION

(a) $\dfrac{200}{40} = 5:1 \text{ ratio}$ (b) $\dfrac{60,000}{26,000} = 2.31:1$

A.11 Below is a condensed balance sheet of the Ed Blanchard Summer Camp:

Balance Sheet

ASSETS

Current Assets	$46,500
Fixed Assets	24,000
Total Assets	$70,500

LIABILITIES

Current Liabilities	$20,000
Long-Term Liabilities	10,500
Total Liabilities	$30,500
Capital	40,000
Total Liabilities and Capital	$70,500

Determine the current ratio.

SOLUTION

$$\frac{46,500 \text{ (current assets)}}{20,000 \text{ (current liabilities)}} = 2.33:1$$

This shows that Blanchard has $2.33 of current assets for every $1.00 it owes in current liabilities.

A.12 The weekly salaries of five employees of the SCC Corp. are as follows: $88.00; $94.50; $106.20; $145.00; $192.30. What is the mean salary of this group?

SOLUTION

$$
\begin{array}{r}
\$\ 88.00 \\
94.50 \\
106.20 \\
145.00 \\
\underline{192.30} \\
\$626.00 \div 5 = \$125.20 \quad \text{Mean salary}
\end{array}
$$

A.13 A glance at a company's payroll reveals the following information:

Salary	Number of Employees	Total Amount Earned
$100	4	$ 400
110	3	330
120	6	720
130	3	390
140	2	280
150	2	300
160	1	160
170	1	170
180	1	180
	23	$2,930

(a) Determine the mean salary.

(b) Determine the median salary.

(c) Determine the mode salary.

SOLUTION

(a) $2,930 \div 23 = $127.39

(b) $M = \dfrac{N+1}{2} = \dfrac{23+1}{2} = 12$ figures down $= \$120$

(c) $120—the most repeated figure

A.14 (a) If the cost of automobiles is 148 percent of the base year, what does this indicate?

(b) In 1985, the base year, 800,000 units were sold. In 1995, 1,500,000 units were sold. What is the index number for year 1985 and year 1995?

SOLUTION

(*a*) This indicates that the cost of the automobile has risen 48 percent since the base year.

(*b*) 1985 = 100%   The base year

1995 = 187.5% $\left(\dfrac{700{,}000}{800{,}000} \times 100 + 100\%\right)$

Glossary of Bookkeeping and Accounting Terms

Account. A record of the increases and decreases of transactions summarized in an accounting form.

Account numbers. Numbers assigned to accounts according to the chart of accounts.

Accountant. An individual who classifies and summarizes business transactions and interprets their effects on the business.

Accounting. The process of analyzing, classifying, recording, summarizing, and interpreting business transactions.

Accounts Payable. A liability account used by the business to keep a record of amounts due to creditors.

Accounts receivable. Amount that is to be collected from customers.

Accrual basis. An accounting system in which revenue is recognized only when earned, and expense is recognized only when incurred.

Additional paid-in capital. Amounts paid in beyond the par value of stock.

Adjusting entries. Journal entries made at the end of an accounting period in order that the accounts will reflect the correct balance in the financial statements.

Articles of copartnership. The written agreement among the partners that contains provisions on the formation, capital contribution, profit and loss distribution, admission, and withdrawal of partners.

Articles of incorporation. A charter submitted to the state by individuals wishing to form a corporation and containing significant information about the proposed business.

Assets. Properties owned that have monetary value.

Authorized shares. Shares of stock that a corporation is permitted to issue (sell) under its articles of incorporation.

Average. A means of presenting large quantities of numbers in summary form.

Balance sheet. A statement that shows the assets, liabilities, and capital of a business entity at a specific date. Also known as the statement of financial position.

Bank reconciliation. A statement that reconciles the difference between the bank's balance and the balance of a company's books.

Bank service charge. A monthly charge made by the bank for keeping a depositor's checking account in operation.

Bank statement. A periodic statement sent by the bank to its customers that presents the current balances of the cash account and provides a detailed list of all the payments made and all receipts received for a certain period of time.

Blank endorsement. Consists of only the name of the endorser on the back of the check.

Board of directors. Elected by the stockholders within the framework of the articles of incorporation, the board's duties include appointing corporate officers, determining company policies, and distributing profits.

Bonds. A form of long-term debt in which the corporation agrees to pay interest periodically and to repay the principal at a stated future date.

Book value per share. The amount that would be distributed to each share of stock if a corporation were to be dissolved.

Bookkeeper. An individual who earns a living by recording the financial activities of a business and who is concerned with the techniques involving the recording of transactions.

Call privilege. Gives an issuing stock company the right to redeem stock at a later date for a predetermined price.

Cancelled checks. Checks that have been paid by the bank during the month and returned to the depositor.

Capital. What an individual or business is worth. Also known as owners' equity.

Capital Stock. The account that shows the par value of the stock issued by the corporation.

Cash disbursements journal. A special journal used to record transactions involving cash payments.

Cash receipts journal. A special journal used to record transactions involving cash receipts.

Certified check. A check whose payment has been guaranteed by the bank.

Chart of accounts. A listing of the accounts by title and numerical designation.

Check. A written document directing the firm's bank to pay a specific amount of money to an individual.

Checking account. An account with a bank that allows the depositor to make payments to others from his or her bank balance.

Closing entry. An entry made at the end of a fiscal period in order to make the balance of a temporary account equal to zero.

Closing the ledger. A process of transferring balances of income and expense accounts through the summary account to the capital account.

Combined cash journal. The journal with which all cash transactions are recorded.

Common stock. That part of the capital stock that does not have special preferences or rights.

Computer. A group of interconnected electronic machines capable of processing data.

Computer hardware. A term that refers to the actual physical components that make up an installation.

Computer programs. A set of instructions developed by a programmer that tells the computer what to do, how to do it, and in what sequence it should be done.

Computer software. The collection of programs and supplementary materials used by personnel to give the computer its instructions.

Controlling account. The account in the general ledger that summarizes the balances of a subsidiary ledger.

Conversion privilege. Given stockholders the option to convert preferred stock into common stock.

Corporation. A business organized by law and viewed as an entity separate from its owners and creditors.

Cost of goods sold. Inventory at the beginning of a fiscal period plus net purchases, less inventory at the end of the fiscal period. Also known as cost of sales.

Credit. An amount entered on the right side of an account. Abbreviation is Cr.

Credit memorandum. A receipt indicating the seller's acceptance to reduce the amount of a buyer's debt.

Current assets. Assets that are expected to be realized in cash, sold, or consumed during the normal fiscal cycle of a business.

Current liabilities. Debts that are due within a short period of time, usually consisting of 1 year, and which are normally paid from current assets.

Debit. An amount entered on the left side of an account. Abbreviation is Dr.

Deposit in transit. Cash deposited and recorded by the company, but too late to be recorded by the bank.

Deposit ticket. A document showing the firm's name, its account number, and the amount of money deposited into the bank.

Depreciation. The cost of a fixed asset distributed over its entire estimated lifetime.

Discounted notes receivable. A term used to describe notes receivable sold to a bank and being held liable for maturity if the maker defaults.

Dishonored check. A check that the bank refuses to pay because the writer does not have sufficient funds in his or her checking account.

Dishonored note. A note that the maker fails to pay at the time of maturity.

Double-entry accounting. An almost universal system that produces equal debit and credit entries for every transaction.

Draft. An order by the seller to the buyer stating that the buyer must pay a certain amount of money to a third party.

Drawing. The taking of cash or goods out of a business by the owner for personal use. Also known as a withdrawal.

Earnings statement. A stub attached to an employee's payroll check that provides the employee with a record of the amount earned and a detailed list of deductions.

Employee. An individual who works for compensation for an employer.

Endorsement. The placing of a signature on the back of a check that is to be deposited or cashed.

Endorsement in full. A type of endorsement that states that the check can be cashed or transferred only on the order of the person named in the endorsement.

EOM. Term used to denote the end of the month.

Expenses. The decrease in capital caused by the business's revenue-producing operations.

Face of note. The amount of a note.

Federal unemployment tax. A tax paid by employers only. Used to supplement state unemployment benefits.

FICA taxes. Social Security taxes collected in equal amounts from both the employee and the employer. These proceeds are paid into a fund that provides disability and old-age payments. FICA stands for Federal Insurance Contributions Act.

Fiscal period. A period of time covered by the entire accounting cycle, usually consisting of 12 consecutive months.

Footing. The recording in pencil of the temporary total of one side of a T account.

Goodwill. An intangible asset that results from the expectation that the business has the ability to produce an above-average rate of earnings compared to other businesses in the same industry.

Gross pay. The rate, arrived at through negotiation between the employer and the employee, at which employees are paid.

Gross profit. Net sales minus cost of goods sold.

Imprest system. A fund established for a fixed petty cash amount and periodically reimbursed by a single check for amounts expended.

Income statement. A summary of the revenue, expenses, and net income of a business entity for a specific period of time. Also known as a profit and loss statement.

Index number. Used to compare business activities during one time period with similar activity during another time period.

Interest. Money paid for the use or borrowing of money.

Interest-bearing note.   A note in which the maker has agreed to pay the face of the note plus interest.

Interest rate.   A percentage of the principal that is paid for the use of money borrowed.

Journal.   The book of original entry for accounting data. It is the book in which the accountant originally records business transactions.

Journalizing.   A process of recording business transactions in the journal.

Ledger.   The complete set of accounts for a business entity. It is used to classify and summarize transactions and to prepare data for financial statements.

Liabilities.   Amounts owed to outsiders.

Long-term liabilities.   Debts that do not have to be paid immediately but are usually paid over a long period of time, normally more than 1 year.

Loss.   The amount by which total costs exceed total income.

Maker.   An individual who signs a promissory note agreeing to make payment.

Markdown.   Downward adjustments of the selling price. Used to induce customers to buy.

Markon.   The percent increase in selling price, when cost is used as a base for markup percent.

Markup.   The difference between cost and selling price.

Maturity date.   The date a note is to be paid.

Maturity value.   The face of the note plus interest accrued until the due date.

Mean.   The most popular method of averaging a group of values. It is accomplished by adding up the values and dividing their sum by the number of values given.

Median.   The number that divides a group in half.

Merchandise inventory.   Represents the value of goods on hand, either at the beginning or end of the accounting period.

Merchandise inventory turnover.   The number of times the average inventory is sold during a year. This ratio shows how quickly the inventory is moving.

MICR.   Term standing for Magnetic Ink Character Recognition. These are numerical characters that can be read by both computers and individuals.

Mode.   The number that occurs most frequently in a series of figures.

Net income.   The increase in capital resulting from profitable operations of the business. It is the excess of revenue over expenses for the accounting period.

Net purchases.   All purchases less returns and purchase discounts.

Net sales.   Total amount of sales minus returns and sales discounts.

Opening entry.   An entry made at the time a business is organized to record the assets, liabilities, and capital of the new firm.

Outstanding checks.   Checks issued by the depositor but not yet presented to the bank for payment.

Outstanding stock.   The number of shares authorized, issued, and in the hands of stockholders.

Par value.   An arbitrary amount assigned to each share of capital stock of a given class. It has no correlation to the market value or selling price of the stock.

Partnership.   An association of two or more persons to carry on as co-owners of a business for profit.

Payee.   The individual that is to receive money from a negotiable instrument.

Payroll accounting.   Accounting for payments of wages, salaries, and related payroll taxes.

Payroll earnings card.   A card that shows payroll data and yearly cumulative earnings, as well as deductions, for each employee.

Payroll register.   A specially designed form used at the close of each payroll period to summarize and compute the payroll for the period.

Payroll tax expense account.   An account used for recording the employer's matching portion of the FICA tax and the federal and state unemployment tax.

Percent.   The relationship between one number and another in terms of hundredths.

Post-closing trial balance.   A trial balance made after the closing entries are completed. Only balance sheet items—that is, assets, liabilities, and capital—will appear on this statement.

Posting.   The process of transferring information from the journal to the ledger for the purpose of summarizing.

Preferred stock.   A class of corporate stock that carries certain privileges and rights not given to other shares.

Prepaid expenses.   Current assets that represent expenses that have already been paid out, though were not yet consumed during the current period.

Present value.   The face amount of the note plus accrued interest.

Proprietorship.   A business owned by one person.

Purchase discount.   A cash discount allowed for prompt payment of an invoice.

Purchase invoice.   The source document prepared by the seller listing the items shipped, their cost, and the method of shipment.

Purchase Returns.   An account used by the buyer to record the reduction granted by the seller for the return of merchandise.

Ratio.   The relationship of two or more numbers to each other.

Real accounts.   All balance sheet items—that is, assets, liabilities, and capital—having balances that will be carried forward from one period to another.

Restrictive endorsement.   A type of endorsement that limits the receiver of the check as to the use she or he can make of the funds collected.

Retained earnings.   The accumulated earnings arising from profitable operations of the business.

Revenue.   The increase in capital resulting from the delivery of goods or rendering of services by business.

ROG.   Business term that stands for receipt of goods.

Running balance.   The balance of an account after the recording of each transaction.

Salary.   Business term used to refer to the compensation for administrative and managerial personnel.

Sales discount.   A reduction from the original price, granted by the seller to the buyer.

Schedule of accounts payable.   A detailed list of the amounts owed to each creditor.

Schedule of accounts receivable.   A detailed list of the amount due from each customer.

Share of stock.   Represents a unit of the stockholders' interest in the business.

Special journal.   The book of original entry in which the accountant records specified types of transactions.

State unemployment taxes.   Taxes to be paid only by employers, with rates and amounts differing among each state.

Stockholders.   The owners of the business.

Subscribed shares.   Shares that a buyer has contracted to purchase at a specific price on a certain date.

Subsidiary ledger.   A group of accounts representing individual subdivisions of a controlling account.

T account.   A form of ledger account that shows only the account title and the debit and credit sides.

Temporary accounts.   Consist of revenue, expense, and drawing accounts that will have a zero balance at the end of the fiscal year.

Time clock.   A clock that stamps an employee's time card to provide a printed record of when the employee arrives for work and departs for the day.

Trade discounts.   This is not a true discount but an adjustment of the price. With it, a business can adjust a price at which it is willing to bill goods without changing the list price in a catalog.

Transaction.   An event recorded in the accounting records that can be expressed in terms of money.

Treasury stock.   Stock representing shares that have been issued and later reacquired by the corporation.

Trial balance.   A two-column schedule that compares the total of all debit balances with the total of all credit balances.

Uniform Partnership Act.   A law used to resolve all contested matters among partners of a partnership.

Unissued shares.   Authorized shares that have not been offered for sale.

Unlimited liability.   The right of creditors to claim any and all assets of a debtor in satisfaction of claims held against the business of the debtor.

Withholding Exemption Certificate.   Known as Form W-4, it specifies the number of exemptions claimed by each employee, allowing the employer to withhold some of the employee's money for income taxes and FICA taxes.

Worksheet.   An informal accounting statement that summarizes the trial balance and other information necessary to prepare financial statements.

Index

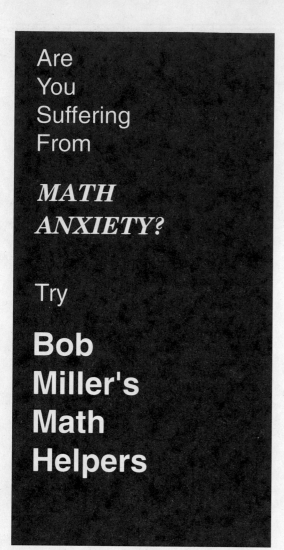

Are You Suffering From

MATH ANXIETY?

Try

Bob Miller's Math Helpers

A unique new series of three class-tested books which will supplement your required texts. Bob Miller teaches Precalculus, Calculus I, and Calculus II in a friendly, personable way. You will learn through creative explanations of topics and multiple examples which are found throughout the text. Here are some comments from students who have used the CALC I HELPER:

"Without this book I'm not so sure I would have come close to passing. With it I not only passed but received an 'A'. I recommend this book highly to anyone taking a calculus course."

■

"Your book is really excellent; you explained every problem step by step. This book makes every topic seem very simple compared to other books."

Bob Miller's **PRECALC HELPER**
Bob Miller's **CALC I HELPER**
Bob Miller's **CALC II HELPER**

Affordably priced for students at $8.95 each. *

Available at your local bookstore or use the order form below.

SCHAUM'S OUTLINES
IN
ACCOUNTING, BUSINESS, & ECONOMICS

Ask for these books at your local bookstore or check the appropriate box(es) and
mail with the coupon on the back of this page to McGraw-Hill, Inc.

❏ **Bookkeeping and Accounting, 2/ed**
order code 037231-4/$11.95

❏ **Business Law**
order code 069062-6/$12.95

❏ **Business Mathematics**
order code 037212-8/$12.95

❏ **Business Statistics, 2/ed**
order code 033533-8/$12.95

❏ **Calculus for Business, Economics, & the Social Sciences**
order code 017673-6/$12.95

❏ **Contemporary Mathematics of Finance**
order code 008146-8/$11.95

❏ **Cost Accounting, 3/ed**
order code 011026-3/$13.95

❏ **Financial Accounting**
order code 057304-2/$11.95

❏ **Intermediate Accounting I, 2/ed**
order code 010204-x/$12.95

❏ **Intermediate Accounting II**
order code 019483-1/$12.95

❏ **International Economics, 3/ed**
order code 054538-3/$11.95

❏ **Investments**
order code 021807-2/$11.95

❏ **Macroeconomic Theory, 2/ed**
order code 017051-7/$12.95

❏ **Managerial Accounting**
order code 057305-0/$12.95

❏ **Managerial Economics**
order code 054513-8/$11.95

❏ **Managerial Finance**
order code 057306-9/$12.95

❏ **Introduction to Mathematical Economics, 2/ed**
order code 017674-4/$12.95

❏ **Mathematical Methods for Business & Economics**
order code 017697-3/$12.95

❏ **Mathematics of Finance**
order code 002652-1/$10.95

❏ **Microeconomic Theory, 3/ed**
order code 054515-4/$12.95

❏ **Operations Management**
order code 042726-7/$12.95

❏ **Personal Finance**
order code 057559-2/$12.95

❏ **Principles of Accounting I, 4/ed**
order code 037278-0/$12.95

❏ **Principles of Accounting II, 4/ed**
order code 037589-5/$12.95

❏ **Principles of Economics**
order code 054487-5/$10.95

❏ **Statistics and Econometrics**
order code 054505-7/$10.95

NAME_____

(please print)

ADDRESS_____

CITY_____ STATE_____ ZIP_____

ENCLOSED IS ☐ A CHECK ☐ MASTERCARD ☐ VISA ☐ AMEX (✔ ONE)

ACCOUNT # _____ EXP. DATE _____

SIGNATURE _____

PLEASE ADD $1.25 PER BOOK AND LOCAL SALES TAX.

MAKE CHECKS PAYABLE TO MCGRAW-HILL., INC. PRICES SUBJECT TO CHANGE
WITHOUT NOTICE AND MAY VARY OUTSIDE U.S.   FOR THIS INFORMATION, WRITE
TO MCGRAW-HILL OR CALL THE 800 NUMBER.

PLEASE SEND
COMPLETED FORM TO:

MCGRAW-HILL, INC.
ORDER PROCESSING S-1
PRINCETON ROAD
HIGHTSTOWN, NJ 08520

OR CALL:

1-800-338-3987